"With *History in the Headlines,* Del Hood has chronicled the history of East County in a unique and interesting way. This is a book to keep on your bookshelf as a valuable reference."

— *Dick Brown, former El Cajon city councilman and Second District supervisor*

"Del Hood has grabbed the 'Headlines' that remind us of the other linked and long-forgotten headlines."

— *Ernie Ewin, former La Mesa city councilman*

"Del Hood's *History in the Headlines* captures the people, places and events that helped make East County the dynamic place it is today."

— *San Diego County Supervisor Dianne Jacob, District 2*

"Invaluable source for serious and just-curious researchers of East County historical information."

— *Eldonna P. Lay, curator of Knox House Museum, historian and author*

"It's fascinating! I loved reading about early days in East County. Anyone who appreciates the history of those who made the area what it is today will enjoy this book."

— *Joan Shoemaker, former mayor of El Cajon*

History in the Headlines:

Half a Century of the Most Notable Events
in El Cajon Valley and Surrounding Areas

1950-2000

Sunbelt Publications
San Diego, California

By Del Hood

History in the Headlines:
Half a Century of the Most Notable Events in El Cajon Valley
and Surrounding Areas

Sunbelt Publications, Inc.
Copyright © 2016 by Del Hood
All rights reserved. First edition 2016

Cover and book design by Kristina Filley
Project management by Deborah Young
Printed in the United States of America

Sunbelt Publications, Inc.
P.O. Box 191126
San Diego, CA 92159-1126
(619) 258-4911, fax: (619) 258-4916
www.sunbeltpublications.com

20 19 18 17 16   5 4 3 2 1

Library of Congress Cataloging-in-Publication Data

Names: Hood, Del, author.
Title: History in the headlines : half a century of the most notable events
    in El Cajon Valley and surrounding areas, 1950 to 2000 / by Del Hood.
Description: First edition. | San Diego, CA : Sunbelt Publications, Inc.,
    2016.
Identifiers: LCCN 2015042916 | ISBN 9781941384220 (softcover : alk. paper)
Subjects: LCSH: El Cajon (Calif.)--History--20th century--Sources. | El
Cajon
    Region (Calif.)--History--20th century--Sources.
Classification: LCC F869.E38 H66 2016 | DDC 979.4/98--dc23 LC record
available at http://lccn.loc.gov/2015042916

Cover photo top: El Cajon Valley High School banner carriers.
Photo: El Cajon Library

Cover photo bottom: 1952 downtown El Cajon.
Photo: San Diego History Center

CONTENTS

Introduction

The idea for this book came to me many years ago when I read *History As You Heard It* by Lowell Thomas, the distinguished radio commentator who had chronicled the procession of World War II by publishing the first paragraph of all his daily broadcasts during that conflict. Compressing events in this way gave the reader a better grasp of the war, which was fought on many fronts for a long time.

When I read in 2012 about the approaching 100th anniversary of El Cajon's incorporation, it occurred to me that residents of the city and surrounding areas might like to know more details about the development of El Cajon Valley in a way that did not require reading vast amounts of material. So, borrowing Thomas' technique, I decided to review all of the papers published by *The El Cajon Valley News* and its successor, *The Daily Californian*, for a 50-year span from 1950 to 2000 and select for publication only the most notable events of that period.

Newspaper reporters are taught to put the major elements of a story – who, what, when, where, why and how – into the first paragraph, which we call the "lead." This provides the reader with a summary of the story and enables him or her to decide if he or she wishes to read to the end. For the sake of clarity, I have taken the liberty to occasionally rewrite the "leads" or to expand them to include more details of the story.

1950 is the starting point for two reasons: (1) That was a watershed year for the city because it hired its first city manager and was quickly being transformed from a rural town to a suburban city; and (2) the source material for pre-1950 events was very fragile, especially the bound volumes of newspapers, and that era already had been documented by Eldonna Lay in her book, *The Valley of Opportunity*, which was published for the city's 75th anniversary. I chose the year 2000 to make it a 50-year span of time due to the fact that *The Daily Californian* was discontinued at the beginning of 2000 and reverted to weekly status under new ownership, thus thorough coverage of local events was severely curtailed in the ensuing years.

I have chosen to introduce each five-year increment of notable events with highlights of the period. If you come across an item of particular interest, don't assume that one entry is the end of the story. Some of the characters who appear in this recitation of events reappear many times in the columns of the newspapers. My advice: Keep reading!

Del Hood

Some highlights ahead:

Tunnel through mountains backed by Col. Ed Fletcher. . . . Lakeside man breaks world javelin throw record. . . . Work starts on El Cajon Valley High School. . . . El Cajon Citrus Assn. puts its plant on the auction block.

Identical triplets – David, Stephen and Robert Gillespie – made national headlines in 1950. *Photo: Thomas Gillespie*

Gillespie triplets as they look today. *Photo: Gillespie family*

1950

Jan. 26 – In an all-day session, El Cajon City Council approved an ordinance setting up a Civil Service system for the city and authorizing the hiring of its first city manager. . . . A ribbon was cut opening a five-mile stretch of Alvarado Canyon Road (Alvarado Freeway) which connected with Mission Valley Road at Fairmount Avenue. . . . Dedication of the National Guard Armory in El Cajon was scheduled for Jan. 29.

Mar. 9 – The building boom in El Cajon required issuing 55 permits for single-unit dwellings in February valued at $361,733, an all-time high.

Apr. 13 – Two new El Cajon City Council members – Bob Steele and Carlos Hull – were elected. Councilman Hovey C. Crandall was re-elected. Claude Kenyon, former mayor, was defeated.

June 15 – El Cajon's first city manager was to be Bernard J. Noden from Mars Hill, ME. . . . El Cajon High School was chosen as the name for the new high school to be built at First Street and Madison Avenue. *(Later the name was changed to El Cajon Valley High School.)* La Mesa High School was chosen as the name for the new school on University Avenue in west La Mesa. *(Later the school was named Helix.)*

June 22 – The birth of identical triplets – David, Stephen and Robert Gillespie — in La Mesa was announced under the headline, "Boy Triplets Gain National Fame."

Aug. 3 – El Cajon had a balanced budget for 1950-51 totaling $217,090.56 – an increase of $19,230 over actual expenditures for 1949-50.

Dec. 28 – Heralding 1950 as the greatest year of expansion in the city's history, the value of building permits for the year totaled $2.2 million. The population of El Cajon had increased 268 percent from 1940 to 1950.

1951 (From the HEART-land News)

Jan. 20 – The value of building permits for the Heartland area in 1950 was put at $25 million. Lemon Grove led the way with permits totaling $8,148,167.

Apr. 10 – An advisory committee to the County Planning Commission recommended that Highway 80 be given future "freeway" status, a switch in the plan which provisionally had designated the Lyons Valley route as a future freeway.

Apr. 24 – The 1950 census showed a population of 49,588 for the La Mesa-El Cajon area, including Lemon Grove, Spring Valley, Crest and Lakeside. El Cajon Valley's population, including Lakeside, was 19,577.

May 8 – An advisory committee reversed its position and recommended that both Highway 80 and Lyons Valley Route be brought to freeway status. Highway 80 was recommended as the priority.

May 22 – M.J. Shelton, chairman of Save Our Water, announced a "consumption check" for all parts of the county against previous use. "There are many easy ways to save water," Shelton said. "Perhaps the best guide is to use it as though it cost you $5 a gallon."

June 5 – The creation of a new municipal court district, called El Cajon Judicial District, was announced, with courtrooms in La Mesa and El Cajon.

July 10 – The detention center at Gillespie Field was "bulging" with illegal aliens, taxing the capacity of the 180-man facility. The Border Patrol was airlifting illegal aliens to El Centro. Illegals had been apprehended as far north as San Luis Obispo.

July 24 – For the first time since it started in 1948, the Mother Goose Parade was to be a daytime event on Sunday, Nov. 18. Previously it had been held on Saturday evening.

Aug. 28 – The San Diego County Boundaries Commission approved formation of the Grossmont Hospital District, subject to ratification by the signatures of 4,000 registered voters. There were about 70,000 residents in the district.

Oct. 9 – Local Western artist Olaf Wieghorst scheduled art shows for Oct. 14 and 21, with 40 canvases to be displayed. He recently had exhibited his work in Los Angeles and Tucson, AZ.

Nov. 13 – A six-column headline, "San Diego Hit by Atomic Aerial Bomb Blast," ran across the front page. Other smaller faux headlines screamed "Downtown Smashed Flat" and "East San Diego Area Burning." Readers were advised: "Go to your nearest Civil Defense Center. Volunteer for a part in the master plan for survival." The paper 'fessed up in an insert: "This didn't happen but it may and we ask: ARE YOU PREPARED?"

Nov. 20 – Attendance for El Cajon's first daytime Mother Goose Parade was put at 200,000.

1951 (From El Cajon Valley News)

Jan. 18 – Dedication of a $600,000 addition to Edgemoor Farm in Santee was announced. The facility was prepared to accept 225 patients transferred from a branch of the county hospital at Camp Elliott.

Feb. 1 – The El Cajon Civil Defense and Disaster Council put out a call for a thousand or more volunteers.

Feb. 8 – Actress Margaret O'Brien led a parade starting at the foot of Broadway in San Diego to Alpine for a ground-breaking ceremony for Alpine Youth Center.

Feb. 15 – El Cajon set a new record for retail sales in 1950: $18,750,504.62. The official census put the population at 5,600. Retail sales per capita was $3,350, about three times the average for Southern California.

May 5 – La Mesa Park Homes, a proposed tract of 2,500 homes, applied for annexation to La Mesa.

July 26 – Burton Jones, president of Grossmont Hospital District Assn., announced his group's goal of building a $1.25 million hospital.

Aug. 9 – Santee Utility and Interest Assn. asked Gov. Earl Warren to halt building in El Cajon until sewage disposal problems were fixed.

Sept. 13 – The paper's banner headline read, "All Local School Building Programs Stopped; Steel Shortage Stalls $7 Million Plans in Area." Construction of Helix High School was affected.

Sept. 27 – Carlyle Reed, publisher of *El Cajon Valley News* and *HEART-land News*, announced the resignation of Emory Thurson, who had been managing editor of the two publications since 1947. Reed took over as editor.

Oct. 18 – More than 400 attended the art show of local Western artist Olaf Wieghorst.

Oct. 25 – Sewer bonds for El Cajon totaling $650,000 were approved, with 461 residents voting out of approximately 2,000 who were eligible.

Nov. 1 – A new Safeway store opened on Main Street. It had 25,200 square feet of sales space, but no windows, and a 55,100-square-foot parking lot.

Sale specials: apples, 6 cents a pound; Edwards coffee, 77 cents a pound; eggs, 63 cents a dozen.

Nov. 15 – It was announced there would be 40 floats in the Mother Goose Parade.

Dec. 13 – Pioneer W.D. Hall, 83, had died. A son of J.P.R. Hall, he had left Ottawa County, Mich., in 1884 to work in southern Texas. He returned to Michigan, sold his farm, settled in Sacramento, CA in 1885 and then was drawn to El Cajon by the fishing stories he had heard. . . . *El Cajon Valley News* announced plans for a new 4,000-square-foot building at 435 N. Magnolia Ave. . . . A.M. Paris, owner of Paris Mortuary, announced plans to build a 5,000-square-foot building in the 400 block of North Magnolia Ave. He had started El Cajon's first mortuary eight years earlier.

1952

Jan. 3 – Construction began on four model homes in a $1.5 million housing project, planned for 122 homes, between Main Street and Broadway near Cuyamaca Street. Prices ranged from $8,500 to $9,200 for a three-bedroom home.

Jan. 10 – Formation of Grossmont Hospital District was approved Jan. 8 by a vote of 3,835 to 1,030.

Feb. 21 – A full-page ad announced that on Feb. 22 the *El Cajon Valley News* would be located at 435 Magnolia Ave. Its previous address was 136 W. Douglas Ave. The move coincided with the newspaper's 60th anniversary. It was started Mar. 12, 1892, by W.H. Somers, an El Cajon Valley Realtor.

Mar. 13 – San Diego County had 43.3 billion gallons of water in various storage facilities, thanks to heavy rainfall.

Mar. 20 – At $21,210,521, El Cajon's sales tax revenue for 1951 had risen $2.5 million above the 1950 total.

Apr. 10 – Voters approved raising the pay of council members from $25 to $40 a month. The vote was 588 to 253.

Apr. 17 – There was to be a Sunday parade marking the dedication of El Cajon Valley Recreation Park on Madison Avenue between First and Second streets.

May 20 – Representatives from seven elementary school districts met to discuss the effect unification would have on the school system.

May 27 – The population of El Cajon Township was put at 62,200 as compared to about 48,000 on Apr. 1, 1950. Included in the township were El Cajon Valley, Lakeside and vicinity and part of the Mountain Empire area.

June 26 – A preliminary census showed El Cajon had a population of 8,658.

July 1 – Unification talks between representatives of 10 elementary districts and Grossmont Union High School District fizzled.

July 29 – The Augmented County Committee on School District Organization turned down, by a vote of 18 to 3, a request for unification by Grossmont Union High School District.

July 31 – *El Cajon Valley News* announced plans to become a bi-weekly publication starting Tuesday, Aug. 5. The paper was to begin publishing Tuesdays as well as Thursdays.

Sept. 9 – W.S. Head, a local historian, published the first of 52 articles in the paper on the topic "Valley History in the Past 2,000,000 Years."

Sept. 11 – Enrollment was expected to reach 8,000 students in new school buildings that had been constructed at a cost of $9 million.

Sept. 25 – Grand opening of Russ's self-service station at 407 El Cajon Blvd. was announced, with regular gas selling for 23.9 cents a gallon and ethyl going for 25.9 cents a gallon. The station was to be open 24 hours a day. Gas station discrimination was in vogue: "We serve the ladies!," the ad boasted.

Oct. 14 – A new post office was to open Oct. 16 on the west side of Magnolia Avenue between Lexington and Douglas. It had three times more space than the existing post office.

Oct. 28 – Western artist Olaf Wieghorst's father, Karl, had been visiting from Denmark. Karl was a respected Danish painter who had permission from the royal family to copy the work of old masters and display them in the national museum in his homeland. . . . Actress June Haver was scheduled to ride in the sixth annual Mother Goose Parade on Dec. 2.

Dec. 4 – City Manager Bernard Noden wrote to the City Council members: "You should sit down with me some night for about three hours and talk about the future. You would find that we are surely unprepared for this tremendous expansion." The city's population was nearing 11,000, and it was expected to vault to 17,000 or 18,000 within a year.

Dec. 9 – Voters by a margin of 3 to 1 defeated a plan to unify the La Mesa-Spring Valley School District.

1953

Jan. 6 – El Cajon's population virtually doubled in less than two years from 5,418 to 11,000. . . . There was speculation that a state correctional facility, likely a state prison farm, would be located in El Cajon Valley or in Santee.

Jan. 13 – First National Bank of El Cajon was to build a $300,000 structure at Magnolia Avenue and Rea Street.

Jan. 15 – John Ballantyne, who came to El Cajon from Scotland in August 1873, died Jan. 14. He helped organize and served as a director of the El Cajon Valley Irrigation District and was a member of the Cajon Valley Union School District Board from 1934 to 1946.

Jan. 20 – The proposed state correctional facility for this area was scratched. . . . Florence Elizabeth Hall, 83, widow of W.D. Hall, founder of W.D. Hall Lumber Co., had died. . . . Metropolitan Water District approved water for 3,000 to 3,500 acres west of Grossmont Summit, setting the stage for bringing water to 6,000 acres of El Cajon Valley land.

Mar. 3 – El Cajon Chamber of Commerce Manager Freeman Durgin suggested that the Padres build a baseball stadium close to Gillespie Field if the team couldn't find a suitable site elsewhere.

Mar. 12 – A proposal to build a low-level highway with railroad access between San Diego County and eastern markets was revived before the Board of Supervisors. The project was first discussed 25 years earlier. The project, requiring a tunnel through the mountains, was backed by developer Col. Ed Fletcher, who said on Mar. 25, 1953: "Next to a bountiful supply of water, this tunnel is the most important project benefiting all of Imperial Valley and San Diego County, as well as Arizona and the East."

Apr. 14 – Planning expert Gordon Whitnall told El Cajon Valley Chamber of Commerce directors that "civic surgery" is the only known cure for El Cajon's growing malignancy – the parking problem. "Either do it or the patient dies," he said. Whitnall said El Cajon was laid out on the "shoestring" concept, which is outdated.

Apr. 16 – El Cajon's gross sales for 1952 hit $21.8 million, a 26 percent jump over 1951. They represented an $8 million increase in two years.

May 28 – Annexation of Bostonia to El Cajon was approved 315-212, adding 3,000 residents to the city.

July 7 – More than 50,000 attended the El Cajon Community Fair during its five-day run, assuring that it would be an annual affair.

July 14 – A full-page ad ballyhooed the new duplex press acquired by *El Cajon Valley News*, which increased printing capacity by nine times what it had been. The newspaper was printing 6,200 copies twice a week.

July 16 – On the recommendation of the County Health Department, the El Cajon City Council asked for withholding dairy permits for Newbanks Dairy on North Johnson Avenue. The dairy was moving to Lakeside, citing population density in El Cajon.

July 28 – El Cajon Valley was put on notice it would be a refuge for San Diegans in the event of an atomic bomb attack.

Aug. 4 – Bourne Products, Inc. signed a 10-year lease on three acres in the industrial area to manufacture aluminum window sashes. It employed 150 workers.

Aug. 13 – Bud Held, 25, a Lakeside native, broke the world record for the javelin throw by nearly five feet in Pasadena. Held, who was studying for the ministry at San Anselmo Presbyterian Seminary in San Francisco, threw the javelin 263.1 feet. The previous record was 258.2 feet.

Aug. 27 – All future building in the eastern part of El Cajon Valley was stopped by the County Health Department pending installation of a sewer system.

Sept. 10 – The new Cajon Valley Junior High School was to open the next week for seventh- and eighth-graders.

Oct. 6 – Simon Casady, former publisher of the *Arizona Republic and Phoenix Gazette*, purchased *The El Cajon Valley News* from the Reed family and assumed the role of publisher. Carlyle Reed remained as editor.

Oct. 29 – Voters had approved an $800,000 bond issue to start construction of Grossmont Hospital. The vote was 7,803 to 1,020. The 100-bed hospital, a $2 million project, was scheduled to be ready for use in late 1955.

Nov. 12 – Harry Hill, a city pioneer, died Nov. 11. He owned a drug store on Main Street and was active in city affairs.

1954

Feb. 4 – The way was cleared for bringing water to 6,731 acres of El Cajon Valley land when the La Mesa-Lemon Grove-Spring Valley Irrigation District Board voted to allow the El Cajon Valley Irrigation District to annex without paying an "inclusion" fee.

Mar. 18 – Charles V. Ferree was to be manager of the new F.W. Woolworth store on Main Street, which was to open before May 20. Ferree, who later became manager of the El Cajon Chamber of Commerce, had been manager of the F.W. Woolworth store in Inglewood.

Mar. 23 – Three inches of rain caused extensive flooding in El Cajon neighborhoods. Lack of adequate drainage was blamed. . . . Two full-page ads announced the grand opening for Big Ace in Lemon Grove. It had 26 departments and gave green stamps.

Apr. 20 – The newspaper warned that "more than one-third of the homes in El Cajon Valley have no protection against fire except that provided by the garden hose and the energies of helpful neighbors."

Apr. 22 – Ground was to be broken soon for a $1.1 million hospital in El Cajon.

May 11 – San Diego County Civil Defense estimated 250,000 people would pour into El Cajon in the event of an atomic or hydrogen bomb attack.

June 17 – Voters in the El Cajon Valley Irrigation District approved $2.75 million in bonds to construct water distribution facilities for 6,700 acres that tie into the existing La Mesa-Lemon Grove-Spring Valley Irrigation District. The vote was 775 to 52.

June 22 – A roundup of Mexican laborers, referred to as "wetbacks," was under way in El Cajon Valley. The roundup had been ordered by U.S. Attorney General Herbert Brownell for Arizona and California. In one day, 120 illegal aliens were apprehended in the El Cajon-La Mesa area.

June 24 – Work began on a new high school for El Cajon.

July 6 – Residents were fighting over how to name the new high school. One faction favored naming it "El Capitan" after the mountain; another wanted to call it "El Cajon Valley" after the area in which it was located.

July 8 – Carlyle Reed, editor and publisher of *The Valley News* from 1938 to October 1953, took a leave to form Carlyle Reed & Associates, a public relations and advertising firm. Publisher Simon Casady assumed the role of editor.

July 22 – By a vote of 4,540 to 330, voters merged El Cajon Valley Irrigation District with La Mesa-Lemon Grove-Spring Valley Irrigation District.

July 27 – El Cajon Valley Citrus Assn. put up its plant for sale, asking $85,000 for four buildings on four acres containing 51,000 square feet of space. The association had been shipping 225 carloads of citrus each year.

Sept. 9 – It was announced that El Cajon would be hiring a dog catcher.

Sept. 28 – The first major convention to be held in El Cajon, the 63rd Southern Baptist Convention, was expected to draw 2,000 delegates.

Oct. 7 – An architect was selected to design a $200,000 regional county administration building at the site of the former Little League ballpark in El Cajon.

Oct. 12 – The San Diego County Department of Public Health imposed a building ban in parts of El Cajon because of extensive use of septic tanks.

Nov. 2 – Mayfair Market was to be built on North Magnolia Avenue, half a block north of Main Street.

Dec. 9 – The Federal Communications Commission granted permission for radio station KBAB, owned by Babcock Broadcasting Co., to locate in El Cajon. . . . An 18-hole public golf course was assured for Gillespie Field.

Dec. 21 – Foodmaster Grocery at Main and Magnolia was robbed at gunpoint of $2,300 by masked gunmen.

A. Milton and Ninie Paris, owners of
Paris Mortuary.
Photo: Yvonne Paris

Bud Held of Lakeside was the first American to
be world-class in the javelin throw.
Photo: Franklin W. Held

Paris Mortuary's first location at 202 N. Magnolia Ave., El Cajon from 1943 to 1952.
Photo: Yvonne Paris

Mother Goose has been strutting down Main Street in El Cajon every year since 1948. This was her 1955 stroll. *Photo: San Diego History Center*

El Cajon was on a growth binge in 1955 when this picture of traffic on Main Street was taken. *Photo: El Cajon Historical Society*

1955-1959

Some highlights ahead:

Last carload of oranges shipped from El Cajon. . . . Site selected for $20 million regional shopping center. . . . A 16-year-old boy charged with the massacre of five members of an El Cajon family. . . . Swift Manufacturing Co. in El Cajon begins building the Pixie, a compact car that got 85 miles to the gallon but had a top speed of only 40 mph.

El Cajon Valley Hospital. *Photo: El Cajon Library*

Councilman Karl Tuttle shaking hands with City Manager Bob Applegate.
Photo: El Cajon Library

1955

Jan. 4 – Right-of-way was purchased to widen North Magnolia Avenue to four lanes from Main Street to Broadway, starting in February. The cost: $290,000.

Jan. 20 – County supervisors approved an 18-hole golf course at Gillespie Field. Construction was to start as soon as weather permitted.

Jan. 27 – El Cajon Chamber of Commerce Board recommended installation of parking meters on downtown streets to raise money to buy property for off-street parking.

Feb. 3 – Grossmont Hospital District Board approved a "heliport" at the hospital.

Feb. 17 – Construction was to begin on the 26,200-square-foot Mayfair Market. It would be the largest retail store in El Cajon.

Feb. 24 – El Cajon and La Mesa were fighting over which city should annex the Fletcher Hills area.

Mar. 3 – "Industrial Boom Hits in El Cajon" was the headline. Six new industries were in various stages of construction.

Mar. 8 – Plans for three new residential subdivisions worth $1.8 million were submitted for approval to the planning commission. They were Joey Manor, Dennstedt Rancho Estates and Denner Park. . . . A front-page editorial made the case for Fletcher Hills annexing to El Cajon.

Mar. 15 – Fletcher Hills residents voted 314 to 295 to annex to El Cajon, and 130 wanted to join San Diego. In a subsequent election, reported on Apr. 19, the vote was 453 to 298 to annex to El Cajon. This time annexing to San Diego was not an option. *(These were unofficial votes.)*

May 12 – Committee on Fly Control set May 15-22 as its "Target Week."

May 31 – A crowd estimated at 100,000 attended the East County Fair and Junior Livestock Show, a record.

July 3 – With annexations, the city was adding 6,500 more residents.

July 21 – Opening of Grossmont Hospital was set for Sunday, Aug. 3.

July 31 – The city's industrial complex included 60 major plants employing 1,177 with payrolls exceeding $4.5 million. A special section printed this headline: "If you must work, why not work nearer heaven?"

Aug. 4 – An entire block on the east side of Magnolia Avenue between Wright and Wells avenues had been reserved for a supermarket and shopping center.

Aug. 11 – A January opening for Singing Hills Golf Course was announced. It would be the fifth golf course in the El Cajon Valley area.

Aug. 21 – A $500,000 recreation center was planned for 70 acres of leased county land. A baseball stadium, restaurant and bowling alley were mentioned as potential tenants.

Aug. 25 – The last carload of oranges was shipped out of El Cajon, bringing an end to the area's citrus industry. El Cajon Valley Citrus Assn. built its packing plant in 1915 and by 1945 the plant was shipping 250 to 300 carloads of citrus a year.

Sept. 1 – It was announced that one of the largest shopping centers in Southern California would be built on 50 acres at the southwest corner of Magnolia Avenue and Broadway.

Sept. 4 – A water emergency was declared when residents of La Mesa, Lemon Grove and Spring Valley Irrigation District used 32,192,000 gallons of water – 8 million more gallons than normally were delivered to the system.

Sept. 8 – A heat wave ended after eight days of temperatures exceeding 100 degrees. The highest was 111.

Sept. 11 – El Cajon Valley High School was scheduled to open Sept. 12 with 1,600 students and 53 teachers.

Sept. 22 – Ground was to be broken Sept. 26 for a new $148,000 county administration center at Lexington and Magnolia avenues.

Oct. 13 – Fletcher Hills voted 450 to 211 to annex to El Cajon. This was the official vote. Previous votes were unofficial.

Oct. 16 – The death on Oct. 15 of Col. Ed Fletcher, 82, real estate developer and former state senator, was announced. . . . The vote was 4,874 to 2,188 for $2.2 million in bonds to build four high schools.

Oct. 20 – Bostonia voted 382 to 277 to annex to El Cajon, adding 3,800 residents and 1,100 acres to the city. Coupled with the Fletcher Hills annexation, El Cajon's population jumped to 21,380.

Nov. 27 – Sears Roebuck announced it would be opening a branch in El Cajon.

1956

Jan. 1 – El Cajon's population jumped from eighth to fourth among the county's nine incorporated cities. The city's population in 1950 was 5,600; this year it was 21,500. Cost of city government grew 300 percent, from $302,532 in 1950 to $882,024 in 1955.

Jan. 12 – Cost of extending the sewer line to Bostonia annexation area was pegged at $552,392.

Jan. 15 – Cajon Valley Union School District rescinded its rule against married couples teaching in the district.

Jan. 19 – Assemblyman Jack Schrade was named El Cajon's first Citizen of the Year.

Feb. 5 – The city is expected to have 699 new occupied homes by the end of the year valued at $10,250,000.

Feb. 9 – The nine-hole Flying Hills Golf Course at Gillespie Field is scheduled to open Feb. 15.

Feb. 12 – Simon Casady, publisher of *The Valley News*, was presented with a citation for his "consistently outstanding editorials" by the California Newspaper Publishers Assn.

Feb. 16 – Santee-Lakeside residents voted 75 to 10 in a straw poll against annexation to San Diego.

Feb. 28 – Voters approved a $5,230,000 bond issue 6,884 to 968 for the La Mesa, Lemon Grove, Spring Valley Irrigation District.

Mar. 4 – More new homes – 1,400 of them – were planned for El Cajon with a value of $18 million.

Mar. 22 – The 18-hole Flying Hills Golf Course was to open Mar. 24.

Apr. 15 – U.S. Sen. Estes Kefauver, running for the Democratic presidential nomination, scheduled a campaign stop Apr. 19 at the El Nadadero Club at 955 W. Chase Ave. It was billed as the first visit by a presidential candidate to El Cajon.

Apr. 26 – A 90-acre site at Broadway and Magnolia Avenue was chosen for a $20 million regional shopping center based on a five-year study that showed 245,000 people, with purchasing power of $260 million, would live within 15 minutes of El Cajon by 1960.

May 20 – Portia Goode was elected to the Grossmont Union High School District Board, the start of a long and distinguished career as a school and community college trustee.

May 24 – Sticks of dynamite were discovered in a student's band instrument case at Cajon Valley Junior High School. Police said the dynamite could have been detonated by static electricity or a slight jar.

May 27 – Six Cajon Valley Junior High School students were taken to Juvenile Hall for their involvement in the dynamite incident.

June 28 – J.C. Penney Co. signed a 20-year lease to build a $1 million store at 131 Main St.

July 2 – Siamese twins joined at the base of their spines were born in El Cajon, an event that drew national publicity because medical records showed only 36 sets of Siamese twins had been separated. The El Cajon twins were successfully separated July 19.

July 22 – Ground was broken for a new plant for *The El Cajon Valley News* on West Main Street.

Oct. 7 – Representatives from 35 El Cajon businesses formed the El Cajon Boosters Club as an agency of El Cajon Valley Chamber of Commerce to attract new business.

Oct. 21 – The attendance estimate for this date's Mother Goose Parade was 400,000.

Nov. 15 – Grossmont Union High School District Board voted to buy 33.5 acres at Fourth Street and Madison Avenue for a junior college site.

Nov. 22 – Voters approved a $1.35 million bond issue for Cajon Valley Union School District. The tally was 1,478 to 336.

Dec. 20 – Written and telephonic warnings of bombs set to explode sent teachers and students fleeing from buildings on three consecutive days at Cajon Valley Junior High School and Holy Trinity Convent School. A 13-year-old student took responsibility for the hoax.

Dec. 27 – The drought was so severe that mayors, the County Board of Supervisors and the Don't Waste Water Committee asked people to attend religious services Saturday and Sunday and pray for rain.

1957

Jan. 3 – El Cajon Valley Home Owners and Taxpayers Assn. revolted against city government, aiming to get City Manager Bernard Noden fired and recall City Council members.

Jan. 24 – El Cajon City Council voted to spend $115,000 to start the development of Wells and Renette parks. Total cost: $500,000.

Feb. 7 – A 100-bed wing was planned for Grossmont Hospital. The Grossmont Hospital District Board had approved more than $1 million to build it.

Feb. 10 – Unification talks were revived for schools in the Grossmont Union High School District whose enrollment was 27,500.

Feb. 28 – Two women members of the notorious "Terrible Williamson" gang of swindlers were arrested here. (*A Saturday Evening Post article said the gang had been operating for 50 years, netting $1 million annually.*)

Mar. 3 – Pepper Drive residents signed a petition which would annex 700 acres to the city.

Mar. 17 – Bids were to be called for a $3.4 million extension of the freeway from Grossmont Summit to Chase Avenue.

Mar. 21 – El Cajon Planning Commission voted 7-2 to permit J.C. Penney Co. to build a $650,000 store on Main Street.

Mar. 24 – The Canadian government confirmed the value of Chemalloy, a metal product made at Gillespie Field which was touted for earlier germination of plants.

Apr. 18 – Fifty-three new businesses had been established in El Cajon since the beginning of the year.

Apr. 25 – The 8,000-square-foot Dupee mansion at Edgmoor Geriatric Facility in Santee, reputed to have ghosts, secret passageways, hidden chambers and a secret room with bars where an alcoholic son had been kept a prisoner, had been demolished at a cost of $100.

Apr. 28 – The test of a rocket at Convair's Sycamore Canyon plant, described as "like a million icicles breaking against the house," had spooked area residents from Lakeside to Jamul. The test began at 1 a.m. Apr. 27 and lasted for 75 seconds.

June 20 – Charlotte Stofer, local music teacher, was found guilty on three counts of violating El Cajon's anti-noise ordinance. Neighbors complained she played the electric organ too loudly. *(Later, Stofer was fined $50 for each of three violations by a court that upheld the constitutionality of the ordinance).*

Aug. 4 – El Cajon police raided a house on El Cajon Boulevard which was described as a clearing house for bookie joints operating throughout the county.

Aug. 25 – An hour-long pageant at El Cajon Valley Junior High School's athletic field portrayed 100 years of El Cajon Valley history. Among the featured events were the first mail delivery from San Antonio, TX, to San Diego and the stop by mail carrier James Mason at the Los Coches Ranch of blacksmith Jesse Julian Ames, believed to be the first white settler.

Sept. 5 – El Cajon Planning Commission voted to extend the right of Fletcher Hills residents to stable horses.

Sept. 8 – Plans were announced to build the third largest arena on the Pacific Coast at Gillespie Field. The arena, to be named "The Pantheon," was to have 70,000 square feet of space and accommodate 5,000. The cost was put at $1 million, with construction to start in 60 days.

Oct. 13 – Population of El Cajon reached 27,710, making it the fourth largest city in the county. La Mesa had been fourth with a population of 23,700.

Oct. 17 – By a vote of 5,898 to 1,061, residents approved a $2 million bond issue for Grossmont Union High School District and authorized borrowing $2.5 million from the state for a third high school in Lakeside.

Oct. 27 – The State Department of Education said a junior college was needed in this area but added a cautionary note about the low property valuation and described it as a "poor" district.

Nov. 28 – The *El Cajon Valley News* announced the start of a "La Mesa edition" to be published Thursday and Sunday. It was described as an "area-wide paper."

1958

Jan. 12 – Chief, the only saddle- and bridle-trained Hereford bull in the world, was saved from the slaughterhouse by restaurant owner George Pernicano. (*Chief marched in many parades with previous owner S.Y. Robbins, who bought the bull at Cuyamaca slaughterhouse when he was three months old.*)

Jan. 26 – Ground was broken on Mission Gorge Road for Fanita Ranch, billed as "the beginning of a new city." It was advertised as an investment of more than $100 million and, when finished, would have 10,000 new residents.

Feb. 20 – *The El Cajon Valley News'* circulation topped 9,000 for the first time.

Mar. 6 – Plans for Grossmont Shopping Center, a $20 million project, were being reviewed. Del Webb, owner of the New York Yankees and builder of a mall in the Clairemont section of San Diego, was among the guests.

Apr. 3 – A tornado swept through Gillespie Field on Apr. 1, flipping airplanes and warping hangar doors. Damage was estimated at $50,000. . . . An industrial survey predicted El Cajon would have 250,000 people by 1988 and an industrial park of 2,000 acres.

Apr. 10 – Bernard J. Noden, El Cajon's first city manager, resigned after eight years. Karl Tuttle, who had won a seat on the City Council, was chosen by fellow councilmen as mayor.

Apr. 20 – The FBI was investigating an anonymous letter threatening Willie Carroll, chairman of the Cajon Valley Union School District Board, with being "blown to bits" for rehiring an unnamed teacher.

May 29 – El Cajon police arrested four "itinerant merchants" for selling new merchandise at Aero Drive-in Theatre, billed as home of the first drive-in swap meet in the United States. It had started four years earlier.

July 27 – Robert M. Applegate, 35, was hired as El Cajon's city manager at a salary of $12,500 a year plus use of a city car. He had been city manager at Baker, OR, where he received $8,400 a year plus expenses. The job had been offered to two other applicants who bowed out.

Aug. 10 – Ron Stacy, star halfback at El Cajon Valley High School, was barred from playing football because he had married at 18. The school's principal demanded a policy change, and Grossmont Union High School District Board voted to permit married students to participate in sports after a county counsel's ruling that it was illegal to ban married students from extracurricular activities.

Oct. 9 – TraveLodge was to build a 50-unit motel costing $350,000 on Main Street just west of Van Houten Avenue. Plans also were announced for a $370,000 professional building on West Main Street.

Oct. 16 – La Mesa-Spring Valley School District voters approved a $5.7 million bond issue 5,034 to 1,366. Another measure seeking authority to borrow $3.7 million from the state was approved 4,972 to 1,386.

Nov. 27 – For the second time in three years, Lemon Grove voters rejected incorporation 2,790 to 2,223. . . . The Mother Goose Parade crowd was estimated at a record 334,000.

Dec. 7 – The Cajon Valley Union School District Board asked Supt. Jens Hutchens to resign but he refused.

Dec. 14 – Carl A. Eder, 16, still on the run, was charged with slaying five members of the Thomas Pendergast family in El Cajon on Dec. 12. More than a month earlier, Pendergast had offered a ride to Eder, who was from Rochester, N.Y., and allowed him to stay in his home on North Second Street. Killed were Lois Pendergast, 37, the wife; children David, 9; Thomas, 6; Diane, 4; and Allen, 2.

Dec. 18 – Murder suspect Carl Eder was captured at Mission Beach in San Diego. He explained to police that he killed five members of the Pendergast family in El Cajon because one of the children, Diane, screamed at him.

Dec. 28 – El Cajon police arrested Daniel W. O'Connor, 34, one of the nation's 10 most wanted fugitives, on an FBI warrant for interstate transportation of stolen property (money from cashing bad checks) and desertion from the Army in 1946. In addition, he was wanted in Canada for severely beating a member of the Royal Canadian Mounted Police. . . . Dr. Donald Eidemiller, assistant professor of geography at San Diego State College, predicted that in five years El Cajon would be as smoggy as Los Angeles, sooner if nothing was done.

1959

Jan. 4 – Plans were announced for a $2 million shopping center on Magnolia Avenue between Wells and Wright streets. DeFalco Market was to be the main store.

Jan. 8 – Another Convair missile test in Sycamore Canyon rattled windows in the area.

Jan. 15 – A local drug store pharmacist was arrested for planting a dynamite bomb outside the bedroom window of a 33-year-old El Cajon woman.

Jan. 18 – John Warburton, 37, principal of Grossmont High School, was named Principal of the Year in a national contest.

Feb. 8 – Swift Manufacturing Co. in El Cajon was building the Pixie, a compact car slightly more than half the size of regular models that was patterned after a vehicle produced in 1903. The plant expected to turn out 30 to 40 cars a week. The Pixie got 85 miles per gallon of gas and had a top speed of 40 mph.

Mar. 5 – Mabel Bryan, the first woman to serve as a member of the Helix Water District Board, was sworn into office.

Mar. 26 – Mount Helix sunrise service was continuing. Started in 1917, the outdoor amphitheater was finished in 1925 at a cost of $90,000.

Apr. 2 – A $4,821,000 capital improvement program was presented to La Mesa City Council by City Manager Dudley Lapham. It included money for a fire and police station, storm drains, streets, traffic signals, public works yard and recreation.

Apr. 23 – A petition drive began to recall all five Cajon Valley Union School Board members for firing Dr. Jens Hutchens, the superintendent.

June 7 – Dr. Jens Hutchens was briefly reinstated as superintendent of Cajon Valley Union School District.

June 14 – Dr. Jens Hutchens applied to continue as superintendent. Thirty-three other applicants wanted his job.

June 28 – The Cajon Valley Union School District Board gave a four-year contract to Dr. Lawrence Magee, superintendent of schools in Santa Cruz, to be head of Cajon Valley schools.

July 2 – Because an election put a reconstituted board in charge as of July 1, Dr. Jens Hutchens was rehired as superintendent for a four-year term at a salary of $17,000 a year. The vote was 3 to 2. Dr. Magee had served for only one day. County counsel ruled Magee's contract was void because it was made after trustees had agreed not to hire a new superintendent before July 1.

Aug. 20 – Burt A. Rees and Celestia Wooters survived a recall vote to oust them for firing Dr. Jens Hutchens as superintendent of Cajon Valley Union School District. Three other trustees lost their seats.

Sept. 27 – Incorporation of Homelands, a four-square-mile area east of El Cajon vying to be the 12th city in the county, was defeated by a vote of 193 to 116.

Oct. 4 – Montgomery Ward announced it would build a large store in Grossmont Shopping Center.

Oct. 18 – Stanford Research Institute predicted El Cajon's population would be 90,000 by 1975.

Nov. 19 – Ground was broken for the 64-bed El Cajon Valley Hospital at Greenfield Drive and Highway 80. Construction of an osteopathic hospital was scheduled to begin soon at Cuyamaca Street and West Main Street. It was to start with 49 beds but eventually have 100.

Dec. 10 – Monte Hall, 56, a television cowboy idol in San Diego County, died of a brain hemorrhage. Hall rode Comanche, his horse, in the Mother Goose Parade.

1958 Grossmont Union High School District Board members Rex Hall, C. H. Foster, Peg Goode and staff. *Photo: Grossmont High School Museum*

El Cajon was a pioneer in the production of small cars. This photo shows the Honey Bee production line in 1958. The next year Swift Manufacturing Co. produced the Pixie here. *Photo: San Diego History Center*

1960-1964

Some highlights ahead:

Two reporters for The El Cajon Valley News arrested within two weeks of each other. . . . El Cajon-La Mesa Northern League wins Little League World Series. . . . PSA jet with 88 passengers aboard makes emergency landing at Gillespie Field, wrecking a landing strip. . . . Both El Cajon and La Mesa celebrate 50 years of cityhood.

Simon Casady took the El Cajon Valley News to daily status. *Photo: El Cajon Library*

1960

Jan. 3 – The temperature dropped to 24 degrees at Gillespie Field, the lowest since Dec. 10, 1956, when a record 22 degrees was recorded.

Jan. 7 – Plans were announced for expansion of Singing Hills Golf Course, a $750,000 project to include a third course and a hotel.

Jan. 21 – *The El Cajon Valley News* ran a full-page ad boasting that its "circulation is growing faster than that of any newspaper in the 11 western states." Paid circulation was 11,645.

Feb. 7 – County Health Director Dr. J.B. Askew warned that El Cajon Valley faced a more critical smog problem than Los Angeles if growth outstripped efforts to control vehicle exhausts.

Feb. 11 – Teenagers collected 21,000 beer cans on a 3.2-mile section of Crest Road.

Mar. 5 – El Cajon City Council called for "urgency" zoning of land at Cuyamaca and West Main streets for a $1.1 million hospital.

Mar. 30 – The Fourth District Court of Appeals unanimously reversed a Superior Court opinion that would have given those working for a recall of Mayor Karl Tuttle and Councilman Walter Boortz a 15-day extension to gather more signatures. This killed the recall effort.

Apr. 3 – A three-day celebration marked the grand opening of Carlton Square in Santee.

Apr. 14 – C. Lloyd Loftus and Robert Cornett were elected to the El Cajon City Council on Apr. 12, providing the necessary votes to ratify a $1 million sewer bond issue that passed by a vote of 3,339 to 1,576. Ballots had to be recounted, but there was no change in the outcome.

June 2 – El Cajon's population had increased 566 percent in the last 10 years, jumping from 5,600 in 1950 to 37,289 in 1960. La Mesa's population was 29,892.

July 7 – TraveLodge announced its intention to build a 35,000-square-foot building and make El Cajon its international headquarters. The company had built 151 motels.

July 21 – El Cajon City Council rejected a plan to put a civic center on city-owned property at Fourth Street and Madison Avenue.

Sept. 18 – Santee Chamber of Commerce voted to oppose El Cajon's annexation of Gillespie Field. Dr. John DeKock, head of Carlton Hills Civic Assn., called El Cajon "an expanding octopus that can't agree on anything from the school board to a sewage plant."

Oct. 2 – Headline: "Construction Skids to New Low." Concrete workers were striking and the valuation of construction projects had tumbled in both El Cajon and La Mesa.

Oct. 9 – More than 20 new industries had started in El Cajon's industrial park, exceeding the number in the previous boom year of 1957.

Oct. 13 – Predictions were that 3,000 layoffs in the aircraft industry would be made by the end of the year.

Oct. 20 – Lakeside Planning Commission approved a plan for an investment of $3 million to $5 million to build an Indy-style racetrack in the Lakeside area.

Oct. 23 – Lyndon Johnson, candidate for vice president, was scheduled to visit El Cajon on Oct. 28, landing at Gillespie Field where he would address a crowd estimated to be between 6,800 and 7,500.

Nov. 3 – U.S. Sen. Edward Kennedy came to El Cajon on behalf of his brother, John, who was the Democratic candidate for president. He spoke at Big Bear Market.

Nov. 10 – Voters gave overwhelming approval for a junior college in the area. The vote was 41,785 to 14,832.

Nov. 24 – Dr. Jens Hutchens resigned as superintendent of Cajon Valley Union School District, effective June 30, 1961.

1961

Feb. 2 – El Cajon City Council voted 4 to 1 to join the Metropolitan Sewer System. Councilman Lloyd Loftus was the lone dissenter.

Feb. 9 – *El Cajon Valley News* reporter Jack Edwin Nevin, 51, who had been on the job for only three days, was arrested by sheriff's deputies on a hold order for Los Angeles County Probation Department. He was wanted on four felony parole violations for writing bad checks.

Feb. 23 – Duane Doug Knoke, 27, a former *El Cajon Valley News* police reporter, was arrested on suspicion of participating in a series of silk-stocking robberies in the region. He was charged with three counts of armed robbery and one count of felonious possession of marijuana. Knoke's brother, Frank, 26, and Alan Cruppie, 25, a painter, also were held. Duane Knoke was on parole from a five-year prison sentence for armed robbery.

Mar. 19 – The retail merchants committee of the El Cajon Chamber of Commerce launched "Operation Survival" to cope with expected competition from large shopping centers. At a meeting attended by 200 merchants, the committee voted to assess members enough to raise $2,000 a month to promote downtown businesses.

Mar. 23 – John Hansen, vice president of instruction at Fresno City College, was named the first president of Grossmont Junior College.

Mar. 30 – El Cajon City Council voted to establish a Housing Commission to hear discrimination complaints in home purchases.

Apr. 6 – Construction of Chet Harritt Dam east of El Cajon was scheduled to start with a big blast on Apr. 18. The dam, built at a cost of $1.7 million and with a capacity of 10,000 acre-feet of water, would hold a six-month supply of water for 125,000 residents.

May 14 – Dr. Peter Bancroft, 44, superintendent of Lincoln Unified School District in Stockton, was chosen as the new superintendent of Cajon Valley Union School District.

May 28 – Mayfair Market closed May 27 after six years in business.

June 8 – The first races for Gillespie Field were scheduled July 8.

Aug. 13 – A 2.9-mile section of Interstate 8 from Magnolia Avenue to the east end of the city was to be ready for traffic Sept. 1.

Aug. 24 – Five minutes before the deadline, legal action paved the way for delivery of $42.5 million in bonds to a New York syndicate for financing of the Metropolitan Sewer System, to which the City of El Cajon recently had been connected.

Aug. 27 – El Cajon-La Mesa Northern League won the Little League World

Series in Williamsport, PA, by defeating El Campo, TX, by a score of 4 to 2. Mike Salvatore hit his second home run of the series with two runners on base in the bottom of the sixth inning.

Sept. 3 – *The El Cajon Valley News* announced it would begin daily publication Oct. 2. Newspapers would be printed five afternoons a week and Sunday morning. The newspaper's circulation was 13,694.

Oct. 11 – An $8 million bond issue to build Grossmont Junior College and Riverview High School in Santee was defeated. La Mesa-Spring Valley School District voters rejected a $4.9 million bond issue.

Oct. 23 – Gov. Edmund G. (Pat) Brown told an El Cajon Elks Club audience a day earlier that "we are going to build a river 500 miles long. We will build it to correct an accident of population and geography which finds two-thirds of our 16.5 million people living in an area which has only one-third of our rainfall." *(This was a reference to the Peripheral Canal which never got built.)*

Nov. 2 – Grossmont Center, with 44 stores, was scheduled to be dedicated Nov. 6.

Nov. 3 – It was announced that a $6.6 million bond issue would be on next April's ballot for El Cajon. The money included $4.9 million for streets and drainage, $1.2 million for parks and recreation, $300,000 for new police and fire stations.

Nov. 6 – A mid-air plane crash out of Gillespie Field killed two Navy men and a female student pilot.

Nov. 28 – Negotiations were authorized to obtain 133 acres in Fletcher Hills for Grossmont Junior College.

Dec. 1 – William Parness, city manager of Livermore, CA, told a civil defense group in El Cajon that 98 percent of the U.S. population would be affected by "saturation" nuclear bombing. Livermore planned to build a community fallout shelter.

Dec. 6 – El Cajon Planning Commission approved a "projected city" of 23 square miles.

Dec. 15 – Unimart announced the opening of its store in El Cajon.

Dec. 17 – A $250,000 parking plan was unveiled for the area bordered by Main, Magnolia, Wright and Julian streets.

Dec. 24 – A full-page ad announced that Washington Merry-Go-Round, a column written by Drew Pearson about national politics, would begin appearing in *The El Cajon Valley News* on Dec. 26.

Dec. 28 – A Pacific Southwest Airlines prop jet with 88 passengers made an emergency landing at Gillespie Field because San Diego Airport was fogged in. There were no injuries, but two port engines and two propellers were damaged. This led to a ban of all planes weighing more than 12,500 pounds at Gillespie. The PSA plane weighed 43 tons – 86,000 pounds.

Dec. 29 – California Supreme Court action resulted in the removal of a blighted World War II-era barracks building in north El Cajon that had been an eyesore for many years. It was to be demolished or torn down and sent to Mexico.

1962

Jan. 9 – El Cajon Boys Club membership passed the 900 mark even though it had opened just seven weeks earlier.

Jan. 11 – El Cajon Chamber of Commerce hoped to triple retail sales and the industrial payroll, increase membership to 1,000 and have a $100,000 budget for the year.

Jan. 25 – The Federal Aviation Agency announced a grant of $263,100 for an instrument landing system and $25,052 for additional land purchases at Gillespie Field. However, the next day it withdrew the news release. On Feb. 1, the FAA said the plan for Gillespie Field is "not officially dead yet."

Feb. 6 – Grossmont Junior College trustees voted 3-2 to propose a $7.5 million bond issue plus $500,000 to purchase a site in Spring Valley for a second campus.

Feb. 16 – Both El Cajon and La Mesa were planning 50th anniversary celebrations of incorporation. La Mesa was planting 2,200 oleander bushes along the railroad right-of-way downtown, and El Cajon was publishing a book and sponsoring a square dance at the Elks Club.

Feb. 25 – Layoffs at General Dynamics, Convair and General Dynamics-Astronautics prompted Gov. Edmund G. Brown to dispatch a task force to San Diego County to alleviate an unemployment crisis. . . . Chamber of Commerce Manager Chuck Ferree and Bill Martin, a public accountant, flew to the Midwest to recruit new industries for El Cajon.

Mar. 15 – The headquarters of General Dynamics Corp. was to be moved to New York "effective immediately."

Mar. 22 – Supt. Peter Bancroft requested the resignations of three principals in Cajon Valley Union School District: Norman Esser, 57, Greenfield Junior High School; J. Cline Slack, 60, Anza; and Conrad Hansen, Crest. None complied with his request.

Mar. 27 – Former El Cajon Mayor James Hunt said he is shocked by what he described as an "unprecedented and completely unwarranted campaign to set up boss rule in our city."

Mar. 28 – Angry parents announced their intention to start a recall of the entire Cajon Valley Union School District Board in reprisal for the firing of three principals.

Apr. 11 – Al Van Zanten, Earl Freeland and Hal Whelply were elected to El Cajon City Council. Three bond issues totaling $6.2 million for streets, drainage and parks and recreation were defeated. In La Mesa, Ray Fellows was elected mayor; J. Robert Helland and Paul Jensen won council seats.

Apr. 22 – El Cajon Mayor Bob Cornett unveiled a plan to move city hall to Johnson Avenue School and let county government take over all of the existing civic center for an inland county headquarters.

Apr. 23 – Highway 80 freeway through La Mesa was to be opened for traffic Apr. 25 from 70th Street to La Mesa Boulevard. The segment had been built at a cost of $3,170,000 and was the last link of a 17-mile stretch of the freeway from San Diego.

Apr. 26 – Four full-page newspaper ads announced the Apr. 27 opening of Handyman on Center Drive in La Mesa.

May 1 – The State Department of Employment announced that 5,000 wage-earners had left San Diego County to look for jobs in other areas. Many were aerospace workers.

May 10 – The first Superior Court session in El Cajon was scheduled June 13.

May 20 – El Cajon Chamber of Commerce asked the city for 65 percent of the business license revenue to promote development.

May 21 – A tanker truck and trailer overturned and dumped 45,000 gallons of sticky road oil at Highway 80 and Broadway, blocking all four lanes of traffic for more than five hours.

June 6 – For the second time, voters rejected a $7.5 million bond issue to build Grossmont Junior College. Also turned down were a $500,000 bond issue for a second college site and $1.8 million for a high school in Santee. Bond issues required a two-thirds majority vote.

July 3 – Unemployment in San Diego reached an all-time high of 8.8 percent during June.

July 18 – A 50th anniversary edition published by *The Valley News* noted there had been three disincorporation attempts since El Cajon was incorporated in 1912.

Aug. 1 – Reconstruction of the east-west runway at Gillespie Field was to begin in the next few months. The Federal Aviation Agency allocated $215,575 toward the $399,250 project. The runway had been damaged by a jetliner that made an emergency landing because San Diego Airport was fogged in.

Aug. 7 – Supt. Peter Bancroft and two other top administrators in Cajon Valley Union School District were urged to resign in a 27-page report by a California Teachers Assn. affiliate. The report recommended reinstatement of three principals who had been dismissed.

Aug. 30 – Huge layoffs were planned by General Dynamics-Astronautics, reducing its work force from 17,402 to 6,000.

Aug. 31 – A secret cache of military rifles, dynamite, homemade bombs and ammunition was found in an abandoned house in the Calavo Gardens area.

Sept. 14 – A $5.25 million contract was awarded to Straza Industries in El Cajon by Aerojet General Corp., adding 80 employees for a total of 450.

Sept. 19 – Voters approved a $7.5 million bond issue to build Grossmont Junior College on a 132-acre site in Fletcher Hills. This was the third attempt, with 37 percent of the eligible voters turning out. Nearly 73 percent of the voters were in favor of the bond issue which required a two-thirds majority vote.

Sept. 26 – Cajon Valley Union School District Board voted 4-1 to retain Supt. Peter Bancroft.

Oct. 22 – Life Line Pet Products, an El Cajon company, was featured in *The Valley News* because it was making Christmas gifts for dogs.

Oct. 25 – The Cuban missile crisis, which took the United States and the Soviet Union to the brink of war, caused a frenzy of buying at local stores. Some markets in Los Angeles reported their sales jumped 400 percent above normal.

Nov. 1 – Unimart opened a 100,000-square-foot store in El Cajon that had 35 departments. It ran 16 pages of advertising in the newspaper.

Nov. 4 – La Mesa-Spring Valley School District Board voted 3-2 to extend by four years the contracts of Supt. Glenn Murdock, Dr. Ted Dixon and Dr. David Pascoe.

Nov. 7 – El Cajon Police Chief Joseph O'Connor was elected county sheriff over incumbent A.E. Jensen.

Nov. 19 – A crowd estimated at 400,000 watched the 16th annual Mother Goose Parade.

Nov. 29 – La Mesa celebrated the installation of the 50,000[th] phone in the city and also the 50th anniversary of its incorporation.

1963

Jan. 8 – La Mesa Post Office sold 20,000 one-cent stamps and El Cajon Post Office sold 8,000. The stamps were needed to supplement four-cent stamps and seven-cent airmail stamps. . . . TraveLodge, whose headquarters are in El Cajon, announced that it now operates 232 motels worldwide.

Jan. 18 – W.D. Hall Co., which had operated in El Cajon for 65 years, had been acquired by an investor group on a sale and lease agreement for $3.5 million.

Jan. 22 – The County Road Department gave the go-ahead for a plan to widen Mission Gorge Road into a four-lane expressway at a cost of $2.5 million.

Jan. 29 – Six students in Grossmont Union High School District schools – El Cajon Valley, El Capitan and the district's adjustment school – were expelled for participating in gang fights.

Feb. 25 – Robert Fenton Garfield, first judge of El Cajon Municipal Court, died of cancer Feb. 24 at Grossmont Hospital. He was 52.

Feb. 27 – Groundbreaking for Grossmont Junior College was scheduled for Feb. 28. The campus was planned for 6,000 students, with 2,500 to enroll in September. First phase of construction cost $9.5 million.

Mar. 5 – The San Diego County Board of Supervisors voted to keep three copies of "The Last Temptation of Christ" on library book shelves.

Mar. 6 – Former Assemblyman Louis Francis filed a $1.475 million libel suit against *The El Cajon Valley News*. An editorial and a published letter had opposed his "anti-subversive" initiative defeated by voters in November.

Mar. 12 – Wallace Dart was appointed chief of El Cajon Police Department, replacing Joe O'Connor who had been elected county sheriff.

Mar. 26 – Annexation of a section of Avocado Boulevard was to take effect in 30 days, increasing the size of El Cajon by 89.4 acres.

Apr. 5 – The State Department of Finance put El Cajon's population at 39,700.

Apr. 8 – The 78-year-old home of Ben Hill, a Lakeside pioneer, was going piecemeal to Mexico. It had 10-foot ceilings and had been kept as a show place on 1,350 acres until 1893 when it was sold.

Apr. 14 – The first membership meeting of Friends of the El Cajon Library was scheduled for Apr. 26.

Apr. 18 –A jury trial was ordered for Ina B. Douse after she allegedly disrupted a civics class taught by John Morgan at El Capitan High School. She faced two counts of violating the state's Education Code and was accused of upbraiding Morgan for the way he taught students. She apologized.

Apr. 29 – A.A. Baxter Corp. of San Fernando Valley, with 45 employees, was relocating to a 7,800-square-foot plant in El Cajon's industrial park.

Apr. 30 – Alpine School District banned classroom visits after a parent allegedly feuded verbally with a sixth grade teacher at Alpine Elementary School.

May 9 – Work started on a 10-acre site at Gillespie Field for the Eastern San Diego County Fair. Basic rent was to be $500 a year for 12 years.

May 31 – Attendance totaled 41,070 for the first two days of the Eastern San Diego County Fair at Gillespie Field. The five-day event drew 95,000 visitors.

June 11 – Daley Corp. submitted the winning bid of $256,603 to reconstruct the east-west runway at Gillespie Field.

June 14 – A federal grant of $1,140,500 was awarded to Helix Irrigation District for its water filtration plant.

June 20 – Zip codes were introduced by post offices in El Cajon, La Mesa, Lakeside and Santee under the Zone Improvement Program (ZIP).

July 1 – A 751-square-foot branch post office opened at Grossmont Shopping Center.

July 5 – *The Valley News* announced that on July 14 it would begin publishing editions Monday through Friday afternoons and on Sunday morning. A weekly edition of the newspaper would be distributed Thursday mornings.

July 12 – The first unit of the 20-acre Mission Industrial Park at 11030 Woodside Ave. was to open Aug. 1. There were 15,200 square feet of space available.

July 23 – Gov. Edmund Brown signed a bill authorizing $900,000 in state aid for fishing and recreation at Chet Harritt Reservoir.

Aug. 7 – The Board of Supervisors voted 4-1 against racetrack development in Lakeside, citing potentially excessive noise and dangerous traffic conditions.

Aug. 16 – El Cajon Valley Chamber of Commerce made a pitch to have a new veterans' hospital located in El Cajon Valley.

Aug. 30 – Raw sewage from El Cajon started flowing into the San Diego Metropolitan Sewer System.

Sept. 3 – The funeral for Theodora B. Ballantyne, 93, member of a pioneer county family and step-daughter of one of El Cajon's founders, was to be held Sept. 4. Theodora rode horseback to teach the first class at Hillsdale School in Jamacha. Her stepfather was A.L. Knox, former San Diego County sheriff and owner of the old Knox Hotel when El Cajon was known as Knox Corners.

Sept. 5 – Record rainfall in El Cajon (.96 at Gillespie Field) pushed masses of wriggling insects from cracks, crevices and ditches in the area. Campo recorded the heaviest rainfall: 1.57 inches.

Sept. 12 – The temperature hit 106 on Sept. 11. Four high schools – Grossmont, El Capitan, El Cajon Valley and Granite Hills – were put on four-hour schedules after several students collapsed from the heat.

Sept. 27 – The heat wave continued, with a high reading of 111 for the week.

Oct. 1 – The El Cajon Chamber of Commerce campaigned to have Gillespie Field designated as "the executive airport of San Diego County."

Oct. 4 – A $2.5 million project to rebuild 7.5 acres of central El Cajon was announced by Art West, president of Hall Co. The plan called for a six-story office building and a shopping center on Hall Co. property at Main Street and Julian Avenue at a cost of $2.5 million.

Oct. 30 – Grossmont Union High School District voters approved a $4.4 million bond issue for a new high school in Santee. Cajon Valley Union School District voters supported a $2.85 million bond issue.

Nov. 19 – A group of parents in Cajon Valley Union School District, organized as the Assn. for Better Schools, demanded that the county grand jury and the State Board of Education investigate the district. School officials were suspected of being involved in land speculation, and there was an accusation that a school board member was obligated to a school administrator for a personal loan.

Nov. 21 – Water stood four feet deep at Ballard and Main streets in El Cajon due to a storm that dumped as much as 1.27 inches of rain on the city.

Dec. 1 – *The Valley News* announced that it had added 187 new subscribers.

Dec. 12 – County Counsel Bertram McLees Jr. ruled that prayers or religious exercises in public schools were a violation of the U.S. Constitution. Trustees of La Mesa-Spring Valley School District had requested the opinion.

Dec. 13 – La Mesa police arrested 10 men, including several San Diego State College students and fraternity brothers, for burglary and conspiracy to commit burglary. Their estimated take was $10,000. The suspect list was increased to 15 the next day.

1964

Jan. 3 – Congress of Racial Equality members in San Diego County were to picket a meeting of the California Real Estate Assn. at the El Cortez Hotel in San Diego. Clergymen for Fair Housing, including El Cajon and La Mesa ministers and other inland pastors, was urging pastors to make statements against attempts to repeal the state's Fair Housing Law.

Jan. 7 – Lewis F. Smith, superintendent of Grossmont Union High School District since 1944, resigned effective June 30. Dr. John Warburton was named his successor.

Jan. 14 – A crowd of 250 attended a four-hour discussion of policies on religious observances in the La Mesa-Spring Valley School District. Three trustees had been threatened with recall, and an "anti-Christ" tag had been put on two of them. The county counsel had ruled that prayer in schools was unconstitutional but teaching about religion was not.

Jan. 22 – Police from El Cajon, San Diego and South County cities arrested 46 suspected dope peddlers in a coordinated raid. One El Cajon man was arrested.

Jan. 24 – Frank Jennings, 78, who joined the El Cajon Police Department in 1920 and retired as chief in 1936, died Jan. 23.

Jan. 28 – La Mesa-Spring Valley School District trustees voted 3-2 for a policy containing these provisions: (1) Students may say prayers in classrooms or graces on their own or with parental permission; (2) teachers may instruct about religion and make clear the contributions of religion to civilization; (3) no prayers or other exercises are to be used as a part of the district's school program.

Feb. 13 – A petition to recall three trustees of the La Mesa-Spring Valley School District was filed with the county school superintendent by the Parents for Prayers Committee. The targets were Robert Andreen, Margaret Burnett and William Johnston.

Mar. 1 – It was announced that the Powder Puff Derby for 1965, an all-women transcontinental airplane race, would start at Gillespie Field.

Mar. 18 – Police Chief Wally Dart announced his department would begin prosecuting "persons selling or giving cigarettes or other tobacco products to youngsters in El Cajon." It was state law.

Mar. 22 – U.S. Sen. Barry Goldwater, running for president, greeted 300 at his campaign headquarters in Fletcher Hills. When Goldwater praised his friend, Si Casady, publisher of *The Valley News* and a devout Democrat, the crowd groaned. "Oh, come off it, Barry, you don't know what you're talking about," a woman shouted. Goldwater replied: "Yes, I do. Si Casady started me in politics. You may not agree with him on what he says, but he's a fine newspaperman."

Mar. 31 – El Cajon City Council junked a plan to turn North Second Street into a six-lane arterial from U.S. 80 freeway to the city limits. Property owners had objected.

Apr. 8 – La Mesa-Spring Valley School District voters approved a $2.9 million bond issue and a $2.1 million state aid proposal. The money was for five new elementary schools and a junior high school plus other facilities.

July 27 – University of the Seven Seas purchased 100 acres about 10 miles north of Lakeside above San Vicente Reservoir. Its proposal was to build an $8 million campus over a five-year period.

July 30 – Dr. Gaylord Parkinson of El Cajon was in line to be elected chairman of the Republican State Central Committee on Sunday, Aug. 2.

July 31 – El Cajon inventor Eugene Horrall was plugging his Television Audio Monitor, a small hand-held device that allowed TV users to adjust the volume to radio earphones.

Aug. 4 – Ground was to be broken at El Cajon Valley Hospital for a $1.2 million expansion that would triple the number of beds from 60 to 180.

Aug. 5 – Vowles Egg and Poultry Co., Inc. launched a project to build a $162,000 cold storage and freezing plant for meat, poultry and eggs at 1105 S. Marshall Ave. in El Cajon.

Aug. 13 – Dr. Charles Collins, dean of curriculum at Grossmont Junior College, and his wife Anna were arrested on a warrant charging violation of a preliminary Superior Court injunction that limited picketing by Congress of Racial Equality members to Bank of America property. Three others also were arrested while protesting alleged discriminatory hiring policies.

Sept. 4 – Dr. Charles Collins and three others began serving 48-hour sentences for contempt of court.

Sept. 23 – In a recall election sponsored by Parents for Prayer, three La Mesa-Spring Valley School District trustees – Robert Andreen, Margaret Burnett and William Johnston – were ousted for their positions on school prayer. Their replacements were the Rev. Lewis Ginn, Geraldine Gill and Dr. William McCandless. Cajon Valley Union School District trustees voted

3-2 against adopting a district policy on prayer in the classroom.

Sept. 29 – Local Agency Formation Commission approved the annexation of Grossmont Junior College and 681 acres to El Cajon.

Oct. 8 – Actor Dennis Hopper, 28, a Helix High School graduate, was to talk to young Democrats in Lakeside on Oct. 10. He played the movie son of Elizabeth Taylor and Rock Hudson in "Giant," and starred or had parts in many Hollywood films, including "Apocalypse Now," "Samson and Delilah," "Easy Rider" and "Rebel Without a Cause," to name only a few.

Oct. 13 – Straza Industries of El Cajon won a $1.66 million subcontract to build parts for the Saturn launch facility at Cape Kennedy, FL.

Oct. 14 – With a new board majority, La Mesa-Spring Valley School District trustees rescinded a district policy banning teacher-led prayers and adopted a new policy by a 5-0 vote which gave teachers authority to direct prayers in the classroom.

Oct. 21 – Publisher Simon Casady announced the sale of *The Valley News* to Richard A. Baker, 32, managing editor of the Eugene (Ore.) *Register-Guard*, effective Nov. 1. Baker served in the Air Force for four years and flew 29 missions as a B-29 gunner in the Korean War.

Nov. 2 – The first issue of *The Valley News* under new owner Richard A. Baker was published. Baker, who was editor and publisher, appointed Ed Beeler, 31, as managing editor and Gordon Smith, 34, as advertising director. Both Beeler and Smith were employees of the *Register-Guard* in Eugene, Ore.

Nov. 17 – Lance Alworth, Earl Faison and Keith Lincoln of the San Diego Chargers were to be grand marshals of the Mother Goose Parade on Nov. 22. James Drury, star of "The Virginian" on TV, was the parade's celebrity guest.

Nov. 23 – The 18th annual Mother Goose Parade drew a crowd estimated at 450,000.

Dec. 2 – Santana, a version of the name given to the "devil winds" (Santa Ana) that come off the desert and heat up San Diego County in the fall, was chosen as the name of the new high school in Santee. Residents of Santee gave 732 votes to Santana, 560 votes to Santee, 114 votes to Fanita, and 64 votes to Rio Seco.

Dec. 7 – The San Diego Chargers beat the New York Jets 38-3, giving the locals the Western Division title of the American Football League for the second year in a row.

Eva Quicksall, school counselor, directed annual Christmas pageant at Grossmont High School. *Photo: Grossmont High School Museum*

Wally Dart, long-time El Cajon police chief. *Photo: El Cajon Library*

Ed Beeler, Daily Californian managing editor. *Photo: El Cajon Library*

John Hansen, first president of Grossmont College. *Photo: Grossmont-Cuyamaca Community College District*

1965-1969

Some highlights ahead:

An 11-foot boa constrictor found in hedge at Grossmont High School....Astronaut William Anders of La Mesa, one of three men to fly around the moon for the first time, was welcomed home....$20 million shopping center to be built at Johnson Avenue and Fletcher Parkway.

Robert Burnham, college district chief executive. *Photo: Grossmont-Cuyamaca Community College District*

Jim Snapp, first popularly elected El Cajon mayor. *Photo: El Cajon Library*

Thousands of young people showed their animals at the Eastern San Diego County Fair at Gillespie Field. Washing Miss America is Chris Pimentel.
Photo: San Diego History Center

1965

Jan. 12 – Harriet Stockwell was appointed to the El Cajon Planning Commission, the continuation of a long career in El Cajon's civic life culminating eventually in her election to the City Council.

Feb. 12 – The temperature in El Cajon dropped to 24, matching a record for this day set 10 years earlier.

Feb. 14 – Effective Mar. 1, *The Valley News* was to be renamed *The Inland Empire Daily Californian* and would be published 365 days a year.

Feb. 16 – The City Council purchased 2.6 acres at Fletcher Parkway and Magnolia Avenue for a new police headquarters building. The property cost $65,000.

Feb. 17 – Fire destroyed the interior of Davis Meat Packer Market at 1152 W. Main St. Faulty wiring was cited as a possible cause.

Feb. 24 – Cajon Valley Union School District Board canceled a contract with Jim's Quality Meat Co. of San Diego after traces of sawdust and excessive fat content were found in the district's supply of ground beef.

Mar. 1 – Souvenir copies of the renamed newspaper were sent to 29,500 subscribers and to 26,000 other households. The name was changed from *The Valley News* to *The Inland Empire Daily Californian*.

Mar. 2 – Supt. John Warburton heralded the fact that Grossmont Union High School District's dropout rate was 1.8 percent, lower than any other district in the state.

Mar. 22 – Simon Casady, former owner of *The Valley News*, was elected president of the California Democratic Council and was preparing to join right-to-vote marchers in Alabama.

Mar. 30 – El Cajon City Council annexed 681 acres in Fletcher Hills, including the $7.5 million Grossmont College campus.

Apr. 6 – County supervisors approved the construction of a girls' rehabilitation center in Santee. The facility, costing $729,800, was to be built on seven acres on the west side of the extension of Cottonwood Avenue near Edgemoor Geriatric Hospital.

Apr. 21 – Anna Dewey and Geraldine Gill, members of the La Mesa-Spring Valley School District Board elected to uphold prayer-in-school policies, were ousted in an election that replaced them with Hardy Kuykendall and Fred Jabusch. Dr. Cyril Padfield was re-elected.

Apr. 23 – Gillespie Field recorded its 500,000[th] landing in the three years since the Federal Aviation Agency's control tower opened.

May 17 – Opposition developed to a proposed state medical and psychiatric prison on the Monte Vista Ranch site at Campo and Jamacha roads. The state had budgeted $1 million to purchase more than 300 acres for the facility, estimated to cost $15 million.

May 18 – El Cajon City Council voted to ban card rooms in the city.

June 30—U.S. Public Health Service expressed an interest in the Santee Lakes percolation project and wanted to convert waste water to other uses, including recreation.

July 1 – Gov. Edmund Brown deleted from the state budget $1.2 million for a psychiatric hospital in East County.

July 31 – El Cajon police raided El Cajon Moose Lodge 1731 for gambling, illegal possession of gambling equipment and violation of liquor license restrictions. The bartender and club steward were arrested.

Aug. 1 – The death of Chet F. Harritt, Santee postmaster and community leader, was announced. He was 56 and had a heart attack. Chet F. Harritt Dam and a school were named for him.

Aug. 4 – Grossmont College trustees voted to continue letting Communists and other controversial speakers address students on campus but intended to seek county counsel's advice on the matter.

Aug. 12 – The County Committee on School District Organization deadlocked three times on plans to unify districts within Grossmont Union High School District. Both a one-district and a two-district plan were defeated. This action moved the controversy to the State Department of Education for a resolution.

Aug. 18 – Zella Crown, 47, a Democratic Party leader and a worker on local political and civic campaigns, died of uremic poisoning. She had been president of the San Diego County Democratic Council and had run unsuccessfully for a seat on the El Cajon City Council and against U.S. Rep. Bob Wilson, R-San Diego.

Aug. 26 – Grossmont College expected to enroll 3,100 students, 600 over its stated capacity.

Aug. 27 – Plans were announced for a $20 million regional shopping center on 20 acres at Johnson Avenue and Fletcher Parkway. The center, with Sears as a major anchor, was expected to generate $35 million a year in sales and have 50 stores.

Oct. 20 – Voters approved a $3.5 million bond for construction at Grossmont Junior College. A two-thirds majority was required for approval. The bond received support from 69.3 percent of the voters.

Oct. 21 – The California Highway Commission allocated $27 million for East County projects, including a 3.8-mile extension of Interstate 8 to a point 2.5 miles east of Alpine.

Oct. 22 – The design for El Cajon's new police station was approved. It would serve a city with as many as 100,000 people and would cost $736,000.

Nov. 15 – John Uzlowski Godwin, 30, of El Cajon returned to his native Poland after an absence of 21 years and was met by relatives he thought had perished at the hands of the German occupation forces during World War II. "I see my home town after so many years, it makes me nervous," Godwin told the Associated Press. "My memories from Poland are terrible. I still see the hangings of boys, one of whom I thought was my brother." John's brother and sister missed his arrival in his homeland but were to join him today in Warsaw. John left Poland in 1944 after the Warsaw uprising against the Germans. Only six years old at the time, John was wounded in the unsuccessful rebellion. He was hospitalized in Angsberg where an American orderly, Troy F. Godwin, decided to adopt him and bring him to the United States.

Nov. 16 – Astronaut Wally Schirra of La Mesa and fellow astronaut Thomas Stafford successfully rode the red-hot Gemini 6 spacecraft to a safe landing in the Atlantic Ocean. Schirra's parents, Mr. and Mrs. Wally S. Schirra Sr., reside in La Mesa.

Nov. 23 – Torrential rains lashed Inland Empire communities, forcing some residents of La Mesa and Santee to flee their homes. Mud and rock slides occurred in El Cajon on Fanita Drive and Navajo Road near Grossmont College and on Fletcher Parkway. Nearly three inches of rain had fallen in El Cajon.

Dec. 27 – As many as 20 homes in the Fanita Rancho Road and Todos Santos Drive areas of Santee were affected by massive earth slippage from recent rains, causing houses to slide off their foundations. Three homes had to be evacuated.

1966

Jan. 4 – A local gas war resulted in a drop to 25.9 cents for a gallon of regular gas.

Jan. 12 – Peter Bancroft, embattled superintendent of the Cajon Valley Union School District since 1961, resigned to accept a higher-paying job in Northern California. He was earning $18,500 a year here and had two more years on his contract.

Jan. 16 – A recall petition was filed with the county superintendent's office to unseat three La Mesa-Spring Valley School District trustees – Dr. Cyril Padfield, Dr. William McCandless and Victor Walton.

Feb. 3 – Electric lights were turned on for the first time at the Deerhorn Valley home of Charles Bratton, 83. A line was installed to the house where he has lived without electricity since 1908.

Feb. 11 – Dr. Cyril Padfield, president of the La Mesa-Spring Valley School District Board and one of three trustees targeted for recall, resigned.

Feb. 20 – Simon Casady, former publisher of *The Valley News*, lost a confidence vote at the California Democratic Council convention and immediately resigned as its president. Casady was involved in a dispute with Gov. Edmund Brown over the Vietnam War, which he opposed.

Mar. 15 – John S. Hansen, president of Grossmont College since its founding in 1961, resigned to be assistant superintendent in charge of education for the State Center Junior College District in northern California.

Mar. 22 – El Cajon City Council stood firm against changing the name of John F. Kennedy Park. The proposal to change the name came from the Park Commission, which claimed that some people refused to donate to a "political memorial."

Mar. 27 – Lt. Cmdr. Ben Cloud, 33, of El Cajon, was serving as the first black military aide at the White House.

Mar. 29 – Harold Hughes, who had a long affiliation with Grossmont Union High School District, was appointed superintendent-president of Grossmont Junior College, effective July 1. He had held a number of administrative posts with the college district since its founding in 1961.

Apr. 12 – Grossmont Junior College District Board voted unanimously against a proposal to bring American Nazi leader George Lincoln Rockwell to the campus to speak to students.

Apr. 13 – Ted Dixon, associate superintendent of La Mesa-Spring Valley School District, was named superintendent of the Cajon Valley Union School District.

Apr. 22 – Lake 5 of the Santee Lakes Project was opened Apr. 21 for one day to welcome the President's Water Pollution Control Board for a tour. An estimated 3,000 area residents visited the park that day.

May 23 – The body of Michael Kiehl, 21, a Lakeside resident killed in Vietnam while serving with the U.S. Army, was interred at Ft. Rosecrans National Cemetery. Raymond Kiehl, his father, is a member of the Santee School District Board.

May 29 – Gov. Edmund Brown, running for re-election, stopped at his La Mesa campaign headquarters and toured the Eastern San Diego County Fair in El Cajon.

June 15 – Voters rejected a one-district unification plan for schools in Grossmont Union High School District. The vote was 13,296 to 10,503. Only Cajon Valley Union School District residents voted for the measure. Voters in eight other elementary districts said no.

July 14 – Citizens United for Recall Election (CURE) called off its campaign to oust La Mesa-Spring Valley School District trustees Victor Walton and Dr. William McCandless.

July 18 – Ground was broken for construction of the Home of Guiding Hands in Lakeside, a $2.2 million facility serving the developmentally impaired.

Oct. 11 – Grossmont Junior College trustees voted to reaffirm their ban of American Nazi leader George Lincoln Rockwell whom two history professors had invited to speak to their classes.

Oct. 17 – An estimated 25,000 to 30,000 people visited Gillespie Field over the weekend to see a display of old-time aircraft. Airplane rides were offered.

Oct. 25 – C.A. Larsen Construction Co. submitted a low bid of $620,000 to build El Cajon's new police station, a two-story, 24,000-square-foot structure at Fletcher Parkway and Magnolia Avenue.

Nov. 23 – The Town Center Project got the ax at a La Mesa City Council meeting. Approval of the $1.8 million beautification project would have required a unanimous vote.

Dec. 5 – Sheriff's deputies and firefighters evacuated eight patients from Townsend Guest Home in the flood-prone area of Via Zapador and Forrester Creek in Santee. El Capitan Reservoir recorded 3.57 inches of rain. The storm dumped 3.99 inches of rain on El Cajon.

Dec. 17 – *The Inland Empire Daily Californian* ran a front-page photo of Virginia O'Hanlon Douglas, now 77, whose letter to the *New York Sun* 69 years earlier had provoked the famous editorial, "Yes, Virginia, there is a Santa Claus."

Dec. 21 – A rash of recently reported UFO sightings over the Inland Empire may have been nothing more than high-flying plastic clothes bags tied together. La Mesa firemen had retrieved one of the bags from a telephone pole wire.

Dec. 22 – Sixty-two doctors on staff at Grossmont Hospital volunteered to take turns so the hospital could provide around-the-clock emergency care.

Dec. 23 – Donald R. Carr, senior mechanical engineer in Lemon Grove, disputed an earlier news report that UFOs sighted in the area were plastic clothes bags. He said the three that he saw were brilliant orange spheres that flickered and then disappeared. Carr reported his sightings to Naval Intelligence.

1967

Jan. 6 – Stromberg-Carlson Corp., a subsidiary of General Dynamics, announced it would open a manufacturing plant in El Cajon within two months. It would provide 200 jobs and have a $1 million annual payroll. . . . Santee Water District was to receive an $800,000 federal grant for demonstrating new methods of reclaiming water for recreational uses.

Jan. 20 – Grossmont Junior College District trustees suspended two students – Phil Decker and Neil Goode – for not reporting the appearance on campus of Communist editor Michael Laski of Los Angeles. The students denied having prior knowledge that Laski would be on campus. The board previously had banned Laski.

Feb. 2 – El Cajon's police force grew to 50 with the hiring of Bernell Hayden, 26, and Michael Perkins, 25.

Feb. 7 – Grossmont Union High School District Board expelled indefinitely five Helix and two Granite Hills students for marijuana use.

Feb. 8 – Dr. William McCandless, a La Mesa-Spring Valley School District trustee, was appointed to the State Board of Education by Gov. Ronald Reagan.

Feb. 22 – Gov. Reagan withdrew his appointment of Dr. William McCandless to the State Board of Education. The nomination was opposed by State Sen. Clair Burgener who represented parts of East County.

Feb. 28 – Dr. William McCandless, who had resigned from the La Mesa-Spring Valley School District Board to accept an appointment to the State Board of Education, was reappointed to the La Mesa board when Gov. Reagan withdrew his nomination to the state board. McCandless had been a member of the state board for only two weeks.

Mar. 6 – Domenick Marsili, 85, of El Cajon, received a patent for a ravioli machine he invented in 1949. He had neglected to file for four patents.

Mar. 12 – Synanon, a drug treatment facility operating on the old St. Francis Seminary property at Madison Avenue and Greenfield Drive, lost its battle to stay there when the El Cajon City Council voted 5-0 to revoke its conditional use permit. The dispute was headed to Superior Court.

Mar. 13 – Synanon gives up its fight to start a school for the children of dope addicts at its El Cajon site.

Apr. 11 – Grossmont Junior College District trustees fired four faculty members for providing beer and wine at an academic retreat Mar. 18. All four were allowed to finish the school year.

July 17 – Josephine Asher Vacher, 97, honored this year as the oldest living native of Old Town in San Diego, died July 15 in a La Mesa hospital. She started teaching in this area in 1890.

July 28 – Ambassador Airlines announced it would offer commuter service to and from Las Vegas with stops between that city and Gillespie Field in El Cajon.

Aug. 16 – El Cajon Valley Hospital was sold for $5.5 million to a Los Angeles corporation, effective Sept. 1. Built in 1960 at 1688 E. Main St., it now has 180 beds and 370 fulltime staffers.

Aug. 19 – San Diego's new $27 million stadium in Mission Valley was to be used for the first time Aug. 20 for a game between the Chargers and the Detroit Lions. Detroit won, 38-17.

Sept. 19 – Ametek, Inc., a Space Age equipment maker, has agreed to acquire Straza Industries for 141,000 shares of Ametek common stock worth about $7.6 million. Straza had 500 employes at its two plants in El Cajon and Carlsbad.

Oct. 14 – Lance Casady, 24, son of former *El Cajon Valley News* publisher Simon Casady, was one of three men indicted for refusing induction into the armed forces. Simon Casady was a bitter critic of the Vietnam War both as a newspaper publisher and later as president of the California Democratic Council.

Oct. 18 – Voters approved a $6 million bond issue to build a new school in Grossmont Union High School District and to improve eight others.

Oct. 19 – A 62-unit motel at 1527 E. Main St. had been completed and would open Oct. 20. A 6,000-square-foot restaurant nearby was to open in February. The motel cost $350,000; the restaurant, $300,000.

Oct. 21 – A recall was started against La Mesa Mayor Ray Fellows. Senior citizens backed the recall.

Nov. 1 – Fire in the Ramona and Julian areas destroyed 26 structures and burned 45,000 acres of brush and grassland. Property damage was estimated at $6 million. The fire started on Halloween.

Nov. 9 – The Walker-Scott Co. of San Diego said it planned to negotiate for space in El Cajon Plaza (later named Parkway Plaza) and hoped to open in 1969.

Nov. 20 – The Mother Goose Parade turned 21 on Nov. 19 and got doused with rain, cutting the crowd size by as much as 150,000.

Nov. 29 – Voters defeated an $8 million bond issue on Nov. 28 to expand Grossmont Hospital. The vote in favor was 6,827 to 5,459, but a two-thirds majority was required for passage.

Dec. 8 – George Wallace, running for president on the American Independent Party ticket, spoke at Veterans Memorial Hall in El Cajon.

Dec. 12 – Grossmont Junior College District trustees approved a free speech area on campus but denied permission for a Communist speaker,

William C. Taylor of Communist Party U.S.A., to use it.

Dec. 15 – Charles Cordell of El Cajon was chosen to be president of the 200th anniversary celebration for San Diego.

Dec. 29 – Sears, Roebuck and Co. purchased the remaining 60 acres of the proposed El Cajon Plaza Shopping Center, giving it control of the 80-acre site.

1968

Feb. 14 – Grossmont Junior College District trustees rejected a second request from the Open Forum Club that a Communist be permitted to speak on campus. The trustees approved an appearance by a member of the John Birch Society. Legal action is possible.

Feb. 19 – A bill was introduced in the Legislature by an Orange County representative to allow Communist speakers on any public school, junior college, state college or university campus in California.

Feb. 20 – John T. Warburton resigned as superintendent of Grossmont Union High School District to join the education department faculty at San Diego State College. He had been superintendent since July 1, 1964, and had a 20-year association with the district.

Feb. 26 – A suit was filed in Superior Court against Grossmont Junior College District trustees asking them to approve a proposed debate on the Vietnam War by a Communist and a member of the John Birch Society. The Faculty Senate and the Associated Student Body backed the faculty's position two days later.

Mar. 7 – Grossmont Hospital abandoned its plan for a 10-story addition in favor of a three-phase wing development.

Mar. 8 – Superior Court Judge George Lazar upheld Grossmont Junior College District Board action denying permission for a Los Angeles Communist, William Taylor, to appear on campus for a debate on the Vietnam War with a John Birch Society member. The matter would be back in court Apr. 1.

Mar. 12 – El Cajon City Council banned open burning of trash, leaves and fields.

Apr. 10 – Jim Snapp became the first popularly elected mayor of El Cajon.

Apr. 23 – Superior Court Judge George Lazar, for the second time in two months, ruled against those challenging Grossmont Junior College District trustees for denying permission for a Communist and a member of the John Birch Society to debate the Vietnam War. Lazar said the Grossmont board had the authority to do what it did.

Apr. 25 – El Cajon Chamber of Commerce Board acknowledged that Grossmont Junior College District trustees had the power to run the district as they see fit but argued they should be "more liberal" in applying the existing policy on campus speakers.

May 21 – The Grossmont chapter of the American Federation of Teachers renewed its plea for adoption of a salary schedule that would permit classroom teachers to earn as much as $18,000 a year.

July 11 – An 11-foot, 40-pound boa constrictor was captured on the Grossmont High School campus. It was found snoozing under a hedge 20 yards south of the science building. The snake had been stolen from Scripps.

Sept. 18 – Some Santana High School classes in Santee had to be held outside because of a space problem.

Sept. 24 – Two teen-age boys in East County had died recently from the effects of sniffing aerosol cans, prompting a community-wide meeting to discuss drug use.

Sept. 30 – A crowd of 200 listened to Carroll Waymon, executive secretary of the San Diego County Citizens Interracial Committee, address the All Faiths Interracial Advisory Council, an arm of People for People that had been started by El Cajon Chamber of Commerce to address race issues.

Oct. 1 – El Cajon was rated as having the dirtiest air in San Diego County. It had recorded 55 smoggy days since Jan. 1.

Oct. 9 – A meeting in Lakeside to discuss how to plan for orderly development of that community drew 700 residents.

Nov. 1 – El Cajon Plaza announced that it would be the first air-conditioned mall in the greater San Diego area. It was an 875,000-square-foot project on 80 acres costing $35 million.

Nov. 13 – Grossmont Junior College District trustees adopted a policy which authorized suspension, expulsion or criminal prosecution of any person who disrupted or aided in the disruption of "normal processes essential to the academic well-being of the college." *(A small group of students had threatened to set fire to a live dog as a protest against the use of napalm in Vietnam.)*

Nov. 14 – Four Black Panthers marched into Room 575 at Grossmont College, but there was no incident. Police kept a close watch on them.

Dec. 11 – The seal of the City of La Mesa was given to retired Navy Cmdr. and Mrs. Arthur "Tex" Anders who were to ask their son, William, to take it with him on his trip to the moon with two other astronauts.

Dec. 17 – Harold Hughes, superintendent-president of Grossmont Junior College District, planned to retire Aug. 1 "for personal and health reasons." He had been an educator in the area for 33 years.

Dec. 24 – Robert Burnham was named the new president of Grossmont Junior College. He had been vice president for student services and formerly principal of El Capitan High School.

Dec. 27 – North Korea released the 82-member crew of the USS Pueblo, including the executive officer, Edward R. Murphy Jr. of El Cajon.

1969

Jan. 7 – Grossmont Union High School District Board expelled 25 more students for various narcotics violations, bringing to 74 the number of students expelled since the beginning of the school year. . . . The site was selected for a new El Cajon Post Office. It will be a 3.4-acre plot at the corner of Lexington Avenue and Van Houten Avenue.

Jan. 9 – Ted Dixon, former superintendent of Cajon Valley Union School District and former associate superintendent of La Mesa-Spring Valley School District, was hired as county superintendent.

Jan. 23 – Air Force Lt. Col. William Anders, one of three astronauts to fly around the moon for the first time, was scheduled to be welcomed home and planned visits to Grossmont and Helix high schools.

Feb. 8 – Anthropologist Louis S.B. Leakey drew 2,700 to the Grossmont College gym where he predicted that the human race might become extinct unless people learned to control their capacity to destroy life.

Feb. 24 – Fire destroyed the Prevost F. Smith Parachute Manufacturing Co. on Cuyamaca Street. It had been there 22 years.

Mar. 21 – Mitchell Gilbert of San Dimas was hired as superintendent of Cajon Valley Union School District, effective Apr. 1. He replaced Ted Dixon who is the new county school superintendent.

Apr. 21 – Parent Action Council was formed in La Mesa to oust Supt. Glenn Murdock and change the sex education program in the La Mesa-Spring Valley School District.

June 2 – Attendance at Eastern San Diego County Fair, which had been in existence for 17 years, set a new record of 121,284 visitors.

June 6 – Rexford L. Hall, 75, retired from El Cajon civic life after 25 years as a trustee of Grossmont Union High School District and Grossmont Community College District, service as the city's first volunteer fire chief, president of the El Cajon Chamber of Commerce and a member of the Selective Service Board during World War II. He was manager of the W.D. Hall Co.

July 1 – Harold Hughes, 62, retired as president of Grossmont College. He arrived in the Grossmont Union High School District in 1936 as a Grossmont High School chemistry teacher, then worked as vice principal of that school, business manager of the district, assistant superintendent, deputy superintendent of Grossmont Community College District, and district superintendent and college president.

July 28 – The Fourth District Court of Appeal reversed a lower court ruling that had upheld Grossmont Community College District Board's authority to bar a Communist from participating in a campus debate. The decision represented a victory for the Open Forum Club on campus.

Aug. 29 – Tommy Buchmann of Lakeside, who clung to life for a record 124 days while in a coma with rabies, died early today at University Hospital, two days after his third birthday. He had been bitten Apr. 1 by a roaming bobcat while playing in his yard. His case drew national attention.

Sept. 11 – A suit challenging the constitutionality of Grossmont Union High School District's policy of expelling students involved in narcotics or dangerous drug offenses was filed in Superior Court. A section of the State Education Code also was challenged.

Sept. 13 – Linda Vista Baptist Bible College and Seminary was to open on a 50-acre parcel bounded by Madison Avenue, Greenfield Drive and Granite Hills Drive in southeast El Cajon. Enrollment for fall classes was 125.

Oct. 22 – Voters in Cajon Valley Union School District approved a $4 million bond issue to build a new school. Avocado School was first in line to be built.

Oct. 29 – County School Supt. Ted Dixon warned East County school districts to start work on getting unified or risk having the state Legislature dictate how schools should be organized in this area. Single-district unification was rejected in 1966 by a vote of 14,354 to 10,530.

Nov. 13 – Victor Perlo, a writer for the Communist newspaper *Daily World*, spoke to about 60 students at Grossmont College at the invitation of the student-run Open Forum Club. A court had overturned district trustees' action to keep Communists off the campus.

Nov. 17 – A car belonging to murder victim LaVelle Frost, 49, former Cajon Valley Union School District trustee and former secretary for *The Valley News* publisher, was found in a bowling alley parking lot at 5593 University Ave. Her slaying was never solved.

Dec. 10 – Santee School District voters approved a $3 million bond issue, with a margin of 84.2 percent voting yes.

Dec. 24 – National Pacific Development Corp. acquired about 10,300 acres in East County, representing all of the undeveloped real estate assets of the Ed Fletcher Co. The property consisted of 106 parcels and was appraised at $15 million. Col. Ed Fletcher came here from Massachusetts in 1888 when he was 15 and died in 1955 at 83.

Navy Lt. Cmdr. Ben Cloud of El Cajon, first black military aide to be assigned to the White House. With him are Luci Baines Johnson, youngest daughter of President Lyndon Johnson and Lady Bird, and her husband, Patrick Nugent. Cloud was 33 at the time. *Photo: Ben Cloud*

Civic leader Charles Cordell worked for
Gillespie Field development.
Photo: El Cajon Library

Ed Murphy of El Cajon was second in com-
mand of USS Pueblo when it was seized.
Photo: El Cajon Library

City Clerk Delight Swain swears in Jim
Snapp, first elected mayor of El Cajon.
Photo: San Diego History Center

Ted Dixon was superintendent of Cajon
Valley Union School District and headed
San Diego County schools.
Photo: El Cajon Library

1970-1974

Some highlights ahead:

*Grossmont High School alum wins Pulitzer Prize for spot photography.
. . . Worst wildfire in San Diego County history drives 7,000 to 10,000
people from their homes. . . . Hundreds of Hell's Angels visit El Cajon
to attend the funeral for two members shot to death in a Modesto bar.*

El Cajon City Council meeting in old building. Left to right: Al Van Zanten, George
Quidort, Jim Snapp, Bob Cornett, Dick Brown. *Photo: El Cajon Historical Society*

Realtor Glenn Mitchel ran a losing
campaign for governor of California.
Photo: El Cajon Library

Glenn Murdock, longtime superintendent
of La Mesa-Spring Valley School District.
Photo: El Cajon Library

1970

Jan. 2 – The 3,365-acre Monte Vista Ranch southeast of El Cajon was sold for $10 million to Carl Olson, owner of Olson Construction Co. of Lincoln, NE. Construction of 6,000 homes, a 100-acre industrial park and a 36-hole golf course was planned. It would be called "Rancho San Diego." Monte Vista Ranch originally was a 9,000-acre land grant known as Jamacha Rancho.

Feb. 10 – State Sen. Jack Schrade of El Cajon was elected Senate President Pro Tem, defeating the incumbent, Republican Sen. Howard Way, in a 23-12 vote....Herbert Marcuse, controversial philosophy professor at UC San Diego, was to speak twice to faculty members at Grossmont College. The Marxist professor was known as "the prophet of the New Left."

Mar. 4 – School district unification was on the table again. An ad hoc committee asked the county school superintendent's office to prepare information on all feasible alternatives to a one-district plan, which was defeated in a 1966 election. A mandatory election was required in 1972. A one-district plan would be on the ballot again unless other plans were offered. The State Board of Education had approved the one-district plan . . . . Voters approved the expansion of Grossmont Hospital by 164 beds in a new, six-story hospital wing.

Mar. 10 – El Cajon City Council approved Goulburn, Australia, as the city's first sister city.

Mar. 17 – A Santee group was trying to persuade the San Diego Chargers to put a training camp in that city.

Apr. 2 – Ninety pints of blood were used to save the life of Richard Morris, 29, who had suffered massive hemorrhaging as a result of his hemophilia and bleeding ulcers.

Apr. 15 – Incumbents Richard Brown, Al Van Zanten and George Quidort were re-elected to El Cajon City Council. Bob Helland was re-elected mayor of La Mesa; Paul Jensen and Mark Uselton won seats on the La Mesa City Council.

Apr. 17 – Monte Vista Ranch was chosen by Grossmont Community College District trustees to be the site for a new community college.

May 4 – El Cajon was declared the winner in a weeklong beautification contest with La Mesa. The payoff: El Cajon Mayor Jim Snapp got a free ride down Main Street in a trash can pushed by La Mesa Mayor Bob Helland.

May 5 – Mount Miguel High School, whose enrollment was nearing 3,000, introduced 10-period days. . . . Steve Starr, former editor of the Grossmont High School newspaper, won the Pulitzer Prize for spot news photography. While working for the Associated Press, he had snapped a photo of armed black militants leaving a Cornell University building which they had been occupying.

May 6 – Dudley "Doc" De Groot, 70, who coached the Washington Redskins to an Eastern Division title in the National Football League in 1945, died of a heart attack at his El Cajon home. He was an All-American senior at Stanford University in 1922.

May 7 – Grossmont College chose to stay open through the weekend despite Gov. Ronald Reagan's order closing state colleges and universities and his recommendation that community colleges do the same. The order came on the heels of the U.S. bombing of Cambodia and the shooting deaths of four students at Kent State University. Grossmont College was the only public higher education institution in San Diego County to remain open.

May 19 – Grossmont Union High School District changed tactics in the drug wars. A revised policy required hiring a director of student services and staff to supervise expulsion cases and mandating an education program to assist in the rehabilitation of students who were expelled for drug violations. This was the first change in three years to a policy which featured quick expulsion of students involved in drug violations.

June 30 – Grossmont College's enrollment is projected to be 12,000, nearly 3,000 more students than are provided for in the budget. The 1969-70 enrollment was about 8,000.

July 6 – Frank L. Hope and Associates, the firm which designed San Diego Stadium, was chosen to draw the plans for a second campus in the Grossmont Community College District.

July 15 – May Co. announced it would join Sears as a major tenant at Parkway Plaza.

Aug. 20 – The San Diego Chargers were to move the team's training site from UC Irvine to an area next to Mast Park in Santee.

Aug. 25 – Greater Grossmont Area Assn. recommended that La Mesa and El Cajon merge as a single city. The proposal was to include also the unincorporated areas of Grossmont-Mount Helix, Lemon Grove, Spring Valley, Casa de Oro, Santee, Lakeside, Alpine, Dehesa and Jamul-Las Flores.

Sept. 25 – Motorists revolted against a speed limit reduction from 35 mph to 25 mph on Severin Drive in La Mesa. Fifty-one cases of speeding on that street had been docketed on court calendars in El Cajon. The 35 mph limit later was restored.

Sept. 28 – The largest wildfire in San Diego County history, ignited when a falling tree snapped a power line in the Kitchen Creek area of East County, had driven an estimated 7,000 to 10,000 people from their homes and ravaged 185,000 acres. Nearly 500 homes had been lost, 115 of them in nearby Crest.

Oct. 8 – J. Clifford Wallace, a La Mesa attorney, had been nominated by President Nixon to be a U.S. District Court judge for the Southern District of California. His nomination was approved by the U.S. Senate.

Nov. 3 – Glenn Murdock, 64, superintendent of the La Mesa-Spring Valley School District, announced he would retire after 42 years as an educator, effective Sept. 1, 1971.

Nov. 4 – John Duffy was elected sheriff of San Diego County in a close race with Chief Deputy Sheriff Warren Kanagy. Ed Miller won his race to be district attorney.

Nov. 12 – An early morning fire caused $375,000 in damage to the fine arts building at Grossmont College. The fire was attributed to use of a gas-fired kiln for making ceramics.

Nov. 24 – Reclaimed water was running through its own pipe for the first time in Santee. It was delivered to Mast Park, to a 28-acre complex of the Santee Youth Assn. and to a tree farm owned by Carlton-Santee Corp.

Dec. 9 – A La Mesa police officer was to be disciplined for comments he made about blacks at a shoplifting clinic. The Coalition of Black Organizations Against Racism took the matter to the City Council. The offending police officer was later suspended for three days, reprimanded and assigned other duties.

1971

Jan. 4 – State Sen. Jack Schrade, R-El Cajon, was deposed as president pro tem of the State Senate. He was beaten by State Sen. James Mills, D-San Diego.

Jan. 5 – The federal government offered 76 acres of surplus Camp Elliott property in the Santee area to the Grossmont Union High School District.

Jan. 8 – City workers were chopping down trees and pulling up sidewalks in El Cajon to lessen pedestrian mishaps. About 250 trees had been cut down in the previous three years. Many of the trees that had been planted in the parkways were the wrong kind, causing bulges in sidewalks.

Feb. 19 – Enrollment was 10,741 at Grossmont College, a 33 percent jump from the previous year. This gave rise to consideration of year-round operation, more off-campus classes, lengthening of the instruction day and Saturday classes.

Mar. 4 – The Rev. Carl McIntire, a fundamentalist radio preacher and promoter of "Marches for Victory" in Vietnam, took control of Linda Vista Baptist Bible College as a training base for "Christian Warriors." The college was to be renamed the Southern California Reformation College. The 50-acre site in southeast El Cajon previously had been a Catholic seminary.

Apr. 27 – El Cajon City Council voted to pay $1,385 a month to subsidize riders going to downtown San Diego on the bus. The subsidy was made necessary by a threat from San Diego Transit Corp. to discontinue service to El Cajon. Riders were paying 90 cents for a one-way trip.

May 4 – Valhalla was chosen as the name of Grossmont Union High School District's ninth high school. Trustee Portia Goode voted against that name because it didn't conform to the tradition of naming schools for their locales. Goode favored "Sequan," the name of a nearby mountain. . . . La Mesa-Spring Valley School District trustees voted to start a pilot year-round plan for their schools.

May 19 – The San Diego Chargers were to begin using a training camp in La Mesa. A plan to put a training camp for the team in Santee had fizzled.

May 21 – The California Highway Commission voted $500,000 for the Baltimore Avenue overcrossing project in La Mesa. That project's cost was $1.8 million.

June 18 – The City of El Cajon announced the start of a sewer service charge on July 1. The minimum bill was to be $1 plus 20 percent of a residence's water bill. It was expected each family residence would be sent a bi-monthly sewer service bill of between $2.80 and $7.

July 6 – Seventh- and eighth-graders at La Presa Junior High School in Spring Valley made state history by returning to classes, giving up their summer vacation. La Presa was the first school in California to have seventh- and eighth-graders on a year-round schedule.

Aug. 6 – The board of People for People, an El Cajon human relations group, voted to send a letter to El Cajon Elks Lodge asking that organization to delete the "white only" clause from its membership rules.

Sept. 28 – A care center for dogs was being discussed as a way to solve the "dog problem" at Grossmont College. Dr. Dale Burke, a trustee, had raised the issue of roaming dogs on campus while their masters or mistresses were attending classes. He estimated there were 20 to 25 dogs on campus at any given time.

Oct. 6 – Vandals desecrated the sanctuary of the Apostolic Church of Faith in Jesus Christ at 514 S. Third St. in El Cajon. The predominantly Mexican-American congregation had experienced three years of intimidation by outside groups. The matter was to be taken to El Cajon City Council.

Oct. 15 – Norman Casserly, an Irish immigrant who claimed to have delivered 3,500 babies over a span of nearly 25 years, was appealing a Superior Court ruling that he stop such deliveries because he didn't have a license. The state stopped issuing licenses for midwives in 1949.

Oct. 20 – Voters defeated a $19.5 million bond issue for Grossmont Union High School District intended for expanding facilities for a growing enrollment.

Nov. 3 – Pete Wilson, 38, who represented parts of East County in the state Assembly, won his race for mayor of San Diego, a job that paid $12,000 a year.

Nov. 5 – El Cajon vaulted to second place among the county's cities in the collection of sales tax revenue. Its take for 1970 was $144.3 million. Chula Vista was third with $133.6 million.

Nov. 17 – El Cajon City Council voted unanimously on 10 separate resolutions and recommendations, paving the way for development of a "Super Block" to spur downtown revitalization.

Nov. 26 – Grossmont Post Office closed its doors after 59 years of service. At the end, it delivered mail to 208 boxholders.

Dec. 1 – Sacred Heart's schools – Greenfield Hills Elementary and High School – were to close at the end of the school year because of looming deficits. The 31-acre campus at 2100 Greenfield Drive served 318 students.

Dec. 10 – San Diego County Board of Education approved a three-way split of Grossmont Union High School District in the latest attempt at unification. The plan had to be submitted to the State Board of Education for its approval. Opposition to the plan was intense.

1972

Jan. 5 – El Cajon City Council voted to oppose all forms of racial discrimination where color is used as the "sole criteria" for membership in any organization. The action avoided direct censure of El Cajon Elks Lodge which had a "white only" membership rule.

Jan. 14 – The State Board of Education voted unanimously for a three-district unification plan for school districts within Grossmont Union High School District. The plan was to go on the June ballot.

Jan. 18 – Leon Lee, 73, co-owner of Main Street Liquor at 401 Cedar St., was shot to death in a robbery witnessed by his wife, Helen. El Cajon police arrested two of three suspects early in March, but they were freed Mar. 14 because of insufficient evidence. The store was the victim of several robberies before and after the shooting.

Mar. 1 – Democrat lawyer Bob Wilson of El Cajon scored an upset victory over favored Republican Jim Ashcraft for a seat in the state Assembly representing the 76th Assembly District. Wilson succeeded Republican Pete Wilson who had won his race to be mayor of San Diego. *(The Wilsons were not related, nor were they related to U.S. Rep. Bob Wilson.)*

Apr. 12 – Mayor Jim Snapp survived an unexpectedly strong showing by antiques dealer Paul Kress to win a second term as El Cajon mayor. Paul Fordem and George Bailey won seats on the La Mesa City Council.

Apr. 26 – El Cajon City Council voted to match $800,000 collected by the Grossmont Community College District for an auditorium on condition the facility be placed in the city's proposed downtown superblock.

Apr. 28 – The State Air Resources Board said it was unhealthy to live in El Cajon for 123 days in 1971 because of air pollution.

May 8 – An estimated 10,000 people were drawn to the Grossmont College campus during a four-day Pleasure Faire featuring Renaissance food, costumes, games, music and jousts.

May 23 – Gov. Ronald Reagan signed a bill appropriating $957,742 for the purchase of a 165-acre site southeast of El Cajon for a second community college campus, which ultimately became Cuyamaca College.

July 13 – El Cajon City Council voted to establish an affirmative action program for hiring, a recommendation of the city's Human Relations Commission.

July 14 – Work had started on the Pine Valley Bridge on Interstate 8, a $10 million project. The tallest column rose 450 feet from the creek bed below.

July 17 – El Cajon's taxable retail sales soared to $44 million in the first quarter of 1972, more than $8 million above sales recorded over the first three months of 1971.

July 25 – Grossmont Union High School District trustees voted 3-2 to approve construction of a major portion of Valhalla High School. The $4.2 million school was expected to enroll 1,200 ninth-graders.

Aug. 15 – Grossmont Community College District Board approved the purchase of a 165-acre site southeast of El Cajon for its second college at $7,500 an acre. The state's share of the $1.2 million cost of the land had been authorized in a $957,742 allocation. The $20 million project was expected to be completed by fall of 1976.

Aug. 16 – Probate Court accepted the city's bid to purchase the historic Knox Hotel at Magnolia and Lexington avenues from the estate of S.H. Mathews, owner, for $4,500. The building was to be moved to Judson Park on N. Magnolia Avenue.

Sept. 13 – Planning and design of a fire training facility on city-owned industrial land was to begin. Lemon Grove had bowed out of the partnership, but La Mesa, Santee, Lakeside and Spring Valley remain as participants with the City of El Cajon. The multi-use facility is to have a communication center, an expanded animal shelter and be the city's largest fire station.

Nov. 8 – El Cajon City Councilman Dick Brown defeated Gene French to represent the Second Supervisorial District. He had the endorsement of San Diego Mayor Pete Wilson.

1973

Jan. 2 – El Cajon and La Mesa announced that 1972 was the biggest year in their histories for new construction. El Cajon's total for the year was $46,198,050; La Mesa's, $19,295,900.

Jan. 9 – For the first time, an elected student representative was given a seat on the Grossmont Union High School District Board. It was a non-voting position, but the student spoke on behalf of the entire student body.

Jan. 11 – A stone monument was erected at the junction of Buckman Springs Road and Oak Drive near Morena Village in East County to commemorate Charles M. ("The Rainmaker") Hatfield, who was hired by San Diego City Council on Jan. 1, 1916, to end the region-wide drought and fill Morena Reservoir. The Hatfields (brothers Charlie and Paul) built a 24-foot-tall wooden tower, released their chemical potion into the air and the result was 40 inches of rain at Lake Morena and the historic flood of 1916 in which 15 people died. Charlie was to have received $10,000, but he got nothing because of the devastation. A court ruled that the flood was an act of God. The Hatfield brothers stopped making rain in 1930 and opened a Singer sewing machine shop in Glendale.

Jan. 22 – Abraham "Abe" Weinstock, who served an unexpired term on the El Cajon City Council in the 1920s and once worked for the Associated Press, died at 96. He had moved here in 1919 and purchased C.C. Clark's Merchandise Store. Abe was credited with pushing for trees to be planted along Main Street and for sidewalks and curbs to be installed. When he retired in 1955, his son, Paul, operated an electric supply store and hearing aid business in what became known as the Weinstock Building.

Feb. 23 – Scott Memorial Baptist Church in San Diego paid $1.3 million for the 31-acre Convent of the Sacred Heart, which had closed a year earlier because of financial difficulties. The property would become the site for the church, Christian High School and Christian Heritage College.

Feb. 26 – Pancontinental Enterprises, Inc. of El Cajon announced plans to produce electricity and desalinated water by harnessing ocean waves. The company said 1,750 of its giant power wheels could produce enough electricity to supply the entire United States.

Apr. 27 – Grossmont Community College District Board voted 4-1 to join with the City of El Cajon to build an auditorium in the downtown super-block. Trustee William Faulwetter was the lone opponent. He called the project a "Mickey Mouse" venture.

June 20 – El Cajon leaders were proclaiming their fiscal savvy by noting that the tax rate for this fiscal year – $1.28 per $100 of assessed valuation – was lower than the $1.35 per $100 of assessed valuation levied in 1919. The City Council cut the rate another three cents – to $1.25 – on June 28.

July 28 – The home of a black Air Force sergeant and his family in Santee was splattered with eggs. Sgt. Donald Rowley and his wife have four children. He was stationed with the 751st Air Defense Group at Mt. Laguna Tracking Station.

Aug. 7 – An editorial tribute was printed in *The Daily Californian* for Florence "Flossie" Beadle of Lakeside who had died recently at 71. In the late '50s, the editorial said, "Mrs. Beadle plopped her canvas chair in the path of a trenching machine and refused to budge until the trees she wanted saved were given sanctuary." When county planners wanted to move the boathouse and bridge from Lindo Lake, the editorial continued, "Mrs. Beadle threatened to use her double-barreled shotgun if insensitive bureaucrats attempted to destroy the landmark." The confrontation ended in a compromise. The editorial concluded: "Flossie Beadle, marching to the beat of a different drummer, made a lasting impact on her community. She proved again that one person, with right on her side, can pierce the armor of the establishment – and win. Her life should be an inspiration to us all."

Aug. 9 – County supervisors voted for a compromise that enabled Edgemoor Hospital in Santee to continue operating with a sharply reduced population. The hospital for the county's indigents served 425 patients, but that number was to be reduced to between 120 and 180. . . . William M. Bowlin, 74, a naval aviator for 31 years and one of two men credited with saving the life of Adm. Richard Byrd during a scientific expedition in Antarctica, died in Lemon Grove. He held the Navy's Distinguished Flying Cross for his participation in the Antarctica expedition.

Aug. 20 – An attempt by a group of El Cajon businessmen to start a new bank was vetoed by State Banking Supt. Donald Pearson, who ruled that economic conditions were not conducive to a successful new banking venture. Mayor Jim Snapp and City Councilman Howard Pierce had been proposed as potential bank directors.

Sept. 17 – Walter Ballard, 77, of Lakeside, who claimed he suffered a light stroke at a hearing on Edgemoor Hospital where smoking was permitted, announced he was taking his anti-smoking campaign to the county grand jury.

Sept. 26 – The City of La Mesa inaugurated a $3 million trial for free bus service. The experiment was to cost the city less than $500 a month.

Oct. 4 – Drivers were warned to fill their gas tanks immediately because 400 gas stations in the San Diego area were threatening to close for four days. The station owners were protesting the federal government's Phase IV price controls.

Nov. 8 – Portia "Peg" Goode, longtime high school and community college trustee, received the M. Dale Ensign Award in New Orleans as the outstanding community college trustee in the nation for 1973. She was a member of the Grossmont Community College District Board.

Nov. 14 – Hundreds of Hells Angels members roared into El Cajon on their motorcycles to attend the funerals of Michael Varner, 28, of El Cajon and his brother, John, 30, of Santee. Both were shot to death in a Modesto bar while en route to San Diego. Michael was president of the El Cajon and San Diego chapters of Hells Angels.

Nov. 30 – El Cajon was about to begin a "grand experiment" in public transit. El Cajon Express would offer 50-cent taxi rides funded by $25,000 in federal revenue sharing money.

Dec. 4 – The City of El Cajon and the county entered a joint powers agreement to build a six-story city hall and adjacent council chamber. The top two floors of city hall were to be leased to the county.

Dec. 5 – El Cajon City Council voted to allow the county to build a $4.5 million experimental solid waste recovery plant on 5.3 acres of industrial land fronting on Bradley Avenue and adjacent to Gillespie Field. (*The experiment failed and eventually the plant was dismantled.*)

1974

Jan. 2 – Chaparral High School was preparing to open in new structures early in February at 1600 Cuyamaca St., abandoning decrepit World War II military quonset huts that had been the instructional site for continuation students. The $1.1 million project would serve 425 students.

Jan. 4 – Glenn Mitchel, local Realtor, announced he would be a candidate for the Republican nomination for governor of California. "Pray for America" and "Back to the Bible" were to be two of his slogans.

Jan. 8 – Parkway Plaza in El Cajon reported that it served more than 14 million customers in its first year. At its opening in 1972, the prediction was for 10 million customers for the inaugural year.

Feb. 22 – Grossmont Community College District trustees voted 4-1 in favor of a plan to put a 1,200-seat auditorium in the downtown superblock, with the cost shared by the City of El Cajon and the college district. Furnishings were to be purchased with a $500,000 fund-raising drive in the community.

Feb. 28 – A memorial plaque was dedicated at Grossmont College for four criminology students killed in a plane crash near Descanso. Names on the plaque were Reese Boldrick, 21; Grant Cunningham, 23; Stephen Stoffregen, 23; and James Morgan, 23.

May 14 – Dick Lee of Santee, 66, was named the Outstanding Democrat of San Diego County for 1973 by the County Democratic Central Committee. He had been involved in Democratic campaigns since working for the election of Franklin Delano Roosevelt as president in Rochester, N.Y.

May 15 – The El Cajon City Council authorized spending $200,000 to buy enough land so the county could build a governmental complex in the downtown superblock.

May 16 – A proposed $100 million condominium project for Rattlesnake Mountain, adding 5,000 people to the area, drew hostile reaction from 100 residents who signed petitions opposing the venture. A few days later, 400 gathered at Pepper Drive Elementary School to oppose the development of 1,800 dwellings on the mountain.

June 5 – Voters passed Proposition E with a 51.5 percent majority, enough to reinstate 29 professional employees, mostly teachers, in the Grossmont Union High School District. The vote added $2.3 million to the district's revenue base, which also saved interscholastic athletics, extracurricular activities and bonuses for coaches.

June 20 – Sharisse Krohn, 25, was cited for keeping "ferocious beasts" – the snakes she used in her dance routine at Boot Hill Bar in Santee. She had to pay $10 per snake to retrieve them from a county animal shelter. Krohn used as many as seven snakes in her act, including boa constrictors, a Burmese python and a New Jersey pine snake.

June 24 – John Weymiller, owner of Jonny Industries at 766 Gable Way, paid his 22 employees in Eisenhower dollars on their last payday. It took about 8,000 clinks of the metallic dollars to make the payment which Weymiller said was a way to show his employees how much they surrendered each payday to the government.

July 9 – Ben and Jim Polak, partners with Coldwell Banker Fund in Community Development Co., won exclusive bargaining rights for redevelopment of 24.4 acres of downtown La Mesa property. The City Council's vote was 3-2....Sharisse Krohn opened a second night club act with her snakes at the In Crowd in Santee. She claimed one of the snakes was wheezing after being released from a county animal shelter. Water and medicine apparently restored the snake to good health.

July 17 – El Cajon Police Officer James Reese declined to accept a 10-year service award from Mayor Jim Snapp, citing his disenchantment with department procedures for handling the grievances of officers. . . . A *Daily Californian* editorial noted that 800 residents of Santee and Lakeside had signed a petition to the San Diego County Board of Supervisors protesting the showing of X-rated movies at Santee Drive-in Theater. What was shown on the screen could be easily seen from nearby roadways.

July 22 – Frank Buck, 36, part owner of Buck Knives, Inc. at 1717 N. Magnolia Ave., died of injuries suffered in a one-car crash July 2.

Aug. 2 – La Mesa Mayor J. Robert Helland pleaded *nolo contendre* to charges of violating the State Election Code while opposing Councilman Paul Jensen's re-election. His plea was equivalent to an admission of guilt. He was accused of failing to properly report campaign contributions.

Aug. 19 – A massive earth slide on a hill at 1601 Galway Place in Fletcher Hills threatened the home of William and Ruth Bucker. An estimated 15,000 tons of dirt were displaced by the slide. The house was not damaged, but a buttress had to be built to protect it.

Aug. 28 – La Mesa Mayor J. Robert Helland resigned Aug. 27, just before he was fined $1,000 and sentenced to three years of probation for his part in working to defeat La Mesa Councilman Paul Jensen in what was determined to be a violation of state election laws.

Sept. 11 – City Councilman Paul Fordem was appointed mayor-designate to serve the final years in the term of former Mayor J. Robert Helland, who had resigned.

Sept. 30 – El Cajon Express, the taxi service funded mainly by taxpayers, recorded its 100,000th passenger since the program started 10 months earlier. The total cost was $118,000. Taxi drivers had amassed 149,000 miles.

Sept. 23 – El Cajon Mayor Jim Snapp, 50, who suffered a major heart attack Aug. 8, asked to be kept on the job despite his illness. The City Council voted to continue his employment until Nov. 12.

Oct. 14 – Carl Eder, 32, convicted of committing the worst mass slaying in San Diego County history at the time, walked away from his unsupervised job at the minimum security California Correctional Institution near Tehachapi. When he was 16, Eder slaughtered five members of the Pendergast family in their El Cajon home on Dec. 12, 1958.

Oct. 18 – Joe O'Connor, who was El Cajon's police chief for 11 years before winning election as sheriff of San Diego County, died at his El Cajon home. He was 59. O'Connor was sheriff from 1963 to 1971.

Dec. 8 – San Diego County's unemployment rate hit 10.3 percent, the highest rate recorded in three years.

Steve Starr, a graduate of Grossmont High School, won a Pulitzer Prize for photography. *Photo: Grossmont High School Museum*

Florence Beadle of Lakeside had a reputation as a fierce defender of the environment. Here she sits on her chair in the path of a bulldozer taking down trees. *Photo: San Diego History Center*

Rubble left by raging wildfire in 1970. *Photo: El Cajon Library*

1975-1979

Some highlights ahead:

Superblock dig in El Cajon unearths mastodon tusk. . . . Son, 12, lifts Impala off his pinned dad. . . . Landmark Communications, Inc. buys The El Cajon Californian. . . . East County residents among fatalities in PSA crash in San Diego.

Lucille Moore was the first woman elected to the El Cajon City Council and the first woman to chair the San Diego County Board of Supervisors.
Photo: City of El Cajon

Peggy Eddy, first woman president of the El Cajon Chamber of Commerce.
Photo: El Cajon Library

Wallace Cohen, first president of Cuyamaca College. *Photo: Grossmont-Cuyamaca Community College District*

Joe Roth, a Granite Hills High School alum, was a standout quarterback for UC Berkeley. He died of cancer at 21.
Photo: El Cajon Library

1975

Jan. 6. – M.H. Golden Construction Co. of San Diego submitted the lowest of five bids for construction of the new El Cajon City Hall and City Council chamber. Its bid was $4,828,000, about $600,000 below architect Art Decker's estimate of $5,428,834.

Jan. 8 – The Rev. Warren Briggs, pastor of Chapel of the Valley United Methodist Church in El Cajon, advocated that suicide should be accepted by society as an option for people suffering from terminal illness.

Jan. 9 – Mel Crain, a San Diego State University political science professor who lived in Harbison Canyon, set off a national uproar with his disclosure that the Central Intelligence Agency in the 1950s opened and read first-class letters sent to some American citizens. Crain, who had been in the Covert Operations Office of the CIA, was bombarded with calls from national newspapers, TV and radio stations and Reuters, a major news-gathering organization in Great Britain. On March 21, 1975, Crain testified about the mail opening before the House Judiciary Committee.

Jan. 20 – A Utotem store clerk, James D, Reed, 38, was shot and killed during a robbery at a store where he was working just off Highway 67 on Morena Avenue in Lakeside. He had been at the store for two months.

Feb. 3 – Mass murderer Carl Eder, who killed five members of an El Cajon family in 1958 when he was a teen-ager and walked away from a minimum security prison in Tehachapi in October 1974, was a suspect in the grisly "slasher" slayings in Los Angeles. Nine Skid Row residents in Los Angeles had been slashed to death and had their throats cut. L.A. police denied Eder was a suspect, but an El Cajon police officer confirmed that LAPD had called here to inquire about the escapee. *(Los Angeles police on Feb. 4 booked a 45-year-old transient named Theodore Lane for investigation into the nine slasher slayings in that city.)*

Feb. 14 – The remains of an ancient village, believed to be more than 900 years old, were discovered near Singing Hills Country Club at the site of a $450,000 tennis club and motel expansion project. The village, called Malamo, was occupied by Kumeyaay Indians sometime after 1000 A.D.

Mar. 10 – A memorial service was planned at United Methodist Church in Mission Valley for Lewis F. Smith, 68, former superintendent of Grossmont Union High School District, who died Mar. 7. Smith worked for the district for 23 years during which time the number of high schools increased from one to seven and enrollment surged from 1,500 to 14,000. Smith had retired July 1, 1964, because of ill health.

Mar. 12 – Ground was broken Mar. 11 for the new $4.8 million superblock in downtown El Cajon.

Mar. 20 – Bulldozers a day earlier had started razing the 78-year-old W.D. Hall Co. building on Main Street to make room for the construction of a new civic center complex. The city paid $1.1 million for the pioneer lumber company's property.

Mar. 31 – Marjorie Berg, 45, ill with terminal cancer, related to *The Daily Californian* how she had checked herself into an El Cajon motel, barricaded the door and swallowed 22 Seconal tablets in an attempt to end her life. She was rescued and now works for "the liberty to die." Her story was sent around the world by Associated Press. Berg reported receiving more than 600 letters in response to the story.

Apr. 9 – John C. O'Laughlin, a bachelor recluse who lived near Santa Barbara and died Aug. 15, 1973, left his entire estate worth $250,000 to the Home of Guiding Hands in Lakeside.

Apr. 11 – Carl Colombo, 19, a student at Grossmont College, is recovering at Kaiser Hospital in La Mesa from severe wounds suffered in a brutal attack in the tropical jungle of southern Mexico. Colombo had wandered for four months alone in the region without any trouble. When he crossed from Guatemala into Mexico, hostile Indians seized him, stripped him naked, used a machete to make deep cuts in his scalp and left him to die. Friendly Indians gave him food and persuaded a truck driver to take him to safety. Albert Colombo, his father and an assistant professor of geography at San Diego State University, flew to Mexico and brought him home.

Apr. 24 – The tusk of a mastodon believed to be between 15,000 and 20,000 years old was unearthed at the excavation site for the downtown El Cajon superblock. It measured 42 inches. The San Diego Natural History Museum sent a representative to the site. He took the tusk with him.

Apr. 25 – Three men entered a Bank of America branch at 845 N. Second St. in El Cajon, herded employees into a room, cut phone lines and escaped in the bank manager's car, which was later found abandoned near a city fire station. The robbers took $24,000 from the vault.

Apr. 28 – Sam Siciliano, 53, a popular humor columnist for *The Daily Californian* for 10 years, was killed Apr. 27 in a traffic accident north of

Escondido on Highway 395. He was en route to Elsinore for a card game when a vehicle crossed the center divider and crashed into his car.

May 21 – Grossmont Community College District trustees voted 3-2 on a financing plan that allows joint construction of a downtown auditorium with the City of El Cajon to move forward. The vote raised the community service tax by 2.1 cents per $100 of assessed valuation.

May 28 – El Cajon Police Department hired its first female patrol officer. She is Sandra Archer, 34, mother of two who attended college for two years and had worked as a secretary and bookkeeper.

June 24 – Two Pacific black brant goslings emerged from their shells in Ron Vavra's yard in east El Cajon, marking the first births of the wild goose in captivity on the North American continent. Vavra, assistant track coach at Grossmont College, and Dick Lantz, a biology instructor there, had started the conservation project seven years earlier. They obtained some brant eggs from the Alaska tundra.

July 2 – El Cajon attorney Don Meloche began his defense of Danny Altstadt, charged with the hatchet slayings of his father, William, 45; his mother, Maxine, 41; and his sister, Nancy, 19, in their San Carlos area home. Meloche, who later was appointed a Superior Court judge, portrayed the father, an aerospace worker at General Dynamics, as a rigid, unbending father who drove Daniel Kent Alstadt to the brink of madness and, finally, to murder. Danny, an honor student and Eagle Scout, set fire to his family's home and also assaulted his younger brother, Gary, with a hatchet, leaving him paralyzed. Danny pleaded innocent by reason of insanity but was convicted and sent to state prison where he committed suicide. Meloche maintained that Danny's treatment by his father caused him to withdraw and become schizophrenic.

July 17 – Property owners were reacting angrily to notices that their property had been reassessed, which meant higher taxes. County Assessor E.C. Williams reported receiving 2,545 phone calls and an average of 10 letters a day.

July 23 – El Cajon City Council voted unanimously to ban smoking in buses, elevators, supermarkets, grocery stores, theaters, City Council chambers and other places. The ordinance exempted restaurants.

Aug. 14 – Elaine Taylor, 7, missing for five days, was found alive near a county refuse site at Otay Lake, about 15 miles from her Spring Valley home where she was abducted. A Mexican alien, 19, who had done yard work for Mrs. Taylor about three months earlier, was charged with several crimes against the girl as well as kidnapping and burglary. Elaine's father, Dr. Philip Taylor, was an El Cajon dentist.

Sept. 26 – El Cajon Mayor Jim Snapp and La Mesa Mayor Paul Fordem agreed to co-chair a community fund-raising drive to raise $366,000 for seats and furnishings for the community auditorium to be constructed in El Cajon's superblock.

Oct. 13 – Gary Forster, 25, father of three and brother of Chicago White Sox pitcher Terry Forster, was fatally stabbed at Boot Hill Bar in Santee while attending a bachelor party for a friend. Three other bar patrons suffered stab wounds during the fracas. Sheriff's officers booked Donald R. McCoy, 21, for the slaying.

Oct. 16 – Greater Grossmont Federation of Teachers adopted a resolution to recall Grossmont Union High School District trustees William Funke and Joseph Drew, alleging their actions were damaging education in the district.

Nov. 5 – El Cajon Mayor Jim Snapp announced that he would not run for re-election. He had suffered a major heart attack 15 months earlier.

Nov. 6 – County supervisors voted unanimously to submit allegations made by Lakeside resident Dick White regarding the death of Michael Nolan, 27, to the grand jury. Nolan died of a skull fracture six days after his arrest July 12 following an incident at a Santee bar. Nolan had fled the bar and was chased by a deputy who struck him with a flashlight when Nolan resisted arrest. White's investigation led him to conclude the original grand jury, which declined to charge the deputy, had been deceived.

Nov. 7 – El Cajon acquired its second sister city, a small municipality in the Black Forest region of West Germany named Sulzfeld. The German American Society of San Diego, headquartered in El Cajon, led the effort to make Sulzfeld a sister city.

Nov. 14 – The oldest dairy in San Diego County, which started in Mission Valley in 1885 and was moved to El Cajon in 1957, announced it would go out of business. Owners of the 43-acre dairy in the Hillsdale section of rural El Cajon cited rising feed costs, marginal profits and unnecessary harassment by regulatory agencies as reasons for closing.

Dec. 3 – Cancer victim Marjorie Berg, 45, who from her bed had led a worldwide drive for the right of terminally ill individuals to commit suicide, died at her El Cajon home. The Associated Press had carried her story to the rest of the world.

Dec. 9 – Sgt. Jerry Hancock, 32, a 10-year veteran of the El Cajon Police Department, was arrested for the alleged burglary of a San Diego barbershop on El Cajon Boulevard.

Dec. 16 – The appointment of G. Dennis Adams, 34, to El Cajon Municipal Court, was described as a "political payoff" for his help in getting Democrat Bob Wilson elected as an assemblyman in 1972. The charge was made by Barry Soper, who served as Wilson's campaign manager in the special election.

Dec. 19 – The San Diego County grand jury let stand an earlier decision that cleared two sheriff's deputies of criminal conduct in the July 17 death of Michael G. Nolan in the aftermath of an incident at a Santee bar.

1976

Jan. 2 – On *The Daily Californian's* editorial page, El Cajon Mayor James Snapp and Santee Fire Chief Elmer Snelson debated the issue of which city should be allowed to annex Gillespie Field. The City of El Cajon eventually won that battle.

Jan. 6 – *The Daily Californian* ran a front-page story about a group of people, mostly young, who claimed to be followers of The Two and who were longing to leave planet Earth in spaceships. Members of the group had been camping at an East County park.

Jan. 22 – Doctors at Grossmont Hospital joined others in the state in a "work slowdown" to protest the high cost of malpractice insurance. Rates for specialists were running from $3,000 to $4,000 a year.

Jan. 24 – Sherri Stout, 17, of Alpine, is the first girl from the Grossmont Union High School District to be recommended for appointment to a military academy. Stout, an honor student at El Capitan High School in Lakeside, chose to attend the Army college at West Point.

Jan. 29 – Dick Mummert, once part-owner of Marck Motors in El Cajon, is to be sentenced Mar. 1 on felony heroin traffic violations. Testimony in court revealed that he had drifted into heroin trafficking to raise money for a new dealership in east El Cajon.

Feb. 5 – A campaign has been launched to raise $380,000 to furnish the East County Performing Arts Center that is under construction in downtown El Cajon. The facility will seat 1,200.

Feb. 11 – Former El Cajon police Sgt. Jerry Hancock, 32, will be sentenced Mar. 31 for a single burglary to which he pleaded guilty. By confessing, he cleared 163 burglaries or attempted burglaries off the books that he had been suspected of committing.

Feb. 23 – Hang glider Steve Spurlock, 29, of Alpine, was killed when his glider plunged to the ground during the 10th annual Gillespie Field Aircade. Witnesses said Spurlock apparently failed to release the tow cord while being towed by a specially equipped van. Spurlock's glider dropped between 200 and 350 feet.

Mar. 1 – Anjac Plastics Division of Reed Irrigation Systems will be relocated from El Monte to El Cajon after construction of one of the largest manufacturing plants in the city's industrial complex. The announcement said the manufacturing plant would be built on 3.5 acres at Bradley and Marshall avenues and will contain 64,164 square feet of space, making it one of the five or six largest plants in El Cajon. . . . Ricky Grill, 12, of Santee, wasn't allowed to lift more than 60 pounds from his weightlifting set, but when a jack broke under the front end of a Chevrolet Impala and pinned his father to the ground, Ricky rushed to the car and raised the front end just enough (six to eight inches) so his father, William, could roll free. The elder Grill suffered a cut on his neck, a split lip and an ankle sprain. Ricky weighs 135 pounds, is 5 feet 4 inches tall and in the seventh grade. He tried to lift the car several times after the incident but couldn't.

Mar. 3 – El Cajon Councilman Bob Cornett was elected the city's mayor by swamping rest home owner Don Coulson, a World War II veteran who spent time in a Nazi prisoner-of-war camp. George Bailey and Walt Slater were elected to the La Mesa City Council.

Mar. 25 – Esther Rachel Weinstock, 97, who came to El Cajon with her husband, Abe, in 1919, died Mar. 24. Born in New York in 1878, she and Abe purchased a general store near Main Street and Prescott Avenue in 1919, operating it until their retirement. Mrs. Weinstock worked with the El Cajon Progress Club, forerunner of El Cajon Woman's Club. Abe Weinstock served briefly on the El Cajon City Council.

Mar. 30 – U.S. Border Patrol agents working out of Gillespie Field apprehended 1,957 illegal aliens during March, setting a record for that month.

Mar. 31 – Attorney Robert Andreen, a Grossmont Union High School District trustee since 1971, was indicted by the county grand jury on conspiracy and bribery charges in connection with alleged bribes in the form of political campaign contributions. Andreen, 49, was named in a two-count indictment along with another El Cajon resident, E. Dene Armstrong, 35, a member of the county planning commission from 1972 to 1974 and president of Fringe Benefit Administration Services, Inc. of San Diego.

Apr. 2 – Robert Andreen and E. Dene Armstrong were among 17 persons, including nine from East County, who were to be arraigned on federal charges related to alleged embezzlement of money held in trust for 6,000 members of a construction union. *(Their earlier indictments had nothing to do with the subsequent filing of federal charges.)* The two men were charged with embezzling about $500,000 from the trust since 1970.

Apr. 14 – Ruth Norman of El Cajon, the 75-year-old leader of Unarius, made headlines around the world by wagering $4,000 with Ladbroke & Co. in London that aliens would land a spaceship in San Diego County in 1976. Norman claims to have established psychic contact with 59 different universes.

Apr. 21 – Steve Jones, 20, a Grossmont College student who lives in La Mesa, won first place in the Lincoln-Douglas debate competition at the National Junior College Speech Assn. tournament in Chicago. He also took second place in impromptu speaking.

Apr. 30 – Dehesa School District was preparing to celebrate its 100th anniversary with a parade, singing, cake walk, square dancing and a pie-eating contest.

May 17 – When two male customers left the Utotem market on Morena Avenue in Lakeside without paying for beer they took, clerk Patrick McCollough fired shots with his pistol at the mag tires on the robbers' truck. CHP officers J.E. Lawson and J.D. Danischen heard the shots, went in search of the suspect vehicle and found it with two flat tires on Willow Road. The occupants were arrested.

May 26 – An eight-part series on the gay subculture in the San Diego area began appearing in *The Daily Californian*, whose staff member researched and wrote the articles after being challenged to do so by a leader of the gay community who argued the local media were biased.

May 28 – Community fund-raising to furnish the East County Performing Arts Center had nearly reached the $100,000 mark. The goal was to raise $380,000.

June 1 – Hoby Erickson of Descanso, chief of that community's volunteer fire department and owner of its Lodestone Café, was planning to reenact his own version of the American colonists' tea party by walking from the county administration building to San Diego Bay harbor at high noon July 4 and then tossing a tea bag into the water. The burly Swede believes he is unfairly taxed and inadequately represented by the county's Board of Supervisors.

June 2 – James Earl Carter III, 26, better known as Chip, came to El Cajon while campaigning for his father, Jimmy, the Georgia peanut farmer and former governor who is running for the Democratic presidential nomination. Chip was interviewed for a story that appeared in *The El Cajon Californian.*

June 5 – Henry Elwood Fleming, 26, of Santee, was sentenced to life in state prison for molesting and murdering 12-year-old Richard Herzig, also of Santee. The boy was abducted by Fleming while he was playing with two of his cousins and 10 days later his body was found in the San Diego River not far from his home. Fleming had been released from Atascadero State Hospital in 1974 after 14 months of treatment as a sex offender.

June 8 – A Vietnamese couple and their nine children were about to observe the first anniversary of their escape from Saigon after the Communist takeover of their homeland. Xuong Nguyen, 53, brought his wife and children to El Cajon where he now works as a custodian for the First Presbyterian Church. The family lives in a house on church property. . . . Owners of The Green Bamboo, a restaurant offering Vietnamese and Chinese food at the corner of Mollison and Washington avenues, worried they no longer will be able to operate their business. Twice the victims of burglary, most recently Dan and Ha Nguyen had to deal with an arsonist's fire that caused $10,000 in damage and a notice from building owner William Sharpe of North Carolina asking them to move out.

June 9 – Santee voters decisively rejected incorporation for their city in the June 8 election. Voters opposing cityhood racked up more than 75 percent of the vote for their position. . . . A 14-year-old boy held sheriff's deputies at bay for nearly two hours June 8 by firing more than 30 rounds with a sawed-off rifle from a canyon hideout near Crest. An argument with his sister apparently led to the standoff. A sheriff's department helicopter participated in the boy's arrest. Family members said the boy has a mental problem.

July 23 – Paul Nanney, 32, of El Cajon, failed in his attempt to set a new globe-circling record for light aircraft. His $15,000 plane, out of gas, went down in frigid waters off the coast of Alaska. Nanney's flight started May 13 from Gillespie Field and had successfully navigated through monsoons between Rangoon and Singapore.

July 29 – El Cajon Mayor Bob Cornett said he would be at Lindbergh Field in San Diego to welcome home Greg Louganis, the 16-year-old Valhalla High School sophomore who won a silver medal in Olympic diving competition in Montreal. Louganis was the first-ever Olympic medalist from El Cajon.

Aug. 30 – Edgar L. Henry, 49, vice principal of Santana High School in Santee, was killed in a traffic accident near Newhall in Los Angeles County. His wife, Phyllis, and the couple's daughters, Pamela, 15, and Patty, 13, were injured in the four-vehicle crash in which three others also died.

Sept. 11 – Tropical Storm Kathleen ripped into three states – California, Nevada and Arizona – leaving four dead and 10 missing and disrupting electrical and communication facilities. Two residents of Ocotillo died as a result of the storm, one by drowning and the other when a four-foot wall of water crushed his house.

Sept. 14 – So many pigeons have established residence in downtown La Mesa that some are being poisoned with strychnine. Downtown merchants are asking for a city ordinance to prevent local residents from feeding the birds.

Sept. 22 – A proposal to stage bingo games one night a week at East County Performing Arts Center received a chilly reception at a meeting of the Grossmont-Cuyamaca Community College District Board. Dr. Dale Burke, a trustee, said it would be "morally wrong" for the board to sanction gambling at the facility located in downtown El Cajon, which is jointly owned by the City of El Cajon and the college district. The matter was turned over to the East County Performing Arts Center Advisory Council.

Sept. 24 – An editorial in today's edition of *The El Cajon Californian* bemoaned the loss of Helix Theater in La Mesa, a community recreation outlet for 28 years. The theater is being razed to make way for the La Mesa Springs shopping center. "Helix Theater has shown the last picture show and that will take a little getting used to," the editorial said.

Sept. 27 – Residents of the area were being urged to get swine flu shots at any of 24 clinics in East County that will be dispensing the vaccine.

Sept. 29 – A 34-year-old wife and mother who had been undergoing counseling for undisclosed problems was being held in county jail after the bodies of her estranged husband and two children from a previous marriage were found in their home at 4670 Mayapan Drive just south of El Cajon. Susan Walsh, also known as Susan Driscoll, was in custody in connection with the deaths of John Walsh, 33, owner of a repair shop for off-road vehicles, and her children – Slade Driscoll, 13, and Dawn Driscoll, 15. All the victims had been shot. She was later charged with three counts of murder.

Oct. 4 – Hugh L. Hudson, 28, of La Mesa, was one of six men killed Oct. 2 when a 190-foot crane collapsed at the site of a San Diego Gas & Electric Co. project at the Encina Power Plant.

Oct. 5 – Harrison Hall, 58, vice president of student personnel services at Grossmont College, collapsed and died of an apparent heart attack Oct. 4 at his home while waiting to take his wife to her doctor's office. He had been with the college since 1969.

Oct. 15 – The county coroner's office said Donald Miles Whaley, the 12-year-old El Cajon boy whose body was found Oct. 1 in a drainage ditch in San Diego, had been sexually molested. Donnie, a victim of strangulation, was found by a crane operator for Daley Corporation near the entrance to the construction company's plant off of Murphy Road.

Oct. 25 – President Gerald Ford addressed a crowd estimated at 25,000 to 30,000 at Grossmont Shopping Center on Sunday evening in his quest to continue as chief executive of the United States. "I won't concede a single state and I won't concede a single vote," Ford told the enthusiastic crowd. *(Ford, who assumed the presidency when Richard Nixon resigned, lost to Jimmy Carter, a Democrat, in the November presidential election.)*

Oct. 27 – State Sen. Jack Schrade, a Republican, has filed a $300,000 slander suit against his Democratic opponent, Assemblyman Bob Wilson. The suit claims Schrade is being slandered by Wilson's campaign charge that Schrade had been investigated in three counties for bribery.

Nov. 2 – Edward George Cammet, 28, manager of Major's Coffee Shop on Interstate 8 in Pine Valley, died of shotgun wounds suffered in an apparent robbery attempt Oct. 18. Two Pine Valley youths, one 16 and the other 17, have been arrested in connection with the murder. Cammet, who was first taken to El Cajon Valley Hospital for emergency treatment of head and neck wounds, died a few hours after he was admitted to University Hospital in San Diego.

Nov. 3 – El Cajon Councilwoman Lucille Moore defeated sheriff's Lt. Walt Kendrick to take a seat on the San Diego County Board of Supervisors representing the Second District. Assemblyman Bob Wilson, a Democrat, ousted 22-year incumbent Jack Schrade, a Republican, to move up to the State Senate. San Diego City Councilman Jim Ellis, a Republican, won the Assembly seat vacated by Wilson.

Nov. 11 – It was announced that movie and television actor and singer Dean Jones will be the grand marshal of this year's Mother Goose Parade. Jones starred in several Walt Disney movies.

Nov. 15 – El Cajon city employees over the weekend moved from their previous work site on Highland Avenue to the new city hall on Main Street. More than 600 pieces of furniture had to be hauled to the new building.

Nov. 19 – Doctors expressed fear that Mt. Miguel High School football player Kip Hayes may be paralyzed as a result of a broken neck and spinal injuries suffered in a recent game at Granite Hills High School. Meanwhile, a public fundraising drive to help pay for Hayes' care has reached nearly $17,000. Area restaurants were pledging to donate some of their proceeds to Hayes, and all of the San Diego Chargers autographed a football that was sent to him.

Dec. 10 – Harriet Stockwell, chairperson of the city planning commission, was appointed to succeed Lucille Moore on the El Cajon City Council. Moore vacated the council seat to run successfully for Second District county supervisor.

Dec. 13 – Myrra Lee, a social sciences teacher at Helix High School in La Mesa, was named Teacher of the Year for California and thus became eligible to compete for the national teacher-of-the-year title. The Associated Press featured Mrs. Lee in a story circulated throughout the state.

Dec. 17 – Unusually dry weather this year has led to a widespread flea infestation in parts of the county. A pest control company in El Cajon was called to fumigate a couple of restaurants, and people living on the upper floors of some condominiums reported being overrun by fleas even though they didn't own any pets.

Dec. 20 – Richard M. Sellers of El Cajon was preparing to go to Naples, FL later in the month to meet a man he thought had been dead for more than 40 years – his own father. Sellers' parents divorced when he was three. His mother brought him to California and told him his father had been killed during World War II. Sellers recently began a search for his father after an unsettling conversation with a great-aunt living in Ramona. With the help of a friend, he sent letters to all the residents of Indianapolis – where the family had once lived – who listed Sellers as their last name. He was contacted by some of them, and that led to the discovery that his father, who had been searching unsuccessfully for his son until about 10 years ago, lived in Florida.

Dec. 28 – Donations for furnishing East County Performing Arts Center amounted to $390,000, short of the goal of $430,000 but close enough to assure the opening of the theater in the spring. Donations and pledges from the public came to nearly $250,000, with additional gifts from the City of El Cajon and the Grossmont-Cuyamaca Community College District adding another $140,000.

1977

Jan. 7 – Joe Roth, who played football at Granite Hills High School and Grossmont College before becoming a high-profile quarterback at the University of California, Berkeley, is battling a virulent form of cancer but still hopes to be chosen by the pros. Roth, a 6'-4" signal caller, was in Hawaii to play in the Hula Bowl and, if well enough, the Japan Bowl on Jan. 15. He has been taking chemotherapy treatments for malignant melanoma.

Feb. 2 – The Grossmont Community College District Board, by a 3-2 vote, stood firm by not allowing a course called "Astrology and Self-Actualization" to be taught as part of its community service program. Opponents of the course were trustees William Faulwetter, Dr. Dale Burke and Dr. Paul Epler. The two trustees on the losing side were Portia Goode and Dr. Sydney Wiener. Supt. Robert Burnham warned the board it was setting a "dangerous precedent" by its decision.

Feb. 10 – Portia "Peg" Goode, 73, well known in education circles at the local, state and national levels, died at Grossmont Hospital after suffering a heart attack at her home. Mrs. Goode's service to education spanned more than 30 years. She was a Grossmont Community College District trustee at the time of her death and had been named the outstanding community college board member in the nation in 1973 by the Assn. of Community College Trustees, a national organization.

Feb. 19 – Karl Tuttle, former El Cajon mayor and councilman, was appointed to serve the unexpired term of Portia "Peg" Goode on the Grossmont Community College District Board. Tuttle had served one term on the board, from 1969 to 1973, but decided not to seek re-election.

Feb. 21 – Joe Roth, 21, quarterback of the UC Berkeley football team, lost his battle with malignant melanoma when he died Feb. 19 at his apartment in Berkeley with his parents, Mr. and Mrs. Leland Roth, and UC football coach Mike White by his side. Roth, who grew up in El Cajon, led the Grossmont College Griffins to a California Community Colleges football championship and in 1975 passed for 1,880 yards and 14 touchdowns to give his Cal team a share of the Pac-8 title. His first cancer operation occurred between his freshman and sophomore years at Grossmont College.

Mar. 16 – Dr. Dale O. Buckwalter, 47, an El Cajon dentist, was one of three persons killed when two small planes collided over the desert. Buckwalter was en route to Needles where he had an office. The other fatalities were two German students training at a flight school in Phoenix. Buckwalter had been making the twice-a-week trip to Needles for 14 years.

Mar. 24 – John Kaelin, owner of Kaelin's Market on West Madison Avenue in El Cajon, is receiving fan mail from near and far for his decision to make good the money orders his store had sold for a company that went bankrupt. The independent market owner so far has paid $136,896 to customers who bought the now worthless money orders and figures he may have to shell out close to $141,000 to cover all of his customers' losses. Congratulatory letters have come from as far away as Germany.

Mar. 28 – Five East County residents were listed as survivors of a fiery collision of Pan American and KLM jumbo jets in the Canary Islands, resulting so far in 562 deaths, which makes it the worst aviation disaster in history. East County survivors were: Anthony and Isabel Monde of La Mesa; Albert and Florence Trumbull of La Mesa; and Edgar Ridout of Alpine.

Mar. 29 – Vera Ballantyne Hughes, who was a switchboard operator in El Cajon during the 1920s, recalled taking a call from a frantic mother in Flinn Springs. "Vera, get me Dr. Knox quick, my baby just ate half a dead frog," the mother shouted. Vera called Dr. Knox and relayed the mother's urgent message to him. "Call her back and tell her to let him eat the other half," said the doctor in an attempt to convey his opinion that this was no big deal. Hughes, now 75, remembers when William Howard Taft, former president of the United States and later a chief justice of the U.S. Supreme Court, came to the small telephone office to make long-distance calls while visiting El Cajon.

Apr. 6 – Pat Evans, 22, an El Cajon motorcycle racer who had been competing at an event in Italy, died of heart failure after suffering massive injuries in a racing accident. Evans, who had attended Monte Vista High School, was a member of the Vesco-Damon Racing Team that had been on the European circuit for four months.

Apr. 18 – Ground was broken for the construction of Cuyamaca College, the second campus in the Grossmont-Cuyamaca Community College District. The project on the 165-acre campus is estimated to cost $50 million. Harold

Hughes, president-emeritus of Grossmont College who now lives in Hawaii, was a surprise guest at the ceremony.

Apr. 29 – Dale Evans, the movie star wife of cowboy actor and crooner Roy Rogers, stopped in El Cajon as part of a promotional tour for her new book, "Trials, Tears and Triumphs." In an interview with *The El Cajon Californian*, she announced that she is on a "witnessing trip" for God. Her latest book is the 16th in a series.

May 2 – Lakeside Theater's decision to show only X-rated films was drawing protests in the form of marching pickets of both adults and young people. The theater is at 10009 Maine Ave.

May 4 – Dr. Wallace Cohen, 54, will be the first president of Cuyamaca College, now under construction south of El Cajon. He comes from El Camino College in Torrance where he has been assistant superintendent and vice president for instruction of a single-campus district. There were 112 candidates for the position.

May 5 – A front-page story featured the forthcoming publication of "The Dubious Dictionary of Wilbur Ballbach." In it, Ballbach, 73, of Alpine, redefines words according to what he thinks they really mean in contemporary usage. Examples: *Copyright* – "The means by which a plagiarist protects his theft." *Orator*: "A speaker who says nothing eloquently."

May 10 – Susan Marie Driscoll, 34, who had been charged with the gunshot murders of her husband and two of her children from a previous marriage, was found guilty of the triple slayings by reason of insanity. Her parents told reporters that Driscoll had a history of suicidal tendencies since 1960.

May 19 – Former El Cajon police Sgt. Jerry Hancock, 33, was released from his five years-to-life prison sentence and was re-sentenced to 10 years of probation, ending his incarceration for committing burglary while he was an El Cajon police officer. Hancock's attorney argued in court that his client had been a target for death threats during the 14 months he was imprisoned. Although he was charged with only one burglary, Hancock was suspected of involvement in more than 160 burglaries while he was a police officer.

May 26 – Two of eight persons convicted in U.S. District Court on a variety of charges involving embezzlement of $500,000 in pension trust funds over six years were from East County. They are E. Dene Armstrong, 36, of El Cajon, a former county planning commissioner, and Robert Little, 51, of La Mesa.

May 28 – Attorney Robert Andreen, 51, a trustee of Grossmont Union High School District, was convicted by U.S. District Court Judge Gordon Thompson of embezzling money held in trust for construction workers. Also convicted of the same offense was Marcus Thompson, 45, of El Cajon, secretary-treasurer of Local 89 of International Laborers Union. Sentencing will be July 18.

June 4 – Mark Goffeny, 8, a second-grade student at Magnolia Elementary School in El Cajon, was featured in an article describing how he uses his feet to write and do a lot of other things because he was born without arms. Principal Dave Hughes said: "Actually, his footwriting is as good as many students' handwriting." Mark, whose favorite subjects are chemistry and physics, plays soccer and piano and dresses himself.

June 18 – Several East County men are named as defendants in an $18 million suit filed in connection with the troubled pension funds of Local 89 of the International Laborers Union. The 18-page suit accused all of the defendants – 17 of them – of conspiracy to defraud the 14,000 pension fund participants on whose behalf the suit was filed.

June 30 – The sale of the *El Cajon Californian* to Landmark Communications, Inc. of Norfolk, VA, was finalized today, ending the 12-year ownership of the paper by Richard A. Baker and the Register-Guard Publishing Co. of Eugene, OR. John Colburn, president of Landmark Community Newspapers, will be the new publisher. Colburn, who has been a newspaperman for 47 years, appointed Ed Beeler, who has been managing editor of the paper, to be editor. Landmark owns dailies in Norfolk and Roanoke, VA, and Greensboro, NC; TV and radio stations in Norfolk; operates 14 TV systems in 10 states; publishes a daily newspaper in Elizabethtown, KY, and two tri-weeklies, four semi-weeklies and seven weeklies in Kentucky, Indiana, Virginia and Maryland.... Lemon Grove officially becomes the 14th city in San Diego County on July 1. It has 23,000 residents.

July 6 – Robert Andreen, a La Mesa attorney convicted of embezzling money held in trust for construction workers, has resigned his seat on the Grossmont Union High School District Board.

July 7 – An El Cajon Chamber of Commerce survey claimed rail users in El Cajon and other East County communities will lose more than $20 million a year in sales revenue and some 800 jobs if San Diego and Arizona Eastern Railway is abandoned by Southern Pacific Transportation Co., its owner. Southern Pacific has petitioned the Interstate Commerce Commission for permission to abandon most of the 145-mile line, including branch lines to El Cajon, La Mesa and South Bay.

July 11 – Twenty-six people were injured, three critically, when a Camaro owned by veteran racer George Esau lost its brakes on the 33rd lap and plowed into a line of pit workers Saturday night at Cajon Speedway. The disabled car struck a crash wall, its throttle stuck and the car climbed a nearly four-foot wall, rode the wall 40 feet and ripped out a huge section of chain-link fence. It was described as the worst accident in the track's 17-year history. *(One of the injured, Ines Valencia, 49, of National City, an official of a Tijuana racetrack, died July 12 at University Hospital in San Diego.)*

July 18 – E. Dene Armstrong of El Cajon, a former county planning commissioner, was sentenced to 10 years in federal prison for his part in a scheme to embezzle pension trust funds of construction workers.

July 22 – Bostonia Ballroom on Broadway in El Cajon has undergone a transformation from a popular country and western music venue to a restaurant and dance hall featuring strolling mariachis and piped-in popular music. The hall, which opened in the 1930s and became one of the hottest spots in the county for country music, has been renamed El Amigo Plaza.

Aug. 1 – Robert Andreen, 51, was sentenced to five years in federal prison by U.S. District Court Judge Gordon Thompson Jr. for his part in a conspiracy to embezzle pension trust money. In a related matter, the Grossmont Union High School District Board appointed Fred Cicalo, director of administrative services for the San Diego County Probation Department, to replace Andreen, who had resigned his seat prior to sentencing.

Aug. 18 – Academy Award-winning song writer Paul Williams is to be the headline attraction for the inaugural event at the recently constructed East County Performing Arts Center. Williams, 36, won an Oscar with singer Barbra Streisand for "Evergreen," which was part of the musical score for the movie "A Star Is Born."

Aug. 27 – El Cajon Western Little League All-Stars were defeated 7-2 by Li-teh Little League of Taipei at Williamsport, PA. The team had racked up 16 consecutive all-star victories before losing to the Taiwan team.

Sept. 6 – Two East County men were killed by a sniper on I-15 while riding their motorcycles near Escondido. The dead: Emerson R. Morris, 29, of Spring Valley, and Raymond L. Smith, 36, of El Cajon. Morris' wife, Dolores, was in critical condition in an Escondido hospital. Smith's wife, Diane, was treated at the Escondido hospital and released.

Sept. 9 – Nearly 700 people attended the opening of East County Performing Arts Center featuring singer-songwriter Paul Williams and comedian Mike Neun. . . . Charles Skidmore, 56, superintendent of Santee School District for nearly 26 years, died at Mercy Hospital in San Diego. He had recently undergone surgery at the hospital. Skidmore stepped down as superintendent in July.

Sept. 16 – Former county planning commissioner E. Dene Armstrong of El Cajon was acquitted of accepting a bribe in 1974 in exchange for a favorable vote on a special use permit. He had been accused of taking the bribe in connection with the approval of a permit for the Dehesa Sand Plant in Dehesa Valley.

Sept. 21 – Former Grossmont Union High School District trustee Robert Andreen pleaded guilty and was fined $500 for a misdemeanor election code violation in connection with an alleged bribery scheme involving Andreen and former county planning commissioner E. Dene Armstrong. The charges of conspiracy to commit bribery and committing bribery were dropped.

Sept. 24 – A La Mesa ordinance enacted to ban nude dancing at the Classic Cat Theater at 5505 Jackson Drive was ruled "unconstitutional" and "void on its face" by Superior Court Judge Wesley Buttermore. La Mesa City Atty. Leroy Knutson is considering an appeal of Buttermore's ruling.

Oct. 1 – *The El Cajon Californian* became *The Daily Californian* again on this date. It was to serve El Cajon, La Mesa, Santee, Lakeside, Spring Valley and Lemon Grove. *The Daily Californian* name had been used for 10 years earlier.

Oct. 2 – Jack Shelver, 42, is to be the first city manager of Lemon Grove. He will be paid $29,000 a year.

Oct. 7 – The president of the San Diego chapter of the Hell's Angels Motorcycle Club was arrested on an indictment charging him with soliciting the murder of members of a rival gang, the Mongols, and attempting to commit murder. Thomas James Renzulli, 29, of San Diego, was taken into custody with 16 other Hell's Angels or their associates. Three of those arrested were East County residents. Tension between the gangs had resulted in a deadly sniper attack on the I-15 freeway near Escondido and a bombing at a Lemon Grove mortuary. Mongols slain in the sniper attack were Emerson Morris, 36, of Spring Valley, who had been a member of the Lemon Grove Chamber of Commerce Board, and Raymond Smith, 36, of El Cajon. Wives of both men were injured in the assault. . . . Neon Seville, 25, of La Mesa, frolicked naked on a jetty of a south Mission Bay beach to protest a new ban on nudity at Black's Beach and all laws outlawing public nudity.

Oct. 10 – A man and his estranged wife were found dead after an eight-hour siege of a house at 712 Terra Lane in El Cajon. The dead: Michael Ray Lowe, 27, of Ramona, and his estranged wife, Cecilia, 27. Their 23-month-old son, Michael Lowe Jr., was in the house owned by Mrs. Lowe's parents, Frank and Dora Korash, but he was not hurt. Police said Lowe, denied entry to the house, broke down a door and entered the dwelling armed with a rifle. Police eventually threw two canisters of tear gas into the house after hearing shots. Lowe had a history of emotional problems, according to his wife's attorney, George Hurst.

Oct. 13 – Brothers Bill and Tom Church of Spring Valley submitted a bid of $65 a ton for 25 tons of used and worn-out books belonging to San Diego Library. The books were destined for the Miramar landfill when the Economic Research Institute protested that such a disposal would be a waste. There were 10,000 books in the first batch the brothers received, requiring quick action to find storage space. Bill Church was thrilled that he had found several books on how to build your own helicopter – something he had always wanted to do.

Oct. 17 – Christine Maria Santiago, 44, of Santee, and her 5-year-old son, Leo, were among 86 persons aboard a Lufthansa jet that had been hijacked by terrorists over France and forced to fly to Dubai on the Persian Gulf. The hijackers were threatening to blow up the plane. Mrs. Santiago, who is recovering from a heart attack and suffers from high blood pressure, had departed Sept. 25 with her son for the Spanish island of Majorca to visit her husband, Antonio, who works for International Telephone and Telegraph Co. The hijackers, who killed the pilot of the plane, were demanding $15 million and the release of 11 imprisoned anarchists in West German jails and two Palestinians jailed in Turkey. *(The ordeal ended when a West German commando team killed three of the four hijackers and rescued all 86 hostages. The rescue occurred at Mogadishu, the capital of Somalia. Mrs. Santiago's blood pressure had soared, so she was hospitalized. Her son stayed with an uncle.)*

Nov. 3 – Harassment of Bus Stop Bar in Lakeside by a faction of the Ku Klux Klan was the focus of a community meeting called by Second District Supervisor Lucille Moore at her Gillespie Field office. The bar had been the target of KKK protests for refusing to fire a black female entertainer and other ethnic minorities. Owners Bob Neal and Don Couture fear they may have to close if the harassment continues. The bar is running a $1,000 deficit. More than 100 people showed up at a rally to support the bar on a Friday evening.

Nov. 5 – Mary Etta's Flinn Springs Café served as a set for "Stunt Man," a movie starring Steven Railsback, who played mass killer Charles Manson in the 1976 television movie "Helter Skelter." The Flinn Springs diner is owned by Larry and Mary Sturholm.

Dec. 1 – Science writer L. Wayne Beemer and his wife, Carol, of Alpine, have filed a claim for the moon, pledging to occupy and develop the planet by 1984. They presented their claim to the Department of Treaties and Documents and to the Department of Space Flight Registry at the United Nations.

Dec. 15 – David M. Copeland, 28, of El Cajon, has been charged with 10 counts of sexual perversion with youths under 18 by using his Foothills Environmental Group as a lure to recruit boys 10 to 14 for homosexual acts. Police say more than 150 boys had become members or affiliates of the club in the two years it is known to have been in existence. The current membership is 40.

Dec. 21 – Simon Casady, publisher of *The El Cajon Valley News* from 1953 to 1964, filed suit in federal court asking that all FBI and CIA files kept on him since 1942 be released. The 70-year-old retired publisher invoked the Freedom of Information Act to obtain hundreds of pages of his files, but they were so heavily censored his attorney says they don't make sense. The attorney, Dan Bamberg, said the two agencies have been interested in Casady since 1942 when he had a newspaper in Texas and wrote a story on Mexican-American servicemen who could not get served in a bar. The files include entries as recently as 1975.

1978

Jan. 12 – Law enforcement officers were trying to solve seven murders that occurred the day before Christmas last year in San Diego County. Victims found in East County: Elizabeth Ann Heidt, 20, whose beaten body was discovered by a Jamul woman walking her dog along Highway 94 near Steele Canyon Road; Jacqueline Lee Greene, 27, of Chula Vista, who was found dead from a shotgun wound to the head in brush east of Santee Lakes; Teresa Ann Weinmann, 43, a teacher's aide who had gone to a corner grocery to buy film and deliver a Christmas present. She had been badly beaten and left on the grounds of Kempton School where she taught. Detectives arrested an 18-year-old neighbor as a suspect. The fourth victim was Raymond D. Powley, 51, of Lemon Grove, who was found dead in his home with several stab wounds in his chest. A Camp Pendleton Marine, Richard Macia, was arrested in Florida and pleaded innocent to murdering Powley.

Mar. 1 – High winds and torrential rain wreaked havoc in East County, flooding roads and causing power outages. Flooding was so bad in the Jamul area that Supt. Jim Turner of Jamul-Las Flores School District canceled classes for a day.

Mar. 2 – An El Cajon couple, Carl and Ann Schneider, who intended to celebrate their 45th wedding anniversary in Hawaii, died when a Continental Airline DC-10 taking them to Honolulu crashed and burned at the end of a runway at Los Angeles International Airport. They were the only fatalities. Carl was 76; Ann, 72. The plane was carrying 117 passengers and crew members. Two tires on the plane blew out. The Schneiders tried to flee the scene by climbing onto a wing and using a chute that put them directly into the flames.

Mar. 2 – A story that first appeared in *The Daily Californian*, and which was distributed nationally by Associated Press, generated a lot of publicity for former San Diego Vice Mayor Vincent Godfrey. The story tells how Godfrey, 64, suffering from degenerative arthritis, turned to exercise and dietary supplements to become Senior Olympics champion in the 110- and 400-meter high hurdles.

Mar. 15 – Insurance agent Bob Cornett resigned as El Cajon mayor because of his job responsibilities. Councilman John Reber was appointed to succeed him.

Mar. 31 – Jack Hanson, 48, was appointed to the El Cajon City Council seat vacated by John Reber when he was appointed mayor to succeed Bob Cornett who had resigned. Hanson had the highest number of votes among unsuccessful council contenders in the Mar. 7 election.

Apr. 12 – The county grand jury indicted 13 members of a gypsy band on charges of burglary, conspiracy to commit burglary, receiving stolen property and contributing to the delinquency of minors. The crimes are alleged to have occurred at four stores in Borrego Springs, six stores in Julian and one store in Brawley. El Cajon Municipal Court has jurisdiction of the case.

May 1 – A front-page story featured the work being done by the Rev. Rocky Oliver and his wife, Karen, who teach at Baptist Bible College in El Cajon and go to Tijuana every Saturday to do missionary work at La Mesa Prison. Besides handing out Bibles and hymn sheets, they take a tin of cookies baked by Karen Oliver to share with the inmates.

May 13 – Comedian George Gobel and singer Gisele MacKenzie were to be the featured entertainers at the El Cajon Boys Club banquet at Hotel del Coronado.

June 2 – Peggy Eddy made history when she was installed as the first woman president-elect of the El Cajon Chamber of Commerce. She is a partner with her husband, Robert, in a company called General Business Services. Peggy will assume the presidency of the chamber next year.

June 7 – Passage of Proposition 13, a statewide measure that sharply limited how much money could be raised from property taxes, drew quick responses from public agencies. Dismissal notices were being prepared today (the day after the election) for Spring Valley Fire Protection District, warning that a minimum 41 of the district's 56 employees will be laid off unless replacement revenue for lost property tax is provided by June 24. Summer school for 3,000 students was canceled by La Mesa-Spring Valley School District on a 4-1 vote.

June 14 – Eight gypsies pleaded guilty to charges of theft at various stores in East County and were fined $3,000 and ordered to repay $455, the estimated value of items taken from stores in Brawley, Julian and Borrego Springs. El Cajon Municipal Court Judge Byron Lindsley ordered the offenders to leave the state within 48 hours. . . . . . Associate Editor Del Hood of *The Daily Californian* won a first-place award in a two-state newswriting contest for his report on the recovery of a badly burned Lakeside boy, Keith Hulin. Hood was in Palo Alto to receive the award from Associated Press news executives. The story was judged best among submissions from newspapers in California and Nevada representing cities under 200,000. More than 50 publications were eligible to enter the contest.

June 21 – Dr. Robert Burnham, 58, superintendent of the Grossmont Community College District since 1970, resigned effective Dec. 29. He had been a teacher and administrator in the Grossmont Union High School District from 1950 until moving to the college district in 1964 as a counselor and later as vice president for student personnel services.

July 1 – El Cajon's First Church of the Disabled was featured in a story that described how about 30 people – all with major disabilities – meet every Sunday afternoon at Chapel of the Valley on East Madison Avenue. Members use Braille hymnals and hear a sermon by the church's pastor, the Rev. Herbert Withey. They come from as far away as Chula Vista, Mira Mesa and North Park.

July 24 – A 13-year-old Spring Valley boy pleaded guilty to the Mar. 17 slaying of Stephen Earl Lewis, a 20-year-old Grossmont College student found shot to death in a pickup truck. The defendant was not identified because he was tried as a juvenile. His plea of guilty to second-degree murder makes the boy eligible for a maximum seven-year term in a

California Youth Authority institution. An 18-year-old companion, Randall D. Larson of Spring Valley, is recovering from multiple gunshot wounds in the chest and faces a murder charge in connection with the shooting death of Rocky Joe Ferguson, a security guard. The 13-year-old later received a nine-year sentence.

July 27 – Seventy-one coaches resigned from 147 coaching assignments in Grossmont Union High School District in response to Supt. Leland Newcomer's ultimatum that coaches either sign up or get out of coaching by Aug. 2.

July 31 – More than 300 people attended a rally at Monte Vista High School at which a petition drive was launched seeking the dismissal of Supt. Leland Newcomer and the reinstatement of all cuts made to athletic programs. The petition asked Newcomer to resign.

Aug. 4 – Sixty-seven coaches in Grossmont Union High School District voted to resign *en masse* unless the district board reinstates three varsity coaches who quit last month. The coaches who resigned were Russ Boehmke of Valhalla, Don Garcia of Granite Hills and Larry Schimpf of Monte Vista.

Sept. 15 – Californian Publishing Co., which publishes *The Daily Californian*, has purchased three buildings on five acres at the northwest corner of Fesler Street and Pioneer Way in El Cajon. The newspaper is to be moved to the new location early in 1979.

Sept. 19 – Paralyzed former Mt. Miguel High School football player Kip Hayes, 19, has left Grossmont Hospital after 18 months of confinement to live in a two-bedroom home that he is renting in La Mesa. Registered nurses will provide 24-hour care at his new residence.

Sept. 25 – A mid-air crash of two planes over San Diego that killed 144 passengers and crew members as well as people at the crash site was described as "the worst ever in the United States" in a story that ran across the top of the front page of *The Daily Californian* in large bold type. A Pacific Southwest Airlines jet carrying 129 passengers and a crew of seven collided with a private plane at 9:20 a.m., then tumbled to the ground in the North Park area, setting at least five homes ablaze. Two persons aboard the Cessna which collided with the PSA plane also were killed. Among the victims with East County ties: Thomas W. Womack II of El Cajon, a 1965 graduate of El Cajon Valley High School; Lisa Golding Davis, 23, a stewardess who graduated from Grossmont High School in 1972; Rosalie Loccoco of El Cajon, mother of five children ranging in age from 14 to 23; Marla C. Scavia, 24, a flight attendant and graduate of Grossmont High School; Robert Fox of La Mesa, first officer on the PSA plane; Dee Anne Young of El Cajon, flight attendant; William S. White of Lakeside, a maintenance worker; Samuel Molinaro of El Cajon; and Jimmie Allen Kelley, 40, of Spring Valley, a PSA pilot. Another victim was attorney J. Michael Taggart, 33, of Palos Verdes, who was aboard the PSA plane en route to represent Grossmont Union High School District and Grossmont Community College District in their negotiations with employees.

Oct. 18 – Roger and Virginia Meyers of El Cajon were featured in a book by Roger's brother, Robert, a reporter for *The Washington Post*. It's entitled "Like Normal People" and tells the story of Roger and Virginia's marriage despite their mental retardation. The book, published by McGraw-Hill, was made into an ABC-TV movie titled "A Very Special Love" starring Shaun Cassidy and Linda Purl. Roger, 30, and Virginia, 27, had bit parts in the movie.

Oct. 27 – La Mesa Police Department is calling for Oktoberfest to end unless changes in its operation are made to lessen drunkenness and brawls. Six people were arrested for drunkenness during the three-day event Oct. 6-8. Minors reportedly were buying and consuming beer.

Nov. 15 – Charles Colson, the so-called "hatchetman" of the Nixon White House and a Watergate conspirator sentenced to prison for his part in the crime, spoke at Cinema Grossmont Theater in La Mesa which showed his film "Born Again," portraying his work in prison ministry. He spoke to reporters in the lobby before the film was shown.

Nov. 18 – Connie Haines, popular singing star from the 1940s when she was with the James and Tommy Dorsey orchestras, is now an ordained minister recently named associate pastor of Christ Church Unity in El Cajon. She will make regular monthly visits to El Cajon to present her musical ministry.

Dec. 1 – An El Cajon man using the single legal name "Tennessee," who was arrested on El Cajon Boulevard for soliciting a prostitute, has hired an attorney and will go to court to contest his arrest for solicitation. Tennessee, 58, owns Tennessee Tree Service. He maintains his solicitation of a prostitute is nobody's business except his and the prostitute whose service he was requesting.

Dec. 12 – Absenteeism in schools was running between 15 and 35 percent, largely because of an epidemic of respiratory ailments.

1979

Jan. 5 – The Swedish Royal Order of the North Star was conferred on La Mesa resident Helge Erickson by Sweden's ambassador to the United States, Wilhelm Wachmeister. Erickson, who came to the United States at the age of 19 in 1929, was cited for "meritorious service to Sweden in promoting good will and good relations in the world." Erickson sold real estate and insurance in La Mesa.

Jan. 8 – An early morning explosion and fire in Lemon Grove destroyed a restaurant, a pinball emporium and the entire stock of a pet shop dealing in exotic birds and other animals. The destroyed businesses were the Marble Machine at 7967 Broadway and Scandia Smorgasbord at 7973 Broadway.

Jan. 17 – Ed Beeler, 45, editor of *The Daily Californian*, was named publisher of the *Carroll County Times* in Westminster, MD, effective Jan. 29. Beeler arrived here in 1964 to be managing editor of *The Valley News* when the newspaper was purchased by Richard A. Baker, part owner of the Eugene (OR) *Register-Guard*. Landmark Communications bought the El Cajon newspaper in 1977 after its name had been changed to *The Daily Californian*.

Jan. 29 – Brenda Spencer, 16, a student at Patrick Henry High School in the San Carlos area of east San Diego, was taken into custody for using a .22 semi-automatic rifle to fire wantonly at Cleveland Elementary School, killing Principal Burton Wragg and head custodian Michael Suchar and injuring at least 10 others. Police said Spencer had between 500 and 600 rounds of ammunition. . . . The funeral for Rexford Hall, 84, El Cajon's first fire chief and later a high school and college district trustee, will be Jan. 31. Hall, a member of the prominent pioneer Hall family which ran a lumber business, took the volunteer fire chief's job in 1923.

Jan. 31 – An elderly woman and her daughter were pulled from their sinking car caught in the rampaging current of rain-swollen Los Coches Creek. Harold Locke, 33, an employee of Riverview Water District, heard the women scream for help. He rescued Leona Fockler of Lakeside and her mother, Frances Van Iwaarden of Holland, MI. El Cajon had received 1.8 inches of rain.

Feb. 21 – El Cajon Mayor John Reber squelched his own proposal to put a rent control measure on the June 5 ballot.

Feb. 22 – *The Daily Californian* was preparing to move from its plant at

613 W. Main St. in El Cajon to a five-acre site at 1000 Pioneer Way. The new site had 83,000 square feet of space in three buildings.

Feb. 27 – Two municipal court judges in El Cajon – G. Dennis Adams and Howard Bechefsky – were elevated to San Diego Superior Court by Gov. Pete Wilson.

Feb. 28 – Dennis Goodell, 34, pastor of Evangel Center in El Cajon, was arrested on suspicion of having unlawful intercourse with a 17-year-old church member he was counseling. Goodell was booked into county jail on 11 counts of unlawful intercourse and five counts of oral copulation with a minor. Evangel Center featured televised healing services.

Mar. 2 – Leland Newcomer, 58, superintendent of Grossmont Union High School District, resigned to take a position as superintendent-president of Santa Clarita Community College District. He had been with the district for four years.

Mar. 9 – On the advice of his doctor, Charles "Chuck" Ferree, 54, resigned as manager of El Cajon Chamber of Commerce after almost 20 years on the job. Ferree suffered a heart attack three years ago. He worked for the growth of the industrial park, annexation of Gillespie Field to El Cajon and the founding of People for People to allay racial divisions. He came to El Cajon to open the F.W. Woolworth store on Main Street.

Mar. 15 – Dennis Goodell resigned as pastor of the Evangel Center in El Cajon after pleading guilty to one count of statutory rape of a 17-year-old parishioner he was counseling. Goodell, 34, spoke to a standing room-only crowd, many of whom asked him to remain as their pastor.

Apr. 5 – Two elderly Alpine women who enjoyed daily walks together were killed when they were struck by a car driven by a 17-year-old girl as they crossed Arnold Way. The victims were Lillian Lyman, 88, the first person to move into the Alpine Village Apartments a decade ago, and Jessie Wievig, 75, who died three days after the accident. A third member of the walking group, Ethel Cole, 73, underwent surgery for internal bleeding and was in stable condition.

Apr. 25 – The Rent-a-Goat business started by Lakeside accountant Harold Norris was attracting national attention. Terry Drinkwater of CBS News was the latest to ask for an interview with Norris. Others who had been here for interviews and photo shoots were ABC-TV, United Press International, Iowa Public Radio and the *Los Angeles Times*. Norris rents his goats to people who want their weeds eaten. . . . A couple that had been divorced for 43 years repeated the vows they had taken more than 53 years earlier. Frank "Hank" Spady and Velta Tennant were remarried in a ceremony at First Baptist Church in Santee. The couple was first married Dec. 27, 1925, in Holyoke, CO, when Velta was 19 and Hank was 17. They divorced after nine years and both had remarried. Their previous partners died.

Apr. 30 – Bella Abzug, the flamboyant former New York congresswoman and activist on women's issues, addressed 300 women and men at the home of Bud and Norma Edelman in El Cajon.

May 2 – A shot fired through a window at a Lakeside home struck a 16-year-old boy in the chest, killing him. Three male juveniles and two girls were being sought for questioning on information that the shooting was the result of an earlier altercation at Lindo Lake Park, across the street from the slain youth's home. The shooting victim was identified as Donny Lloyd Hale.

May 7 – Three East County residents were among the five people killed in a plane crash near Mt. Laguna possibly caused by strong winds. East County victims were Linda Quinci, 23, of La Mesa; Michelle Carroll, 19, of Spring Valley; and Margaret Boettcher, 29, of Spring Valley.

May 18 – Barbara Freer, co-owner with her husband of the Flinn Springs Inn east of El Cajon, outplayed 52 women to win the Seven-Card Stud crown in the 10th annual World Series of Poker in Las Vegas. She won $12,720.

May 29 – Greg Dionne, 25, of El Cajon, fell 2,500 feet to his death May 28 during a parachuting demonstration at the National Air Festival at Brown Field in Chula Vista. His chute failed to fully open, a malfunction that was captured on film. Dionne had made 500 jumps.

June 4 – Statistics were published showing that a 19-mile stretch of Highway 67 from Maplewood Street in Lakeside to Highway 78 in Ramona accounted for 14.6 percent of the automobile fatalities in East San Diego County, according to the California Highway Patrol. The same road had 6 percent of the area's traffic injury accidents and required 12 percent of CHP's manpower to patrol.

June 12 – The death of actor John Wayne from cancer led to a front-page story in *The Daily Californian* featuring reminisces by Lillian Bowman of El Cajon, who served as governess for Wayne's daughter, Marissa, and cooked for the Waynes on their yacht in the late 1960s. Lillian and her husband, Wayne, worked four years for the famous actor and his family.

July 13 – Buck Knives, Inc. announced it would begin construction on its new $2.5 million world headquarters in El Cajon. The construction had been opposed in a lawsuit by the Fletcher Hills Highlands Homeowners Assn.

Aug. 2 – A 69-year-old Englishman dying of terminal lung cancer saw his wish fulfilled to return to his native land. Norman Brown of El Cajon had lived in the United States for 20 years. He was to board a plane accompanied by an El Cajon Valley Hospital nurse within a few days and fly to his new home at a hospice near Liverpool. He had been guaranteed immediate admission at the Liverpool hospice.

Aug. 6 – Steve Kell, 34, of El Cajon, whose nationally syndicated cartoon strip "The Captain and Mandy" was appearing in 30 newspapers across the country, including the *Los Angeles Times* and the *San Francisco Chronicle*, lamented the cancellation of his work in the wake of two jetliner crashes that killed more than 300 persons. Kell, a PSA pilot, is defiantly promoting a new cartoon strip and writing a book. His cartoon strip was canceled after the PSA jetliner crash in San Diego and the DC-10 crash in Chicago.

Sept. 1 – This headline appeared on the front page of *The Daily Californian* ahead of Labor Day: "Traveling this weekend? You'll probably have to pay more than $1 a gallon for gas"

Sept. 5 – Richard Laemmle, who lives with his 11 dogs – seven puppies and four adults – in a 1960 Mercury station wagon, was in trouble with local Humane Society officials who have charged him with animal cruelty. Humane officers say Laemmle has been feeding his pets bananas and tacos, giving them skin problems. Laemmle told police his uncle, Carl Laemmle, founded and operated Universal Studios, and his father, Louis Laemmle, once owned a string of Chicago theaters. Laemmle said he worked at the studio for 10 years earning $2,500 a week but left because he couldn't keep his mouth shut.

Sept. 10 – Mark Lyons, 17, a Grossmont High School student, was featured in the "Living" section of the newspaper after being named "San Diego's Best Built Teen-Ager." Lyons bench presses 310 pounds and aspires to the title of "Mr. Olympia."

Oct. 1 – Brenda Spencer, 17, pleaded guilty to murder in the sniper killings of two persons – a principal and a janitor – at a San Diego elementary school in the San Carlos area on Jan. 29. Earlier she had pleaded innocent by reason of insanity.

Oct. 20 – Former County Supervisor Jack Walsh posted bail for Richard Laemmle, an itinerant homeless person who had been convicted of animal cruelty for keeping 11 dogs in his Mercury station wagon. Walsh thought El Cajon Municipal Court Judge Thomas Duffy was too harsh in sentencing Laemmle to jail and ordering that his dogs be euthanized. "I think that's outrageous," Walsh said, offering his own home as a refuge for Laemmle and his dogs. Laemmle had been sentenced to 40 days in jail and two years on probation.

Nov. 23 – A ranch house built in 1866 at 905 Fourth St. in El Cajon sustained $15,000 in damage when its roof caught fire. The owners said they would repair the roof.

Nov. 27 – A $49 million suit has been filed against the City of La Mesa by the controversial Classic Cat Theater alleging violations of the civil rights of 18 nude dancers during two raids by police. Sixty-seven criminal charges of lewd behavior were filed against 15 of the dancers and charges of running a house of prostitution were lodged against two of the owners. Photographs of 18 of the theater's male and female dancers were taken during Oct. 16 and 17 raids.

Nov. 28 – La Mesa City Council suspended City Manager Gayle Martin and asked the district attorney's office to investigate alleged improprieties. Martin was accused of blocking a fire department memorandum from reaching the city's redevelopment agency. The memorandum expressed concern about the fire safety of La Mesa's planned senior housing project to be constructed at 8100 Orange Ave.

Nov. 29 – An early morning residential fire killed a young couple and their infant daughter in Lakeside. The victims were Jessie Sims, 27; his common-law wife, Grace Carter, 22; and their six-month-old daughter, Esther. They lived on Golden Ridge Road. A malfunctioning wall heater was cited as a possible cause of the deadly blaze.

Dec. 1 – Larry Pierce of La Mesa was a free man after the district attorney dropped charges that he had killed 30-year-old Dale Huffington in the back room of Pierce's gas station on Jan. 24, 1976. Pierce's first trial on a first-degree murder charge ended in a mistrial; jurors deadlock on the verdict in his second trial; and his third trial ended when charges were dropped. The ordeal, besides taking three years of Pierce's life, also ended his marriage. Pierce, a former Marine Corps MP, claimed a robber intent on stealing the gas station's receipts killed Huffington when he (Pierce) went to the front of the store to report the crime.

Dec. 28 – A 25-year-old orphan abandoned by his American parents in Korea was to arrive today at Los Angeles International Airport to meet his new parents, Robert and Doye Fannin of Spring Valley. Doye Fannin had met James Daniel Bronson while on a tour of duty in Korea in 1968. James, whose parents both were Caucasian Americans, had been treated as an outcast and left to fend for himself. U.S. Rep. Lionel Van Deerlin assisted with the adoption. Robert Fannin is a retired Army major.

George Bailey served on the La Mesa City Council and the San Diego County Board of Supervisors. *Photo: El Cajon Library*

School board trustee Robert Andreen imprisoned for embezzlement. *Photo: El Cajon Library*

Disgraced pastor Dennis Goodell pleaded guilty to statutory rape. *Photo: El Cajon Library*

Newly elected El Cajon mayor Bob Cornett shares a laugh with City Clerk Delight Swain in 1976. *Photo: San Diego History Center*

Some highlights ahead:

Son of former Chargers linebacker Emil Karas shot and killed at a Santee party....Ku Klux Klan leader wins a shot for a congressional seat representing East County....Mother Goose Parade to stay in El Cajon....Big Oak Ranch owner, running for Second District supervisor, arrested in connection with the shooting death of his son-in-law.

Grant Thompson, 15, piloted stolen plane that crashed at Gillespie Field, killing him and four others.
Photo: El Cajon Library

Donald Walker, chancellor of Grossmont Community College District, on list of 100 most effective college bosses.
Photo: Grossmont-Cuyamaca Community College District.

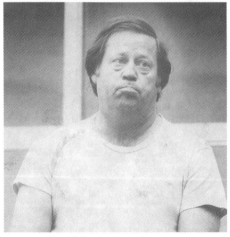

Herman "Rock" Kreutzer, former owner of Big Oak Ranch, was sent to prison for killing his son-in-law. *Photo: El Cajon Library*

Jan Claussen of Santee was the first woman mayor of an East County city. *Photo: El Cajon Library*

1980

Jan. 8 – La Mesa City Manager Gayle Martin resigned his $42,000 a year job, calling himself a political "scapegoat." He had been suspended with pay for three weeks. Martin was the city's sixth city manager since 1953.

Jan. 10 – Tom White was appointed editor of *The Daily Californian*.

Jan. 18 – U.S. Rep. Bob Wilson, 62, announced that he would not seek a 15th term in office. Wilson represented much of East County during his 28 years in the House of Representatives.

Feb. 4 – Alvin Lou, 25, a 1972 honor graduate at El Cajon Valley High School, won the Rolaids Open, his first Professional Bowlers Assn. title, in Florissant, MO. He posted a 277-211 score over top-seeded Gip Lentine to claim the $15,000 first-place prize in the $100,000 event.

Feb. 21 – East County was bracing for its seventh rainstorm since Feb. 13. Mt. Laguna received 14.94 inches of rain; El Cajon got 5.73 inches since that date. The latest storm flooded trailer parks, caused dams to overflow and flooded roads. Three hundred people were evacuated from a La Mesa trailer park near Interstate 8. Three Graveline brothers from El Cajon – Mike, 19; Scott, 16; and Gary, 14 – were swept away in a rubber raft they were using to ride fast water through one of the city's concrete-lined drainage channels.

Mar. 1 – Chloris Scott wrote about Alice Mabel Knox, 95, daughter of Amaziah Knox, who built the first commercial building in El Cajon, which was then named Knox's Corner. The hotel that was constructed first identified the area that is now Main Street and Magnolia Avenue.

Mar. 3 – The body of Mike Graveline, 19, of El Cajon was found in a river basin in Santee, several days after the bodies of his two younger brothers were discovered. All three brothers boarded a raft in El Cajon during a downpour that filled drainage channels through El Cajon and were swept away in the rushing water.

Mar. 24 – Emil Steven Karas, 19, of El Cajon, son of former Chargers all-star linebacker Emil Karas, was shot and killed during a wild melee at a Santee party. The shooting happened in the 9400 block of Halberns Boulevard. James Louis Buckel, 20, was arrested on suspicion of murder. The elder Karas died of cancer in 1974.

Apr. 1 – Deadly cyanide was being added to jars of pickles and teriyaki sauce at Safeway stores in the region. No instance of food poisoning had been found in East County stores, but such tampering had occurred in La Jolla and Pacific Beach. An extortionist was demanding 50 diamonds from the nation's largest supermarket chain in exchange for identifying what food on store shelves had been laced with cyanide. Several days later, Richard Q. Williams, 46, a horse trainer, was charged with the crime.

Apr. 15 – A recount showed that Harriet Stockwell had defeated Thomas Manning by only three votes for a seat on the El Cajon City Council.

May 14 – National University lost its bid to establish a branch on Van Houten Avenue in El Cajon to serve its 800 students in the area. Nearby businessmen, including Tom Kozak from Kozak's Restaurant, opposed the university campus, citing parking and traffic problems it would create. . . . A restored Model A Ford became a death trap for a Lakeside couple, Jeffrey and Patti Wright, both 26. Their antique car was struck by another vehicle traveling 60 mph on a highway in Imperial Valley. The accident orphaned the Wrights' daughter, Kimberley, who was 17 months old.

June 2 – A record number of prospective voters – 909,880 – had registered for the June 3 primary election in San Diego County. Registrar of Voters Ray Ortiz predicted 72 percent of them would use the new voting system that relied on punching ballots. The decision of U.S. Rep. Bob Wilson, a Republican first elected in the 1952 Eisenhower landslide, not to seek re-election was credited with causing the unusually high predicted voter turnout as lower-level officeholders tried to move up the political ladder.

June 4 – The most shocking result of the June 3 primary was the election of Tom Metzger, leader of the Ku Klux Klan in California, as the Democratic nominee for the 43rd Congressional District whose occupant represents parts of East San Diego County, Riverside County and Imperial County. Metzger won by 318 votes over Ed Skagen, chairman of the San Diego County Democratic Central Committee. He was a loser in San Diego County but won the nomination with large majorities in Imperial and Riverside counties.

June 10 – Patti LuPone, 30, won a Tony for best actress in the musical "Evita" on Broadway, inspiring great joy for her proud father, Orlando "Chick" LuPone of La Mesa and her stepmother, Saralyn. Chick LuPone retired from the New York City public school system in 1964 and was a professor of elementary education at San Diego State University until his retirement in 1974.

June 23 – Lance Russell Spetter, 15, of El Cajon, died June 22 when a batted baseball hit him in the side of the head while he was playing pitch-and-hit with friends at Kennedy Park. It was the second fatality within seven months resulting from playing ball. Michael Mueller, also 15, died Dec. 6 when struck in the chest with a softball.

June 26 – James Lewis Buckel, 21, charged with murder in the death of the son of the late San Diego Chargers' linebacker Emil Karas, was cleared of the crime on grounds of justifiable homicide and self-defense. Investigation revealed that Buckel was being assaulted when he fired the shot that killed Emil Karas Jr. after a party in Santee.

June 30 – Roy Rogers and Dale Evans, billed as the King of the Cowboys and the Queen of the West, were in El Cajon on June 28 for the opening of the new Far West Savings branch at 1235 Avocado Ave. More than a thousand people greeted the movie stars.

July 1 –Air Bahia, a La Mesa-based air carrier service, launched its first commercial flight between Gillespie Field and Los Angeles. Daily flights of the twin-engine, nine-passenger aircraft are scheduled to leave El Cajon for Los Angeles International Airport at 8 a.m. and return at 8 p.m. A one-way ticket costs $30. . . . Gunther Pool at Gillespie Field closed and about 70 "mourners" were on hand to pay their respects to the pool which had served area swimmers since it opened in the 1940s.

July 15 – Figures released by the county planning department showed that the county's population had reached 1,711,811 – 453,957 more than the 1970 figure of 1,257,854. El Cajon's population increase during the decade was 38.9 percent, up from 52,273 in 1970 to 72,621 in 1980. La Mesa grew from 39,178 to 49,058 in the same period, an increase of 25.2 percent.

Sept. 24 – Santee Youth Recreation Center was trying to break a Guinness Book of World Records mark for lap sitting. The current record is held by Cranbrook, B.C., and was set May 14, 1978, when 3,394 Canadians sat on laps.

Sept. 26 – An El Cajon mother who slashed her 3-year-old son's throat after arguing with him about what he could have for breakfast was found innocent of his murder by reason of insanity. Margaret Jean Walters, 38, was expected to be sentenced to a mental hospital. Walters had been diagnosed as a chronic schizophrenic, and all psychiatrists who examined her agreed she was insane. *(On Oct. 30 the newspaper reported that Walters was sentenced to Patton State Hospital.)*

Oct. 1 – The cost of halting a landslide along Fletcher Parkway in El Cajon was put at more than $600,000 by an engineering company that had studied the problem. Engineers cautioned that inactive slides in the area could be triggered by another bout of heavy rains.

Oct. 17 – The Lyn-Vette Guest Home in El Cajon had its license revoked by the State Department of Social Services after an administrative law judge found that residents of the facility had been "physically and verbally abused and not afforded diagnosis on several occasions." The facility was on Taft Avenue.

Nov. 7 – El Cajon florist Jennie Lee Irey was one of 30 florists from around the country invited to decorate the White House for Christmas. Irey owned Colonial House of Flowers on Second Street.

Nov. 12 – Armed robbers had struck three homes in East County in recent days, one of them resulting in the death of a 36-year-old El Cajon man, Robert Edward Hurley, who was fatally shot while taking trash to the curb. Robert and Mavis Perry of Spring Valley were terrorized for four hours as robbers – one armed with a handgun – ransacked their home. Two masked men interrupted a family dinner in La Mesa, stealing cash, jewelry and other items.

Nov. 15 – La Mesa attorney Edwin Meese III, 49, was chosen to be a counselor for President-elect Ronald Reagan. Meese had been Reagan's chief of staff in the California governor's office and subsequently served as Attorney General in the Reagan Cabinet.

Nov. 25 – A La Mesa woman, Barbara Middleton, 39, was identified as one of the 84 victims who died in the MGM Grand Hotel fire in Las Vegas. Her fiancé, Dell Hanks, 47, who had been with her at the hotel, was still listed as missing.

Dec. 2 – Santee officially became a city today, and the first city council meeting was held at the Santana High School gym. Council members were Gene Ainsworth, Woodie Miller, Jan Claussen, Roy Woodward and Jim Bartell. . . . An editorial in this issue noted the achievements of El Cajon resident Bernard "Rocky" McGale, who grew up on the Pine Ridge Indian Reservation in South Dakota. Orphaned at 9, he was sent to live with foster parents in New York. When his foster mother died, he left home at age 11 and wandered alone. In Baltimore he was hired as a trainer and groomer at a racetrack. When he was old enough, he made his way to San Diego and joined the U.S. Marine Corps. Court-martialed for shooting a man while on guard duty, he was ordered to China where he taught guerrillas to use explosives against the invading Japanese. With that experience, he was selected as a member of the famous Carlson's Raiders, an elite unit whose guerrilla activity was heralded by World War II historians.

Dec. 23 – President Jimmy Carter signed into law a bill that will enable James Daniel Fannin of Spring Valley to become a permanent resident alien and eventually apply for U.S. citizenship. Fannin, 26, was born in Korea to a U.S. Army lieutenant and a Women's Army Corps (WAC) sergeant who abandoned him in Korea when their tours of duty ended. Left with a Korean family, his parents promised to return for him but never did.

James was shunned by most of his countrymen because of his Amerasian status. Two years ago, Doye Fannin spotted the 6-foot, 5-inch man while working for the Red Cross in South Korea and began the lengthy process of bringing him to this country. James has been adopted by Robert Fannin, a retired U.S. Army major, and his wife. He has a scholarship to study at San Diego Technological Institute.

1981

Jan. 2 – A 15-year-old Santee youth who had no flight instruction stole a twin-engine aircraft on New Year's Day that crashed into a furniture warehouse near Gillespie Field Airport, killing him and four passengers. The unlicensed pilot, Grant Robert Thompson, was a student at Santana High School where he had taken an aeronautics class. Other victims were Joseph A. Gerulaitis, 32, and Roberta Elizabeth Gerulaitis, 35, the youth's stepfather and mother; Edward Allen, 35, a family friend; and Chief Petty Officer Richard Pehl, 37. The plane, bound for Las Vegas, crashed at 1903 Friendship Drive, about a half-mile southwest of the airfield. It was the worst aviation disaster at Gillespie Field in its history.

Jan. 10 – El Cajon Superior Court Judge Elizabeth Zumwalt found 14-year-old Jeff Auer responsible for the death of his 9-year-old brother, Andrew. Zumwalt ruled: "I find beyond a reasonable doubt that he struck the (fatal) blow in the heat of passion." Andrew disappeared from his Santee home the night of Aug. 15, and his body was found nearby on Aug. 18 buried under brush. A dog being taken on a walk by its owner discovered the body. Sentencing for Jeff Auer was set for Jan. 30.

Jan. 19 – *The Daily Californian* celebrated the release of 52 American hostages held by Iran, framing the front-page story headlined "Coming Home" with small photos of all the hostages inside two thick black borders.

Jan. 29 – Kurt Anderson, 26, died less than two hours after he was bitten by a pet albino cobra in his Lemon Grove home. Investigators found 89 reptiles at the home, including 57 snakes, 31 lizards and a 14-inch alligator.

Feb. 2 – Larry McCraw, 28, a karate instructor at Tracy's Karate Studio, did 27,225 sit-ups over a span of 11 hours, hoping to land a spot in the Guinness Book of World Records. The current record is 26,000.

Feb. 3 – Former Valhalla High School diver Greg Louganis finished a distant second behind Eric Heiden as the country's top amateur athlete. Heiden, who received the Sullivan Award given by the U.S. Amateur Athletic Union, set five Olympic speed-skating records and won five gold medals at the Winter Olympics in Lake Placid, N.Y. (*Louganis would go on to win multiple gold medals in Olympic competition at Los Angeles (1984) and Seoul, Korea (1988).*

Feb. 23 – Stephen R. Thatcher, 35, of Antioch, CA, was named the first city manager for the new city of Santee. He will be paid $38,000 a year.

Mar. 10 – Extension of the San Diego Trolley to El Cajon was approved in a 5-0 vote by the Metropolitan Transit Development Board despite objections by some La Mesa homeowners. The completion date for the 176-mile trolley system is 1986.

Mar. 12 – El Cajon Police Chief Wally Dart, 52, who will retire April 30, gave a farewell interview to *The Daily Californian* in which he recalled a confrontation with a Doberman pinscher guard dog at a junkyard. Dart scrambled over a six-foot fence to escape the growling watchdog. He had been with the department for 29 years, 18 of them as chief. There were only six officers in the department when he started in 1952. The department now has 152 employees.

Mar. 29 – U.S. Census Bureau reported that La Mesa's population had jumped to 50,342, which will qualify it to receive at least $2 million more over the next 10 years in federal revenue sharing funds.

Apr. 1 – The entire front page of *The Daily Californian* was devoted to the assassination attempt against President Ronald Reagan by John Hinckley Jr., 25, described as a wealthy oilman's son and an "irresponsible drifter" from Evergreen, CO who was under a psychiatrist's care.

Apr. 6 – The controversial book, "Our Bodies, Ourselves," was cleared by Supt. Robert Pyle for use in Grossmont Union High School District schools after it had been challenged as "pornographic" by an unidentified district resident. Evangelist Jerry Falwell of the Moral Majority has led a national effort to have the book banned in schools. Pyle said the book, though very explicit, is not pornographic because it does not appeal to prurient interest. The book focuses on women's health issues.

Apr. 14 – Columbia, an 80-ton U.S. rocket ship, ended its 36 orbits around the Earth by landing at Edward Air Force Base. Two El Cajon firms – Ametek-Straza and Chem-Tronics, Inc. – helped build the space shuttle.

Apr. 17 – F Street Bookstore on Main Street in El Cajon closed down its peep shows today and threw covers on its narcotics paraphernalia to appease the El Cajon City Council, which next week will decide if the X-rated bookstore should have its license revoked. (*The City Council voted April 21 to close the store, but its order was challenged by the bookstore's attorney, Thomas Homann, who said he was drafting an "impressive lawsuit" against the city. A federal judge later granted a preliminary injunction, preventing the license from being revoked.*)

May 1 – Ruth Norman, the 80-year-old leader of Unarius in El Cajon, lost her bet that space beings would land somewhere on Earth by April 30, 1981.

The wager, which made headlines around the world, had been placed with Ladbroke and Co., Ltd. in England. Norman claimed she maintained psychic communication with the leaders of 32 other worlds. . . . The firing of Tom Barton, 41, principal of Christian High School, set off a firestorm of charges about the influence of Pastor Tim La Haye on school affairs in the aftermath of a story published in the *Los Angeles Times.* Barton thinks he was fired because he allowed two Roman Catholics to be on the high school's staff as substitute aides. Full-time staff members are required to be members of Scott Memorial Baptist Church where La Haye is the pastor.

May 6 – Conservative author and newspaper columnist Phyllis Schlafly brought her campaign to prevent the adoption of the Equal Rights Amendment to Grossmont College. At an assembly sponsored by Associated Students of Grossmont College, Inc., she opposed conscription of women into the armed forces, saying that women cannot go 28 days without a bath, which is sometimes required of men in combat.

May 14 – Capt. Darwin Sinclair, 50, who has been a police officer for 25 years in El Cajon, was named the city's police chief by City Manager Bob Applegate. Sinclair replaces Wally Dart who retired at the end of April.

May 31 – The Rev. David Jeremiah, pastor of Black Hawk Baptist Church in Fort Wayne, IN, has been hired to replace controversial Tim La Haye as senior pastor of three congregations in El Cajon, the North Park section of San Diego and Solana Beach. La Haye, senior pastor at Scott Memorial Baptist Church in El Cajon, resigned to devote his time to Family Life Seminars, a fundamentalist education and counseling ministry that he operates with his wife, Beverly. La Haye was California chairman of the Moral Majority, a national group led by evangelist Jerry Falwell.

June 4 – A Superior Court jury found Donovan Leistico, 39, of San Diego, guilty of murdering his estranged wife, Ellen, 37, an El Cajon Municipal Court traffic clerk, by hitting her with his truck on Blossom Valley Road. Leistico, a real estate agent and a former Lutheran elder, maintained in court that the collision between his truck and his estranged wife was an accident. (*On July 1, Leistico was sentenced to 26 years to life in state prison.*)

June 9 – Stoney's Rock "N" Roll Market, which opened May 3, 1952, at the junction of Jamacha Road and Granite Hills Drive in El Cajon, was closing. Owner Buell "Stoney" Stone cited the cost of doing business as the reason. Long-time customers held a wake to mark the occasion.

June 13 – Daniel Alstadt, 24, who with a hatchet murdered three members of his family in 1975 and set fire to their San Carlos area home, has asked to be declared legally sane so he can eventually be released from prison. A jury had ruled that Alstadt, then 18, was sane when he killed his father and insane when he killed his mother and 19-year-old sister. Judge William

Low has asked four court-appointed psychiatrists to examine Alstadt, who is housed at the men's colony in a San Luis Obispo facility. *(Judge Low on July 10 found that Alstadt is now sane, but there will be no immediate change in his status as an imprisoned felon.)*

July 1 – Sheriff's deputies and marshal's deputies in San Diego County were on strike over the amount of their pay increase, which affected law enforcement in a 4,200-square-mile area with 535,000 people. About 800 deputies stayed away from their jobs. County supervisors declared a state of emergency, which allowed the use of city police agencies to assist with law enforcement in county areas.

July 3 – Willie Carroll, a prominent El Cajon businessman who owned seven health-care facilities in the area as well as a mortuary, died of a heart attack today at Grossmont Hospital. He was 61. Carroll had been in El Cajon since 1937 when his mother and father loaded their large family into a trailer and made the move here from Texas.

July 4 – A bulldozer struck a rock while grading in Wildcat Canyon near Lakeside, creating sparks that set off a range fire which destroyed at least one home, threatened dozens of others and spread over 3,300 acres.

July 7 – Quadruplets – all boys – were born July 6 to Laurence and Janna Wagner of La Mesa at Mercy Hospital in San Diego. The quadruplets were described as unusually healthy. The Wagners own Yamata Music School which caters to small children.

July 27 – Van Hanh Buddhist Temple – the only one of its kind in San Diego County – opened at 8617 Fanita Drive in Santee. It will serve the Vietnamese community.

Aug. 5 – Ruth Krell, 82, of El Cajon, recalled how as a young Pacific Telephone Co. operator she had overheard President Woodrow Wilson tell Adm. Caperton, commander of the Pacific Fleet, that he had declared war on Germany at the start of World War I. The call came to her station at the Hotel del Coronado where Caperton was staying. How did she overhear what President Wilson was saying? She pulled the plug that connected the two men halfway out of its socket.

Aug. 18 – A quadriplegic left to die last month in his El Cajon apartment by his ruthless caretakers has become a service project for the Santee Kiwanis Club. Melvin Spooner, almost totally paralyzed from the neck down, was robbed of $500 by the couple hired to care for him. When he was found three days later, he was dehydrated and having difficulty breathing. The Kiwanis club bought him a new color television set, provided him a telephone extension cord that he could use to summon help, built a counter so liquids were always available and promised him a special typewriter. Friends and neighbors also were assisting Spooner.

Aug. 19 – Classic Cat Theater in La Mesa, a nude dance club, lost its bid to remain at its present location on Jackson Drive where it had been since 1977. Nine employees, both women and men, were convicted on 22 charges involving obscene conduct during performances and sentenced to probation and ordered to pay fines.

Sept. 2 – Three teenagers – two of them from Santee – set a new world record for continuous roller skating by bettering the previous mark of 13 days, 10 hours and 20 minutes posted last year by an Australian team. The new record holders: Rob Zorn, 18, of Santee; Cory Cube, 17, of Santee; and Ken Morris of Chula Vista. They added five hours to the previous record.

Sept. 14 – *The Daily Californian* ran a post-prison interview with former El Cajon police officer Jerry Hancock who recently was released from prison where he had been held for 15 months for committing burglary while a member of the police force. Hancock, whose employment as a cop was cited as a factor for his release because of death threats while imprisoned, had been in three institutions – Chino, Sierra Conservation Camp and San Quentin. In the interview, Hancock said his motive for committing burglary was to make his department "look bad" because of a conflict he had with a lieutenant in the department. He is now living in a small Idaho town and selling auto parts. Hancock, whose first marriage ended in divorce, has remarried but said he returns to El Cajon occasionally to see his two sons. Although Hancock was convicted of only one burglary, the district attorney agreed not to prosecute him for 183 other burglaries he was suspected of committing on condition that he plead guilty to one charge.

Sept. 21 – U.S. Rep. Clair Burgener, 60, announced he would not seek re-election to his 43rd Congressional District seat when his term ends in 15 months. Burgener, whose district includes much of East County, won his most recent election by swamping Democratic challenger Tom Metzger, leader of the Ku Klux Klan in California, a race that drew national attention because of Metzger's political extremism. By the end of his current term, Burgener will have served in public office for 24 years. He was a San Diego city councilman before his election to Congress.

Nov. 4 – An advisory vote showed that 62.5 percent of the respondents favored extending the San Diego trolley line to El Cajon. The vote was 32,488 to 19,470.

Nov. 16 – The "Best in the West" rodeo in Lakeside drew 11,000 spectators over two days.

Nov. 19 – Long-time civic leader and former El Cajon Councilman Howard Pierce died at 64. He had served as a trustee of Cajon Valley Union School District and was a city planning commissioner before being elected to the City Council.

Nov. 24 – The San Diego County Board of Supervisors voted unanimously to endorse the proposed East County trolley to El Cajon and Santee. It also voted to apply for $85 million in state grants to fund the $89 million light-rail system.

Nov. 26 – Friends of the El Cajon Library launched a library expansion project to cost $2.2 million.

Dec. 2 – Dean Waite, 33, publisher of *The Daily Californian*, announced he would leave the paper Dec. 22 to accept a position with the new 24-hour cable TV weather channel in Atlanta, GA. Circulation of the paper had increased from 13,000 to 20,000 since his arrival here in October 1978.

Dec. 9 – It was announced that El Cajon's city clerk, Mildred Kennel, would retire Jan. 1 after serving in that office for 28 years.

Dec. 12 – A helicopter crash on Interstate 8 during the evening rush hour killed the pilot, Walter Napieralski, 30, and his 6-year-old son. It was believed the pilot was trying to avoid a patch of fog.

1982

Jan. 14 – Cajon Plaza, Inc. filed an industrial development plan for Gillespie Field land that includes Cajon Speedway, which averages 100,000 fans a year for stock car races. The racetrack began operating in mid-1961.

Jan. 22 – Buck Knives, El Cajon's second largest employer, laid off 76 workers because of a sales slump and planned to terminate 10 more. The firm employs nearly 500 at its 1900 Weld Blvd. plant.

Jan. 26 – Mother Goose Parade Assn. directors discussed moving the parade to San Diego for possibly higher attendance. *The Daily Californian* editorialized against the move and there was an outcry from local businesses. The parade had been held annually for 35 years.

Feb. 4 – Grossmont Hospital District's plan for a $58 million expansion drew opposition from the Health Systems Agency which claimed that East County didn't need 134 additional beds and a 700-car garage. The agency said the district needs only 21 more beds by 1990.

Feb. 6 – Editor Tom White explained why *The Daily Californian* was getting smaller. He wrote that it cost 53 cents to produce each paper, but subscribers paid only 12 cents of that amount and if readers chose to buy the paper from a vending machine they paid only 25 cents.

Feb. 9 – Directors of the Mother Goose Parade Assn. voted 19 to 12 against moving the parade to San Diego.

Feb. 11 – Buck Knives laid off 67 more workers because of slumping sales.

Feb. 23 – The San Diego Assn. of Governments (SANDAG) reported the first drop in the overall crime rate in 10 years for San Diego County.

Feb. 26 – Trusthouse Forte, Inc., parent company of TraveLodge International and the Colony Kitchen restaurant chain, announced its plan to move its corporate offices from El Cajon to San Diego. Twenty-five workers were laid off.

Mar. 1 – Santee tenor Jonathan Welch won second place and $2,000 in the 1982 Western Regional Finals of the Metropolitan Opera auditions. Welch, 31, missed a chance to compete in the national finals but eventually sang opera on the international circuit, mainly in Europe.

Mar. 3 – A contest to select a slogan for El Cajon drew 1,100 entries. The winner: "El Cajon – It's winter sun and summer fun." Mary J. Hayward submitted the winning entry, but the City Council delayed giving its official approval.

Mar. 6 – Seventeen homeowners in Santee won more than $17 million in damages in Superior Court because the Oakhills subdivision was built on unstable ground. The jury deliberated 12 days before returning its verdict.

Mar. 18 – San Diego Humane Society offered a $250 reward for information leading to the arrest and conviction of those responsible for alleged "ritual slayings" of sheep south of El Cajon near Grove Road. *(It was later determined that cougars probably were responsible for the slayings.)*

Apr. 1 – Clifford Graves, chief administrator for San Diego County, warned supervisors they were facing the most severe revenue shortfall in the county's history. The projected revenue gap would be $73.9 million unless there were sharp cuts.

Apr. 2 – Buck Knives, Inc., once El Cajon's second largest employer, announced the layoff of 104 workers, the third major job reduction since 1980.

Apr. 5 – El Cajon City Manager Robert Applegate announced that he will retire July 9 after 24 years on the job.

Apr. 27 – The Santee City Council approved a major use permit to build a $2 million eight-plex theater at the corner of Mission Gorge Road and Olive Lane. The 26,878-square-foot structure is the second of its kind to be built in the county. Oceanside is the only other city with an eight-plex theater.

Apr. 28 – C&M Airlines, based in the Mojave Desert, was given approval by the County Board of Supervisors to fly to and from Gillespie Field to Los Angeles. The airline offered four flights a day.

Apr. 29 – FedMart Corp. announced it will shut or liquidate all 46 of its retail discount stores in three states within two months. The closures will put 3,500 people out of work in 12 San Diego County stores, including four in East County.

May 19 – San Diego County placed first in the country for measles cases despite a 90 percent immunization rate. Health experts were stumped as to the cause, but an audit showed that 10 percent of the immunization records for elementary students in three East County districts – Cajon Valley, La Mesa and Lemon Grove – were incomplete.

May 20 – East County buses operated by the County Transit System carried a record 57,311 passengers in March. It was the highest ridership in March since 1975 and a 12.5 percent increase over the same month in 1981.

May 24 – The La Mesa Cannonball rolled down the track for the first time in 54 years as a passenger train. It went to Lemon Grove and El Cajon, a 15-mile journey. Paying passengers totaled 950. . . . An attempt was made on the life of Kip Hayes, 23, a quadriplegic paralyzed while playing football for Mt. Miguel High School in 1976. A distraught acquaintance tried to turn off Hayes' respirator. The acquaintance, 22, was booked into county jail on suspicion of attempted murder and burglary.

June 4 – Susan Driscoll, 41, who served five years in Patton State Hospital for shooting to death her husband and two teen-age children, was released from the hospital with assurances her sanity had been restored.

July 6 – The Wagner quadruplets of La Mesa – Ben, Brett, Chad and Kyle – celebrated their first birthday. Larry and Janna Wagner were expecting triplets when the quads were born.

July 7 – Robert Acker, who had been serving as acting city manager since the retirement of Robert Applegate, was appointed city manager of El Cajon.

July 10 – Bill Lewis, 49, vice president of Pathway Bellows, Inc. of El Cajon, was among 149 passengers believed to have perished in a July 9 air-liner crash minutes after takeoff from New Orleans airport. It was the sec-ond-worst plane crash in U.S. history to that point.

July 12 – A Santee family was trying to cope with the loss of five family mem-bers who died in the Pan-Am crash in New Orleans while flying here to attend the funeral of Lawrence W. Cummings, who had been killed when his motor-cycle collided with the draw bars of dump trucks in Santee. Two of Cummings' sisters and three of their children were among the plane crash fatalities.

July 13 – El Cajon Mayor John Reber, 50, was arrested on suspicion of drunken driving and misdemeanor hit-and-run driving. Reber hit a wooden fence on Old Chase Avenue. He was later sentenced to two days in jail and was placed on three years' probation.

July 26 – Scott Meese, 19, son of President Nixon's adviser Ed Meese, who later was appointed Attorney General of the United States, was killed in an automobile accident in McLean, VA. The Meese family lived in La Mesa. Scott Meese had attended Valhalla High School and was an honor student majoring in government and politics at Princeton University.

Aug. 12 – Herzog Contracting Co. began drilling at the Sycamore Canyon landfill in Santee to determine if methane gas could be extracted from county dumps. County officials estimated it would cost $10 million to build a power plant at each of the county's four landfills.

Aug. 16 – *The Daily Californian* carried a feature story on Helen Hall, 85, a La Mesa woman called "Queen of the Road" who claimed to have walked 16,000 miles through 50 states to promote various causes, including wel-fare reform. She was writing her memoir.

Aug. 25 – Supt. Walter Yuhl of the Grossmont Community College District took a $4,000 a year pay cut to dramatize the fiscal plight of his district, which had only $95,000 in its reserve fund for the 1982-83 fiscal year.

Aug. 27 --The county's jobless rate hit 11 percent in July. There were 91,200 San Diegans without jobs.

Sept. 1 – Ten businesses on El Cajon Boulevard protested a decision by the El Cajon City Council to grant a business license to the Okinawa Massage Parlor at 557 El Cajon Blvd. In the last three months, the city has received applications for three additional massage parlors. The objecting businesses wanted Okinawa Massage Parlor's license revoked.

Sept. 11 – Some parents in the Jamul-Las Flores School District had pulled their children from public school, allegedly because they had been harassed for their opposition to "secular humanism" being taught in the district. Eleven children had been taken out of the school. Parents complained their children had received death threats and threatening phone calls. One parent claimed to have been run off the road by a district employee. At issue was Project LAUNCH, a federally funded program developed by the Newport-Mesa Unified School District in 1978.

Sept. 15 – A two-year battle by the El Cajon City Council against the F Street Bookstore on Main Street came to an end when the council approved an agreement that allowed the controversial, X-rated book store and peep show to operate. The city had spent more than $25,000 opposing the business.

Sept. 24 – Fire destroyed Captain Kidd's Galley Restaurant at 530 N. Second St. in El Cajon. The fire was attributed to the lack of a metal hood over the deep-fat fryer.

Oct. 14 – A record number of San Diego County residents had registered to vote in the Nov. 2 statewide general election. The total was 952,214, of whom 42.9% were Democrats; 42.1%, Republicans; 12.2%, non-partisan; 1.6%, American Independent; .3%, Peace and Freedom; .7%, Libertarian; and .2%, miscellaneous.

Oct. 20 – Paul Robert Pitts, 26, who killed his 2-year-old stepson by putting him in a toy box with a blowing hair dryer, was sentenced to 25 years to life in prison, the maximum. Jared Cartwright died Jan. 29 of asphyxiation and heat stroke after being in the toy box for more than 20 minutes. Pitts was convicted of first-degree murder and felony child abuse.

Oct. 22 – El Cajon painter Olaf Wieghorst, 83, celebrated as one of the greatest living Western artists in the world, sold his "Navajo Madonna" painting for $450,000.

Oct. 27 – Thousands of East County residents were among 263,000 in the county who were without power for 46 minutes the previous day when San Diego Gas & Electric Co. lost its connection with Southern California Edison. Power was interrupted at 3:49 p.m. and was not restored until 4:45 p.m.

Nov. 3 – Republican Pete Wilson, who began his political career as an assemblyman representing parts of East County, defeated Democrat Jerry

Brown for a seat in the U.S. Senate, winning 51 percent of the vote to Brown's 45 percent. Wilson had been mayor of San Diego. . . . Voters turned down a proposed tax to raise $150,000 a year for the Mother Goose Parade over the next three years.

Nov. 24 – Former State Sen. Bob Wilson is being paid $750 a month by the city of El Cajon to represent its interests in Sacramento, plus travel-related expenses.

Dec. 1 – An Alaska-based storm tore through East County with winds in excess of 57 mph, uprooting trees, wrecking patio roofs and downing phone poles. More than a half-inch of rain had doused most areas of the county, and 150,000 residents lost power.

Dec. 3 – Two East County residents were arrested in a crackdown by federal agents on an international cocaine-running operation known as "The Corporation." In all, 13 persons were taken into custody in New York and San Diego, including a lawyer for the California Department of Transportation, a sports promoter and a law student. The operation was making $200,000 a month in San Diego.

Dec. 6 – Ron Ballard, 40, assistant city manager of National City, was hired to be city manager for Santee at $46,000 a year. There were 140 applicants.

Dec. 7 – Kahl Scientific Instrument Corp. in El Cajon, which manufactured devices for the study of weather and water, became the first business in California to win the presidential E-Star award. The award was given for increasing its sales overseas. The company had 50 employees and was started in 1958 at Gillespie Field by Joseph Kahl. His son, Gerald, was in charge of the El Cajon plant.

Dec. 9 – The $38 million county building in El Cajon's superblock is to be occupied by 8 a.m. Monday, Dec. 20. Three hundred workers will take space in the 10-story building, the city's tallest structure.

Dec. 14 – Walter Yuhl, 51, resigned as superintendent of the Grossmont Community College District effective Jan. 3 and will return to teaching. He had guided the district for four years.

1983

Jan. 5 – Pigeons were being trapped in El Cajon and exiled to other venues because there were too many of them befouling the downtown area. A

San Diego newspaper columnist had recommended spiking their drinking water so they would fall from their perches and die.

Jan. 6 – With the Home of Guiding Hands in Lakeside threatening to close within 30 days because of financial difficulty, the community rallied to raise $45,000 for the 14-acre residential and educational facility that served 296 mentally and physically challenged individuals. The facility said it needed to raise $1 million to pay off debts and avoid closure.

Jan. 12 – Target was planning to open two stores in East County in facilities abandoned by FedMart Corp. One was to be at 345 N. Magnolia Ave. in El Cajon, the other at 8000 Grossmont Blvd. in La Mesa. The East County stores would employ 450. Target had eight stores in San Diego County.

Feb. 2 – Ralphs planned to open three stores in East County employing 210. The stores were to be in La Mesa, the San Carlos section of San Diego and El Cajon.

Feb. 17 – Grossmont Hospital District Board approved a $58 million expansion plan that would add 150 beds, a neo-natal intensive care unit and facilities for a cardiac catheterization lab and open heart surgery to the 400-bed hospital by 1990.

Feb. 18 – A 15-year-old El Capitan High School student was expelled until at least September for lacing the brownies he gave to his teacher with marijuana. Wanda Ishmael, the teacher, ate three of the brownies at a school party welcoming her back from surgery for the removal of a malignant tumor.

Feb. 23 – An out-of-court settlement could mean $7.2 million for Kip Hayes, the Mt. Miguel High School football player who was left a paraplegic as a result of an injury. Hayes had filed a $20 million product liability suit again Riddell Corp. of Los Angeles which made football helmets. Hayes suffered his injury in 1976.

Feb. 26 – Using an 1872 law protecting the public from "mischievous animals," an El Cajon Municipal Court jury found pit bull owner Rex Harvey of Ramona guilty of involuntary manslaughter and death by a mischievous animal. Harvey's two pit bulls attacked the Harveys' landlord, 68-year-old George de Martini, who died Aug. 21 from his injuries. Harvey, 25, said he would appeal.

Mar. 9 – El Cajon City Council rejected a proposal to declare March 13-19 as "White History Week." The designation had been requested by Winston

W.P. Burbage of Lemon Grove, who was San Diego political director of the White American Political Assn. Burbage made his proposal in response to the council's declaration of Feb. 13-19 as Black History Week.

Mar. 14 – In what was referred to as a sting operation, more than 100 illegal aliens jumped into a furniture van parked near Jacumba driven by Border Patrol agents, thinking they had hitched a ride to Los Angeles.

Mar. 19 – Sam, a 1-year-old Yorkshire terrier left behind when his family moved from Colorado to Santee in January, showed up on their doorstep after an apparent 841-mile trek through the plains, mountains and valleys of Colorado, New Mexico, Arizona and California. The dog, owned by Ray and Debbie Foltz, was described as "unbelievably weak and filthy and covered with grease." It was suffering from malnutrition, muscle spasms and blistered paws. Sam had been separated from his family for two months and 12 days.

Mar. 21 – Three teen-age girls were being held as suspects in the death of a disabled Vietnam veteran, 37-year-old Dick Sherwood, who was stabbed, beaten and dumped in the mountain area east of Alpine, possibly suffering fatal exposure to several nights of extremely cold temperatures. Deputy District Attorney Craig Rooten described Sherwood's death as a "torture murder." A 16-year-old girl faced murder, robbery, kidnapping and auto theft charges. Her friends, 14 and 17, were held as accessories to the crime. Later, a 13-year-old girl was implicated.

Mar. 22 – Border Patrol agents apprehended 2,442 illegal crossers Sunday and another 2,115 Monday in the San Diego County sector. The March count of apprehensions during the first 21 days was 31,801 – up 45 percent from the 21,953 taken into custody during the first 21 days of March 1982.

Mar. 30 – Drunken driving was blamed for 40 percent of the fatalities in March in the area of East County patrolled by the California Highway Patrol. Fourteen people had died in 10 accidents so far this month.

Apr. 18 – Parents swamped Santee School District's office with calls because of anxiety over reports that a physician was testing a Hill Creek substitute teacher for Legionnaire's disease. Some children were temporarily withdrawn from school by parents or taken to doctors for medical checkups. Supt. Douglas Giles challenged a physician's conclusion that the ventilation system at Hill Creek was the probable cause of respiratory problems experienced by kindergarten teacher Barbara Martin. OSHA, the government agency in charge of workplace safety, had found no health hazard.

Apr. 22 – Grossmont Union High School District Board voted to require students to maintain at least a "C" average in a minimum of five classes to be eligible for athletics, band, specialty corps and cheerleading squads. It was to be a one-year experiment.

May 3 – Santee City Council voted 4-1 to reject a plan from Chilcote Inc. for up to 1,404 condominiums on 105 acres of flat land along the western edge of Cuyamaca Street and north of the San Diego River.

May 11 – Santee School District Board voted 4-1 to lay off one nurse and 37 instructors, a move the Santee Teachers Assn. described as the "darkest moment in a school district dedicated to excellence . . . a step backward." The district was trying to slice $1.2 million from its budget.

May 20 – A Juvenile Court judge found a 13-year-old girl implicated in the death of a disabled Vietnam War veteran guilty of second-degree murder. Dick Sherwood, 37, had been kidnapped, stabbed, beaten and left to freeze to death in the mountains east of Alpine after an all-night party with several teen-age girls.

June 4 – Dr. Donald Walker, 61, a former instructor and administrator at San Diego State University, was appointed superintendent of the Grossmont Community College District. He had been president of Southeast Massachusetts University and Idaho State University.

June 9 – A 14-year-old Alpine girl pleaded guilty to second-degree murder in the death of Dick Sherwood, 37, a paraplegic Vietnam War veteran who froze to death in the mountains east of Alpine after being beaten, stabbed and burned with a cigarette lighter.

June 18 – Wickes Furniture in El Cajon, the company's only outlet in San Diego County, announced it would go out of business, a victim of difficult economic times.

July 8 – Rose Christine Gonzalez, 14, was sentenced by Juvenile Court Judge Judith McConnell to 15 years to life in California Youth Authority for her part in the death of disabled Vietnam War veteran Dick Sherwood, 37. Timothy Slade Elliott, 38, of Campo faced a preliminary hearing in Municipal Court to determine if there is enough evidence to try him on charges of murder and kidnapping in the same case. Two other girls – Joyce Renee Largo, 16, of Campo and Marguerite Benjamin, 18, of Alpine – face a Sept. 19 trial in Superior Court for Sherwood's death. Nicolosa Aguilera, 13, of the Logan Heights area of San Diego, was convicted in Juvenile Court on May 20 of second-degree murder and was sentenced to the California Youth Authority.

July 14 – Don and Cynthia Watkins found their dream home in Santee after a six-month search, but they were forced to give it up because of an act of vandalism. Don, 31, a San Diego police officer, is black; Cynthia, 26, is white. They have two sons, 17 months and two weeks. Escrow was to close Aug. 1, but the couple abandoned the house when "KKK," the abbreviation for the notoriously racist Ku Klux Klan, was painted across the front of it.

July 20 – Grossmont Community College District Board voted to ban smoking at its meetings.

July 21 – The American Avenue area of La Mesa is infested with rats and residents were warned to take care of the problem or risk potentially serious health hazards.

Aug. 3 – El Cajon City Council unanimously approved stricter smoking regulations, passing an ordinance requiring restaurants that seat 20 or more persons to designate smoking and no-smoking areas. Restaurants seating fewer than 20 have the option of designating no-smoking areas or prohibiting smoking. Smoking also is banned in elevators, restrooms, waiting rooms and public halls of every private or public health care facility. Separate waiting rooms for smokers are permissible.

Aug. 5 – Raleigh Hills Hospital in El Cajon, an adult alcohol treatment facility, gave its employees their last paychecks and is to reopen Sept. 1 as a treatment center for adolescent substance abusers. The entire staff of about 20 was fired.

Aug. 18 – County supervisors shut down the Big Oak Ranch in Dehesa Valley, citing complaints about noise, illegal camping and parking, litter and crowds in excess of the legal limit attending country music concerts. Owner Rock Kreutzer vowed to sue to remain open.

Aug. 20 – Former Faith Chapel youth pastor Michael Frank McMahon, 32, was sentenced to five years and eight months in prison for having sex with three girls, 15 to 17, who attended his church. . . . Santee Sam, the Yorkshire terrier that drew national attention for his 72-day, 841-mile trek across four western states to rejoin his family, was struck and killed by a truck. The celebrity dog dug a hole under a fence and darted in front of a passing truck. The family had received nearly 4,000 letters and publicity in the *National Enquirer, USA Today* and on CBS Evening News with Dan Rather.

Aug. 23 – Charles Decker, 67, the real estate developer described as the driving force behind the development of Parkway Plaza, died of a heart attack.

Aug. 25 – SRI International recommended that El Cajon's deteriorating downtown be turned into an "urban village" with high-density housing, institutional and office buildings, retail stores and cultural attractions. Its study cost $73,000.

Sept. 2 – Grossmont Union High School District Board voted 4-0 to reinstate the six-period day on a one-year trial basis starting Sept. 12.

Sept. 12 – Rock Kreutzer, 46, owner of Big Oak Ranch in the Dehesa Valley area, was arrested and jailed for defying an order to close down his ranch for concerts. Neighbors had complained of excessive noise and traffic congestion. Kreutzer filed a $40,000 claim against the county for his arrest for not having a valid entertainment license.

Sept. 28 – Park rangers at Santee Lakes Regional Park and Campground were given the authority to fire "bird bombs" above the roosting spots of cormorants to chase the birds away. More than 600 cormorants were reportedly seen in one day. If the "bird bombs" didn't work, rangers were to use "cracker shells" to accomplish their eviction.

Oct. 24 – Superior Court Judge Sheridan Reed issued a preliminary injunction stopping the county from enforcing its ordinance requiring a license to stage entertainment events. He said it was unconstitutional. This affected the case of Big Oak Ranch owner Rock Kreutzer, who had been arrested and jailed for disobeying the ordinance.

Oct. 25 – A pioneer Dulzura couple – Oli Sperry, 81, and his wife, Hazel, 87 – were found dead at their home, bound and gagged with bed clothing. Law enforcement investigators suspected illegal immigrants because their vehicle was missing.

Nov. 1 – A 56-year-old East County woman was in critical condition after surviving the first liver transplant ever performed in Southern California. Her family asked that her identity not be revealed. The operation at Sharp Memorial Hospital took 21 hours, cost an estimated $70,000 and the patient used at least 270 units of blood. . . . John Somerville, 79, of El Cajon, a retired philosophy professor at U.S. International University, had launched a statewide campaign for an initiative requiring the United States to declare it would not be the first to use nuclear weapons. He had to collect 393,835 signatures of registered voters to qualify the initiative for the state ballot in November 1984.

Nov. 2 – The third murder in less than a week had occurred in the tiny East County community of Dulzura. Catherine Garland, 50, had been shot in the head in her home....Kory Wolf of El Cajon was selected as the November Playmate centerfold in *Playgirl* magazine. Wolf, 22, was a 1980 graduate of Granite Hills High School.

Nov. 4 – Florence Ellen Marano of El Cajon was identified by her family as the first adult in Southern California to undergo a liver transplant. She and her husband, Victor, have eight children. Doctors said Marano was making progress and her liver was functioning.

Nov. 8 – Liver transplant patient Florence Marano died, eight days after undergoing the rare operation. She suffered from biliary cirrhosis, a disease not related to alcohol consumption.

Nov. 9 – Joan Shoemaker, in her first try for elective office, unseated incumbent Dona Foster for a seat on the El Cajon City Council. She later was elected the city's mayor.

Nov. 10 – Three Mexican citizens were in custody in connection with three murders in the Dulzura area. They were to be tried for murder in Mexico.

Nov. 15 – Jan Claussen, appointed mayor of Santee, became the first woman to fill that position in an East County city.

Nov. 18 -- Joyce Largo, 16, was convicted of first-degree murder in the torture death of a paraplegic Vietnam veteran near Alpine in mid-March. Sentencing will be Dec. 16. The victim, Dick Sherwood, 37, of Yuma, had been paralyzed in an automobile accident in Germany.

Nov. 19 – East County's jail is to open Dec. 12 with 100 prisoners.

Dec. 1 – Two Mexican nationals charged with the slayings of three Americans in the Dulzura area of East County confessed to the killings. Defendants Pablo Hayes, 25, and Ricardo Sandoval, 18, said they robbed and suffocated an elderly couple Oct. 24 and shot and killed Catherine Garland, 50, during robberies. Two other defendants – Jesus Escobedo, 20, and Antonio Alba, 35 -- were accused of helping the murder suspects cover up the crime.

Dec. 2 – Kory Wolf of El Cajon is Playgirl's Man of the Year for 1983.

Dec. 7 – Douglas Timothy Slade Elliott, 38, is the fourth of five defendants and the first adult to be convicted in the death of Richard Sherwood, 37, of Yuma, AZ. Elliott was found guilty of first-degree murder, robbery and kidnapping. He claimed he was drunk and in the back of the van when his girl companions tortured Sherwood and left him to die in the mountains east of Alpine.

Dec. 9 – Margaret Ann Benjamin, 18, pleaded guilty to auto theft and being an accessory to robbery in the death of Vietnam War veteran Dick Sherwood. Murder and kidnapping charges against her were dismissed . . . . Dr. Joel Warner, who had resigned as administrator of El Cajon Valley Hospital, is now president and chief executive officer of newly formed Medical Surgical Centers of America, which plans to start a chain of outpatient surgery centers.

1984

Jan. 5 – Three elderly men from Santee and San Diego pleaded innocent to more than 50 counts of committing lewd acts with three girls aged 13 to 15. Those accused were Calvert John Mack, 56, of Santee; his neighbor, Kenneth J. Norton, 69; and Don Winegar of San Diego, 63. Sheriff's officers had seized more than 1,000 photos of under-age girls having sex with adult men in Mack's apartment.

Jan. 11 – La Mesa City Council climbed on the no-smoking bandwagon, passing an ordinance 3-2 which restricts smoking in various places and is similar to San Diego's rules.

Jan. 19 – Robert Charles Hartt Jr., 29, was arrested in connection with the child pornography ring in Santee on suspicion of unlawful intercourse with a minor and oral copulation with a minor under 14. Another suspect, George Earl Walker, 27, of Santee had pleaded innocent to the same crimes.

Jan. 23 – Archie Moore, former world light-heavyweight boxing champion, planned to attend a Santee City Council session to oppose Councilman Jim Bartell's request for a ban on boxing in the city. The call for a ban came after boxer Stewart "The Hawk" Darden fell to the canvas and lapsed into a coma 33 seconds from the end of a junior welterweight match at RollerSkateLand in Santee. Darden regained consciousness but was listed in serious condition at Grossmont Hospital.

Jan. 26 – Because of zoning restrictions, Santee City Council limited to 500 the number of spectators allowed to attend boxing matches at RollerSkateLand. The facility could accommodate 2,000.

Jan. 20 – The first jail escape attempt at El Cajon Detention Facility fizzled. Two hefty prisoners kicked out a cell window on the eighth floor, made a rope out of a bed sheet and greased themselves with something akin to petroleum jelly. They were too large to wiggle out of the small window. Eventually, they summoned a jail guard because they were getting cold.

Feb. 2 – Raymundo Salazar, 28, of San Diego, became the seventh man arrested by sheriff's deputies in connection with the Santee child pornography ring. He faces charges of unlawful sexual intercourse with a minor and oral copulation with a minor under 14.

Feb. 15 – La Mesa City Council unanimously rejected a request by Cindy Harken of Horton Drive to keep a pet cougar in her triplex home, even though she promised to have her pet declawed, neutered and its teeth capped. . . . Pan American Airlines offered $1.3 million in an out-of-court settlement to the family of William Lewis Sr., 40, of El Cajon, who was one of 154 passengers who died in a July 9, 1982, crash near New Orleans. Lewis was vice president of marketing for Pathway Bellows.

Feb. 16 – Eric N. Starr, 46, owner of Eric's Rib Place in Old Town, was sentenced to a year in county jail, fined $5,000 and placed on probation for five years after pleading guilty to one count of solicitation to commit arson at his failing El Cajon restaurant.

Feb. 18 – Mayor George Bailey of La Mesa, 64, announced he would run against incumbent Supervisor Paul Fordem for the Second District seat on the San Diego County Board of Supervisors.

Feb. 27 – Golden Star Promotion has given up its fight to stage professional boxing matches in Santee and will move the matches to Skyline Rollarena in Spring Valley.

Feb. 28 – Kenneth J. Jordan, 69, of Santee, pleaded guilty to three counts of oral copulation with a minor and child molestation. Donald Winegar, 63, of San Diego, pleaded guilty to two counts of oral copulation with young girls. Calvert John Mack, 66, was bound over for trial on charges of oral copulation, unlawful sexual intercourse with minors, soliciting lewd acts from minors, sexual exploitation of children and contributing to the delinquency of minors.

Feb. 29 – William Sanford Sr., 54, of Santee, was arrested on suspicion of murder in the death of his son, William Troy Sanford, 20, who died of a single gunshot wound to his head. The father and son had been feuding for about four years, according to a neighbor.

Mar. 2 – Classic Cat, a La Mesa night club that featured nude male and female dancers for five years before it closed, resurfaced as The Cat on College Avenue in San Diego.

Mar. 17 – Helix High School graduate John Hoagland, working on contract for Newsweek magazine, was killed Mar. 16 in El Salvador while covering the fighting between army troops and rebels. Hoagland, 36, had graduated from Helix in 1965.

Mar. 19 – Jonathan Welch, 33, an operatic tenor from Santee, was one of 11 winners chosen from 26 semi-finalists in the Metropolitan Opera Auditions for Young Singers in New York. All finalists were invited to a joint recital at the Metropolitan Opera House on Apr. 1 with the Met orchestra.

Mar. 23 – Cyril Leigh Smith, 73, a retired aircraft mechanic from Lakeside, became the eighth man arrested in the Santee child pornography investigation.

Mar. 31 – Faith Chapel youth minister Michael McMahon's term in state prison was reduced by 16 months in an appearance before Superior Court Judge Kenneth Johns. McMahon had been sentenced to a term of more than five years for having sex with girls who attended his church.

Apr. 12 – James Ray Spencer, 32, son-in-law of Big Oak Ranch owner Rock Kreutzer, suffered a fatal gunshot wound to his chest. Kreutzer, who was running for the Second District seat on the county Board of Supervisors, had been involved in a fight with Spencer on Mar. 24. Investigators said part of Spencer's finger had been bitten off.

Apr. 18 – Kip Hayes, 25, crippled in a Mt. Miguel High School football game eight years ago, is suing an insurance company and a federal employee health benefit program for $10.5 million. The suit alleges that Prudential Insurance Co. and the National League of Postmasters of the United States had acted in "bad faith" by modifying his insurance policy and placing a $10,000 limit on payment for nursing care. Hayes needed round-the-clock nursing care because he was paralyzed from the neck down. Last year's tab for his care was $191,000.

Apr. 20 – The cost of extending San Diego trolley service to Santee might be $217 million, according to environmental reports approved by the Metropolitan Transit Development Board.

May 1 – Herman "Rock" Kreutzer, owner of Big Oak Ranch, withdrew from the Second Supervisorial District race in the wake of his son-in-law's death caused by a shotgun blast to his chest.

May 4 – The first of eight men accused of lewd behavior with under-age girls in Santee was sentenced. Kenneth Jay Norton, 60, was sent to jail for 270 days. He was given credit for 189 days already served.

May 5 – Pathway Bellows of El Cajon had laid off 60 workers – or 30 percent of its employees – in the last eight months. The company makes bellows, expansion joints and other pipe components for the world market.

May 10 – Santee City Council voted 4-1 to keep its $500 limit on campaign contributions for ballot measures and propositions despite a ruling by the U.S. Supreme Court that the limit was unconstitutional.

May 12 – Donald Winegar, 63, of San Diego was sentenced to four months in jail, fined $300 and placed on three years of probation for his part in the Santee child sex scandal.

May 14 – Herman "Rock" Kreutzer rejoined the race for the Second District seat on the County Board of Supervisors.

May 17 – Earl Reeves, 51, former minister of Lighthouse Baptist Temple near the La Mesa city limits, was sentenced to 28 years in prison after pleading guilty to two felony and two misdemeanor charges involving child molestation.

May 30 – Demolition of El Cajon's oldest home began despite efforts by El Cajon Historical Society and a private corporation to save it. The 115-year-old house, built by El Cajon founder Amaziah Knox for early-day pioneer Isaac Lankershim and his family, was located at 630 Trenton St.

June 1 – Excavation work at the site of the Lankershim house turned up nothing of value. Workers dug in the area they believed had been the site of the outside toilet, but all they found was a piece of iron whose use and origin could not be determined. Pioneers often disposed of items they didn't want by dropping them into toilet holes.

June 15 – Santana High School in Santee was recognized as one of the best high schools in the nation. There were 202 high schools in the country that had been given that designation.

July 2 – The Rev. Dorman Owens, pastor of Bible Missionary Fellowship Church in Santee, was arrested over the weekend for violating a court injunction against picketing at one of two San Diego clinics which provide abortions. He spent three hours in jail for picketing the Birth Control Institute at 4228 El Cajon Blvd.

July 17 – Chem-tronics Inc., an El Cajon firm manufacturing precision engine components for commercial and military jet engines, announced the sale of its outstanding stock to an Illinois company for $51.23 million. Interlake Inc. was the buyer.

July 26 – Pablo Hayes, 25, of Ensenada, was sentenced to 35 years in prison and fined $375 for his part in the slayings of three Dulzura residents. Two others – Jesus Escabedo, 20, and Antonio Alba, 35, both of Tijuana -- were convicted of covering up the murders and both were sentenced to one year and eight months in prison.

July 27 – William Troy Sanford, 55, of Santee, was sentenced to three years in prison for shooting his son and only child in the head following a series of arguments. He pleaded guilty to voluntary manslaughter for killing William Troy Sanford Jr., 20.

July 28 – A black 8-year-old boy will remain with a white homosexual La Mesa man for the time being after the California Supreme Court refused to hear San Diego County's appeal protesting the arrangement. Harold L. Doerr, 49, who has custody of the boy, noted the child's therapist and psychiatrist had testified that removal of the child would have been detrimental to his welfare.

Aug. 2 – Design drawings were approved for a $76 million, seven-level addition to Grossmont Hospital.

Aug. 3 – El Cajon City Councilman Jack Hanson asked for proof that there was a rat problem in the city. He got the evidence when 40 rats were put into pails and left on his front porch. The council voted to spend $3,753 to hire the county Bureau of Vector Control to conduct a survey of the rat population.

Aug. 4 – Barona Indian Reservation opened its $2.5 million bingo hall in Lakeside.

Aug. 20 – El Cajon Valley Colt League team defeated an East Peoria, Ill., team 4-3 to win the Colt League World Championship.

Aug. 27 – Arthur Lopez, Jr., 18, of Escondido, died of injuries suffered when he tried to escape from the El Cajon jail. He broke out of his eighth-floor cell and fell four stories, landing on a platform. He was facing a burglary charge.

Aug. 28 – A San Diego judge let stand a decision by the Grossmont Union

High School District Board to expel a 17-year-old student from El Capitan High School for having five unopened cans of beer in his truck at a night basketball game. The judge said he lacked jurisdiction to overturn the decision.

Aug. 29 – Joyce Renee Largo, 17, of Campo, was sentenced to 25 years to life in state prison for her part in the slaying of paraplegic Dick Sherman of Yuma, AZ.

Sept. 4 – Democratic vice presidential nominee Geraldine Ferraro visited El Cajon on a campaign swing and toured Kahl Scientific Instrument Corp. on West Main Street.

Sept. 18 – Betsy Sneith, 23, of Spring Valley, gave birth to a healthy girl, making history because the baby was the first born to a mother who had received a heart transplant. Sneith had the transplant in 1980, receiving the heart of a man fatally injured in an accident.

Sept. 29 – A racially mixed couple filed separate suits of $7 million each against San Diego County and the State of California because of a racially motivated attack against them a year ago in Dulzura. Luther and Rita Moore had gone to a restaurant for breakfast where they were insulted by men who later attacked Luther Moore, 38, a black man, outside the restaurant with knives, chains and a bullwhip.

Oct. 2 – The cost of eradicating roof rats in El Cajon was put at more than $500,000 by the County Bureau of Vector Control. It would take five years to complete the project.

Oct. 5 – A *Daily Californian* editorial commented on the publication of "Joe: His Fight for Life," a book about standout quarterback Joe Roth who played at Granite Hills High School, Grossmont College and the University of California at Berkeley but died of cancer at 21. The book was written by his mother, Lena, now a resident of Idaho. The editorial concluded: "Those who knew Joe Roth admired him greatly. Those who did not know him, but who read of his courageous but losing battle against cancer, will admire him, too."

Oct. 15 – An unidentified woman won $114,000 in a bingo game at Sycuan Indian Bingo Palace. It was the largest jackpot awarded since the opening of the 1,400-seat casino last winter.

Oct. 18 – El Cajon resident Nilda Pisculli, 47, won $4.1 million in a New York lotto game.

Oct. 23 – Herman "Rock" Kreutzer, owner of Big Oak Ranch in Dehesa Valley and recently defeated in a run for Second District supervisor, was arrested at dawn today on suspicion of murdering his son-in-law. Also arrested were Kreutzer's wife, Lynne, 33; son, Kurt, 19; and another son, Jerome, 26. The four were arrested in connection with the April 11 shooting death of James Ray Spencer, 32. Rock and Jerome later were charged with murder; Lynne and Kurt Kreutzer were charged as accessories to the slaying.

Oct. 29 – Sheriff's vice squad detectives raided three homes in the Jamul area in a weekend crackdown on cockfighting. Six people were arrested and nearly $20,000 worth of fighting birds and equipment were seized along with illegal drugs.

Nov. 7 – Jack Doyle, a member of the Padre Dam Water District Board, pulled off a surprise victory to become the first popularly elected mayor of Santee. He defeated Councilman Roy Woodward, Councilman Gerry Solomon and incumbent appointed Mayor Jan Claussen.

Nov. 15 – Grossmont Hospital was to break ground for a six-story, $12.6 million medical office facility and outpatient surgical center.

Dec. 3 – Pathway Bellows, Inc. announced it will close its plant at 1452 N. Johnson Ave., resulting in the loss of 60 jobs. The company's manufacturing operations were to be consolidated with its plant at Oak Ridge, TN, as of Jan. 1, 1985.

Gunther Pool at Gillespie Field closed and about 70 "mourners" were on hand to pay their respects. *Photo: El Cajon Library*

PERFECT PARTNERS

STAN HONDA
PHOTOGRAPHY

Pigeons posed a problem for both El Cajon and La Mesa. Photo: El Cajon Library

Switchboard operator Ruth Krell overheard President Woodrow Wilson talking
to an admiral at the start of World War I.
Photo: El Cajon Library

Jack Doyle in his naval officer's uniform.
He was Santee's first popularly elected
mayor. *Photo: El Cajon Library*

The Rev. David Jeremiah was hired to replace controversial pastor Tim LaHaye at Scott Memorial Baptist Church in El Cajon. *Photo: El Cajon Library*

"Old Main" building on Grossmont High School campus. *Photo: Grossmont High School Museum*

Ku Klux Klan leader Tom Metzger was jubilant when he won the Democratic nomination in 1980 for a congressional seat. *Photo: El Cajon Library*

Paul Fordem served both as a La Mesa city councilman and as San Diego County Supervisor, District 2. *Photo: El Cajon Library*

Stephen Thatcher, first city manager of the newly incorporated city of Santee. He was 35 when he was hired. *Photo: El Cajon Library*

Kozak's Restaurant opened on Main Street in El Cajon in 1964. Henry Kozak opened the first Denny's in San Diego. *Photo: El Cajon Historical Society*

1985-1989

Some highlights ahead:

Two East County men – David Lucas and Toufic Naddi – charged with multiple murders. . . . CHP Officer Craig Peyer convicted of killing Cara Knott of El Cajon. . . . Pilotless jet fighter crashes into hangar at Gillespie Field, causing a devastating fire. . . . Student leaders at Grossmont College caught using credit cards (not their own) to finance an expensive stay at a Hollywood hotel.

El Cajon City Council members, left to right, Harriet Stockwell, Jack Hanson, Mayor John Reber, Richard Smith and Joan Shoemaker. *Photo: City of El Cajon*

1985

Jan. 9 – La Mesa City Council approved in concept a $4.5 million plan to improve and beautify Fletcher Parkway.

Jan. 11 – Oscar Olear, 28, of Jamul, was sentenced to 90 days in county jail for drawing a knife on a black man who was with his white wife at the Dulzura Café on Nov. 28, 1984.

Jan. 18 – Grossmont Union High School District Board approved building a new high school – to be called West Hills – at the western edge of Santee. The 70-acre campus, previously federal property, would be the 10th high school in the district.

Jan. 24 – Pastor Dorman Owens and 13 members of his Bible Missionary Fellowship in Santee were found guilty of civil contempt of court for disobeying a court order limiting their anti-abortion picketing at a birth control clinic. Owens was given a 10-day suspended jail sentence, fined $150 and placed on one-year probation. . . . A federal judge granted a request by Prudential Insurance Co. of America to limit its home nursing care benefit for paraplegic Kip Hayes to $10,000 a year. Hayes, 25, a Mt. Miguel High School football player paralyzed from the neck down during a game, required fulltime nursing care. His lawyer, Harvey Levine, planned to appeal.

Feb. 13 – TV reporter Larry Himmel aired a segment on downtown El Cajon that drew the wrath of civic leaders because it focused on thrift shops, Pussycat Theater, the F Street Bookstore and seedier parts of the city. The East County Economic Development Council authorized Gordon Austin, executive vice president of the La Mesa Chamber of Commerce, to write a scathing response and send it to Himmel's bosses. ECEDC considered Himmel's report to be a distorted portrayal of El Cajon.

Feb. 21 – Betsy Sneith, 24, of Santee, who made medical history five months ago by becoming the first recipient of a heart transplant to risk her life by giving birth, died of cardiac arrest at UCSD Medical Center. . . . John Grunstad, president of El Cajon Chamber of Commerce and a leader in downtown redevelopment, died of cancer at Grossmont Hospital. He was 48.

Mar. 1 – El Cajon Mayor John Reber saw fiscal health for the city and announced the forthcoming construction of a three-level, 20,000-square-foot fire station at Magnolia and Douglas avenues, building of a 9,400-square-foot neighborhood center to seat 350 in the same area at a cost of $4.2 million and the opening next month of a $4.25 million transit center on Marshall Avenue.

Mar. 2 – Developer Richard A. McKee, 59, of El Cajon, was sentenced to 32 months in state prison after pleading guilty to six counts of real estate fraud. McKee also was ordered to pay $640,000 in restitution. . . . Forace Boyd, one of the founders of Grossmont Hospital and past president of its board of directors, died at 83.

Mar. 14 – David Lucas, 29, a self-employed carpet cleaner from Casa de Oro, who earlier had been charged with slashing the throats of three victims, faced three additional charges of murder committed in the same fashion. His latest alleged victims were Suzanne Jacobs, 31, of Normal Heights and her son, Colin, 3, and Roberta Garcia of Spring Valley. His earlier alleged victims were Rhonda Strang, 25, of Lakeside and Amber Fisher, 3, whom Strang was babysitting, and University of San Diego student Anne Swanke, 22, of San Carlos.

Mar. 16 – Brothers Phillip Wallace, 45, and Thomas Wallace, 47, working together on the roof of an apartment building in Lemon Grove, died within an hour of each other when both of them suffered heart attacks.

Apr. 1 – San Diego police agent Thomas Edward Riggs, 27, of El Cajon, was slain while on duty March 31. Another El Cajon resident, agent Donovan Joseph Jacobs, 28, was wounded. Sagon Aahems Penn, 23, of San Diego, was booked into county jail on suspicion of murder, two counts of attempted murder and auto theft. A ride-along passenger from San Diego also was wounded.

June 3 – Toufic "Tom" Badih Naddi, 44, a Lebanese immigrant, was in custody for the weekend slayings of his wife, Aida, 26; his father-in-law, Habib Sabbagh, 73; Sabbagh's wife, Lillian, 58; and Naddi's two brothers-in-law, Osama Mashiri, 38, and Michal Sabbagh, 38, all Jordanians. The murders occurred on Carlow Way in the Fletcher Hills area of El Cajon. Domestic problems were believed to be the cause of the killings. Naddi's two small children – Nabil, 5, and Cathy 3 – were unharmed.

June 8 – Betty Pettit of Santee was to fly to Portland, OR, for a chance to win $5 million in the Oregon state lottery. *(I saw no subsequent headline announcing that she had won, so her one spin must have been a loser.)*

June 18 – East San Diego County was identified as a haven for illegal drug labs by Bill Hansen, a federal Drug Enforcement Agency agent. North County was fingered, too. The illegal labs were making methamphetamine.

June 24 – Former El Cajon Mayor Karl Tuttle, 71, died of cancer June 23 at his home. Tuttle had been an El Cajon councilman, mayor, trustee of Grossmont Community College District at two different times and chairman of San Diego County Airport Commission. His civic contributions spanned 25 years.

July 2 – Johnny Massingale, a Kentucky drifter who spent 10 months in San Diego County Jail for two 1979 murders now charged to David Lucas, said he confessed to the throat-slashings because "I wanted to stay alive." Massingale originally was charged with the murders of Suzanne Jacobs, 31, and her son, Colin, 3, and the 1981 slaying of real estate agent Gayle Garcia, 32, whose body was found in a Spring Valley home she was showing. Massingale, who has a fourth-grade education and cannot read or write, said he confessed in 1984 because a Kentucky state police investigator threatened him with the death penalty if he did not take responsibility for the killings.

July 8 – Rocky Home, a longtime dairy in Lakeside, announced its closing after 25 years in retail sales. Owner Harry Buckel cited higher costs of operating the dairy, including the expense of maintaining a fleet of 21 delivery trucks.

July 13 – Kiddie cults – teenagers interested in the satanic influence of heavy rock music – were a concern of some East County law enforcement officers. One officer described the problem as "out-and-out devil worship by these kids."

July 19 – Municipal Court Judge Tom Duffy became the first Superior Court judge in El Cajon.

July 20 – Staging of the annual Mother Goose Parade in November was in doubt when the parade's sponsors fell $25,000 short in their fund-raising efforts. The county had contributed nothing to the parade coffers.

Aug. 2 – Barona Indian Reservation near Lakeside opened its $2.5 million bingo hall. More than 800 people had to be turned away from the 2,000-seat facility.

Aug. 14 – Elbert "Thad" Poppell was denied a license to operate a nude spa by a unanimous La Mesa City Council. The city officially adopted the findings of hearing officer Robert Rice, who advised that the Between the Two spa would be contrary to public morals.

Aug. 15 – A computer glitch left *The Daily Californian* unable to process copy and today's edition was published only with the assistance of *Israel Today*, a specialty publication.

Aug. 23 – Grossmont Hospital District scrapped its $77 million plan for a seven-level expansion project in favor of a more modest proposal. Low occupancy rates were cited as the reason.

Aug. 24 – *The Daily Californian* announced it would begin publishing a Sunday edition, but there would be no Monday paper. Tuesday through Friday publications would arrive on doorsteps in the afternoon; Saturday and Sunday issues would be delivered in the morning.

Aug. 30 – Sale of the historic Lakeside Hotel was announced. The new owner is Isachael Corp., which paid $250,000 for the building.

Aug. 31 – Calvert John Mack, 67, a paraplegic and reputed ringleader of a teenage pornography and sex ring in Santee, was sentenced to 20 years in state prison.

Sept. 11 – Nan Couts, 96, who campaigned for the establishment of the Grossmont Hospital District starting soon after World War II, died at her El Cajon home. She came to this country with her parents from Yorkshire, England, in 1890.

Sept. 20 – Three members of Herman "Rock" Kreutzer's family pleaded guilty to lesser charges stemming from the fatal shooting of Kreutzer's son-in-law at the Big Oak Ranch in Dehesa Valley. Jerome Kreutzer, 28, a son, had a murder charge dropped when he pleaded guilty to voluntary manslaughter in the April 11, 1984, shooting of James Spencer, 32, in a garage on the Harbison Canyon ranch. Rock's wife, Lynne, 35, and his youngest son, Kurt, 20, both pleaded guilty to being an accessory to a felony. Rock Kreutzer was found guilty of second-degree murder on Sept. 3.

Sept. 25 – Second District Supervisor Paul Fordem confirmed that he ended his campaign for re-election two weeks ago because he is suffering from acute hypertension.

Oct. 1 – El Cajon Municipal Court Judge Michael Brennan, 43, died Sept. 29 of brain cancer at Mercy Hospital. In an interview two weeks before his death, Brennan counseled: "Avoid materialism. He who dies with the most toys is not the winner."

Oct. 3 – Timely and hefty donations by Channel 51 and Mazda dealers in San Diego County will enable the Mother Goose Parade to continue its annual march down Main Street in El Cajon. This year's parade had been in doubt because the county declined to make a requested $25,000 contribution.

Nov. 16 – Hundreds of students at Grossmont High School staged a brief walkout in support of teachers who were at odds with the Grossmont Union High School District Board over salaries and other benefits. Two trash cans were set afire by the students. . . . An overturned 20-ton truck and trailer carrying 15 tons of powdered cement mix snarled traffic for four hours on Interstate 8 near Grossmont Summit.

Nov. 20 – Ron Dahlgren, administrator of Grossmont Hospital, was asked to resign by the Grossmont Hospital District Board, allegedly because of his stormy relationship with the medical staff. Dahlgren was to stay on the job until Dec. 31.

Nov. 27 – A security guard struck a 1-year-old girl in the mouth and a striker in the face during a melee that broke out at the back of a Vons store at Fletcher Parkway and Navajo Road. It was the first major outbreak of violence in the month-long strike by meatpackers and Teamsters.

Nov. 30 – Ralph E. Winkler of Lakeside, a retired Air Force major, announced that he would be a candidate for the Republican nomination for California's secretary of state.

Dec. 1 – Ben Polak, Jr., 67, a well-known East County civic leader, died Nov. 29 of lung cancer at Alvarado Community Hospital. He was best known for his leadership role with San Diego County United Way. . . . Lois Clark McCoy of El Cajon became the first woman to be elected president of the National Assn. of Search and Rescue, which was comprised of 1,500 organizations involved in life-saving activities.

Dec. 5 – Convicted murderer Herman "Rock" Kreutzer asked for a new trial, claiming that his attorney, C. Logan McKenzie, had been ill and could not adequately defend him.

Dec. 7 – Herman "Rock" Kreutzer, 49, was sentenced to 17 years to life in state prison for the shooting death of his son-in-law, James Spencer, 32, on April 11, 1984, at the Big Oak Ranch in Dehesa Valley.

Dec. 14 – Jerome Kreutzer, 28, son of Herman "Rock" Kreutzer, pleaded guilty to voluntary manslaughter and was sentenced to six months in county jail and a fine of $1,500 for his part in James Spencer's death. Kurt Kreutzer, 20, another son, was ordered to serve 90 days in a work furlough program and spend nights in jail for his part as an accessory to the murder. Lynne Kreutzer, 35, wife of Rock Kreutzer, had her felony conviction as an accessory reduced to a misdemeanor and was required to complete 200 hours of community service. . . . An unconfirmed report said court transcripts revealed that a man accused of biting an El Cajon police officer has the AIDS virus. The lawyer for Blaine Prairie Chicken called the report "hearsay." Prairie Chicken faced trial Jan. 27 in El Cajon Superior Court for felonious assault on a peace officer and a misdemeanor count of resisting arrest.

Dec. 31 – Geraldine Lafferty, 48, of Spring Valley, won $2 million in the year's final Big Spin of the California Lottery.

1986

Jan. 4 – Four people killed Jan. 2 in a single-engine plane crash in a steep, fog-covered canyon near Crest were identified as Frederic Nemes, 29, a San Diego bakery owner; his wife, Olga, 27; and Mrs. Nemes' parents, Claude and Jacqueline Bridier of France. The victims were returning from Las Vegas when the crash occurred. . . . Genstar Southwest Development of La Jolla purchased the 2,400-acre Fanita Ranch site in Santee. The property was for a proposed 8,000-unit residential development. The purchase price was not announced.

Jan. 14 – A sheriff's deputy trainee and mother of two, Kelley Ann Bazer, 28, was shot and killed in Spring Valley, allegedly by robbers who wanted her car to flee the scene of an armed robbery they had committed at a Safeway store. The three suspects, all from San Diego, were in custody. Bazer was visiting relatives in the area when she was shot.

Jan. 23 – El Cajon City Council ordered a moratorium on zoning changes, effectively halting new apartment construction for at least nine months. Nearly half of the city's population of 80,000 (49%) lived in apartments.

Jan. 25 – Three Grossmont College instructors were awarded the George Washington Honor Medal for excellence in economics instruction by the Freedoms Foundation of Valley Forge, PA. They were Bruce Barnett, Larry Smith and Dr. Wilford "Bill" Cummings, who were cited for providing to students over the past 12 years a comprehensive view of the various theories of economics.

Feb. 4 – Paul John Boileau, 45, was convicted of 171 counts of grand theft and corporation-codes violations stemming from $1 million in losses sustained by real estate investors in his El Cajon company, Boileau & Johnson. An employee, Lillian Stagliano, also was convicted of 171 counts. She was in charge of the trust deed investment department. Stagliano later was sentenced to serve five years in state prison. Boileau's trial was still pending.

Feb. 7 – Two female residents of an El Cajon board-and-care home for the developmentally disabled died in a fire at 1280 Clarendon St. The victims were Pietra Carrao, 47, and Patty A. Melton, 33. An investigation revealed the fire alarm system had been turned off. Nearby Bostonia Fire Department was unable to respond because it did not have a mutual aid agreement with El Cajon.

Feb. 14 – A brother and sister, Jacob Jerome Herron IV, 13, and Laura Anne Herron, 16, died as a result of a single-car crash on Jamacha Boulevard. With Laura driving, the car went out of control, veered into the oncoming lane and collided with another vehicle. Jacob died at the scene; Laura died three hours later at Mercy Hospital in San Diego.

Feb. 20 – Hazel Sperry, 81, former curator of the Knox Hotel Museum and an authority on pioneer life in El Cajon, died in Tustin where she had been living with relatives. She came to El Cajon in 1941, taught at Bostonia School and was named Citizen of the Year in 1979.

Feb. 21 – David Allen Giles, 19, who was hailed as a hero for knocking on doors and alerting fellow residents of a fire at a home for the developmentally disabled on Clarendon Street in El Cajon, was arrested on suspicion of arson and murder. He faced three counts of murder since another resident of the home had died from his injuries.

Mar. 1 – A Mt. Miguel High School math teacher accused of furnishing drugs to an undercover sheriff's officer was suspended without pay from his $25,000 a year job pending a formal dismissal hearing. The teacher, Larry Wilson, maintained his innocence and claimed his arrest was racially motivated because he was the only black teacher on the staff.

Mar. 18 – Toufic Naddi, 45, charged with killing his wife and four members of her family in their Fletcher Hills home, was declared mentally incompetent to stand trial and was committed to a state mental hospital for treatment. Five court-appointed psychiatrists diagnosed Naddi as paranoid and incapable of cooperating with his attorney. He was committed to Patton State Hospital for three years.

Apr. 2 – The manager of a fire-ravaged home for developmentally disabled adults was arrested and charged with three counts of involuntary manslaughter. Nayoma Raleigh managed the Linda Turman Home on Clarendon Street in El Cajon where three adults died as a result of a fire the night of Feb. 6. The manslaughter charges were based on the fact that the home's fire alarm system had been turned off. Patty Ann Melton, 33; Mark Buis, 33; and Pietra Corrao, 47, were the fire victims.

Apr. 3 – Stewart Siegel, 48, former bingo games manager at Barona Indian Reservation north of Lakeside, pleaded guilty to rigging games in the year that he supervised them. Losses to bingo players were estimated to be as high as $500,000.

Apr. 10 – Grossmont Union High School District trustees voted to expel 66 students arrested in an undercover drug bust in February. The expelled students were permitted to participate in a county Department of Education program that allows them to work their way back to their schools.

Apr. 30 – A $62 million plan to add three major department stores, upgrade and nearly double the size of Parkway Plaza by August 1990 was put before the El Cajon City Council. The city was asked to build a $7.7 million parking garage for 830 vehicles. The expansion project was expected to boost sales tax revenue for the city by $800,000 a year.

May 9 – Bingo games at Barona Indian Reservation were closed down permanently by a vote of tribal members. The games were shut down Apr. 23 for reorganization and remodeling. A former manager had pleaded guilty to rigging the games.

May 16 – Accused murderer David Lucas, 31, lost his bid to have his trial moved out of San Diego County because of pre-trial publicity. Lucas is accused of six murders. . . . Joanna Roche, 8, seriously injured when she ran into the street in front of her Spring Valley home and was hurtled 46 feet through the air by a passing car, was reported to have made an amazing recovery, considering the extent of her injuries. She spent 15 weeks in the hospital, according to her mother, and reverted to a fetal position. With therapy, she had now reached the developmental stage of a 5-year-old.

May 29 – Big Oak Ranch in Dehesa Valley was purchased by Steven and Alice Keyser from the Small Business Administration for $345,000. The 27-acre ranch formerly belonged to Herman "Rock" Kreutzer, who was convicted of killing his son-in-law and is serving a 17 years-to-life sentence in state prison.

June 18 – Drug stores and supermarkets in East County were pulling Extra-Strength Excedrin capsules from their shelves. Bristol Myer, manufacturer of the over-the-counter painkiller, asked stores nationwide to discontinue selling the pills after authorities in Auburn, WA, confirmed that a cyanide-laced capsule caused the death last week of a 40-year-old woman in that city.

June 20 – La Mesa Mayor Art Madrid repeated his demand for a public apology from Councilwoman Jeri Lopez who at a council meeting asserted that ethnic weddings at a city recreation center could be damaging to a neighborhood park. Lopez refused, saying her comments were not meant to have racial implications and she did not think an apology was necessary.

June 24 – Grossmont Hospital signaled it would raise patient rates by 36 percent in July, the largest annual rate increase in its 31-year history. The rate hikes were blamed on underfunding of Medicare, Medi-Cal and the East County Medical Services program.

July 11 – Sagon Penn, acquitted of murdering San Diego police officer Thomas Riggs of El Cajon and the attempted murder of Officer Donovan Jacobs, also of El Cajon, was ordered to stand trial on lesser counts that had not been resolved at the first trial. The shootings occurred Mar. 31, 1985, in the predominantly black area of southeast San Diego.

July 20 – Jerry Watson, 44, a former police officer who is the new owner of a painting and maintenance service in El Cajon, was trying to get backing for a test of what he believed is a "cure" for a particular type of cancer contained in a letter written in 1922 to his grandfather, William A. Watson. The "cure" consisted of blending four herbs into a paste and applying it to cancer sites. Watson said he had seen evidence that the remedy worked.

July 29 – East County apartment owners, faced with a vacancy rate that nearly tripled in one year, were enticing renters with all kinds of special offers: free rent, free lottery tickets, microwave ovens, rent reductions, and custom colors for wallpaper and paint.

Aug. 1 – Santee Fire Department evacuated 1,400 employees and customers from the Mission Gorge Plaza shopping center after fumes from an unknown chemical sickened several employees. Paramedics treated and released three people who complained of dizziness, headaches and chest pressure. The chemical later was identified as perchlorocthylene, a degreasing agent, but its source was not immediately determined. . . . Marty Ray Flint of El Cajon was indicted by a federal grand jury on a charge of possessing Molotov cocktails and making threats against President Reagan. Flint wanted the president to help him become a jet pilot. If that help did not come by Sept. 10, Flint said he would go to Washington, D.C., to kill the president. . . . Jesse Lee Stuart, 20, was convicted of first-degree murder for the shooting death of sheriff's deputy trainee Kelly Bazer in the aftermath of a robbery in Spring Valley. Bazer, 28, of El Cajon, was shot in the back Jan. 13 while visiting in the Spring Valley area and her car was stolen.

Aug. 6 – Grossmont College received a $31,256 grant from the county's

Regional Occupation Program (ROP) to start a class to train nannies. Calls about the class were coming from all over the country.

Aug. 15 – A federal grand jury indicted current and former officials of Jet Air, Inc. of El Cajon on charges of falsifying inspections and the theft of gold in airplane parts repairs. Those indicted were former president George T. Straza and current company vice president Joao Jaime Costa. Straza and his wife owned all of Jet Air's corporate stock. The 31-count indictment involved a U.S. Air Force contract with Jet Air for the refurbishing of air seals on the F-100 jet engine.

Aug. 27 – Clarence Jones of Spring Valley found a six-foot python resting on the engine of his pickup truck. Animal control officer Charlene Ranger undraped the snake from its cozy dwelling place, with TV cameras recording the event.

Sept. 11 – El Cajon police raided the largest clandestine drug lab ever found in the city – and it was right next to an elementary school. Lt. Randy Narramore, chief of detectives, said the lab had made a new batch of meth oil that would have yielded millions of dollars in illegal sales. The raid was at 1079 Merritt Dr., next to Anza Elementary School. Authorities later put the street value of the meth at $44 million.

Sept. 12 – Jesse Lee Stuart, 20, was sentenced to 35 years to life in state prison for killing sheriff's cadet Kelly Bazer, 28, in Spring Valley and for two robberies that preceded the murder.

Sept. 13 – Among Grossmont Hospital's 3,200 employees, more than 40 languages are spoken. There are 279 staff members who can be pressed into service as translators when patients are admitted who cannot speak English.

Oct. 2 – Volunteers of America in El Cajon won a $4 million federal loan to build a 75-unit apartment complex. This was the third federally subsidized project for East County to house low-income individuals. The Salvation Army was awarded a $4.3 million loan from the U.S. Housing and Urban Development Department last year for 75 units. The first federal assistance loan was for Senior Towers, an 88-unit complex near City Hall which opened in January 1981.

Oct. 7 – The case of an El Cajon woman charged and jailed for neglect of a fetus drew national attention. Pamela Rae Stewart, 27, gave birth Nov. 23, 1985, to a baby with massive brain damage caused by the mother's use of amphetamines during her pregnancy. Stewart had a condition called *placenta abruptio,* a tendency for the placenta to separate from the uterine wall. She had been advised to get medical attention immediately if she started hemorrhaging, but she waited 12 hours and her infant was in distress by the time she arrived at the hospital.

Oct. 10 – Buck Knives in El Cajon and a research and development firm in Oceanside were awarded a $15 million contract by the U.S. Army to manufacture a multi-purpose bayonet. . . . Lucky Stores, Inc. announced it would be closing all of its Gemco stores and selling them to Target stores for an estimated $700 million. There were 80 Gemco stores with 14,000 employees in three southwestern states. La Mesa and El Cajon both had Gemco stores.

Oct. 25 – The former manager of a board-and-care home for the developmentally disabled in El Cajon was found guilty of two counts of involuntary manslaughter resulting from the deaths of two residents who died in a fire at the facility. Nayoma Raleigh, 41, was acquitted of a third count of involuntary manslaughter for the death of another resident at the Linda Turman Guest Home. The fire alarm system at the home had been turned off.

Nov. 1 – An El Cajon man, Benjamin Ross, 27, was one of four painters electrocuted when their scaffolding touched a 12,000-volt high tension wire at the San Diego Submarine Base. Edward Illig, 37, of Lemon Grove also was killed. The other two victims were from San Diego.

Nov. 5 – Dr. Donald Walker, chancellor of Grossmont Community College District, was on a list of 100 rated the most effective chief executives at higher education institutions in the United States.

Nov. 13 – John Russell, whose 16-year-old daughter is a sophomore at El Capitan High School, launched a campaign to ban "The Color Purple," a Pulitzer Prize-winning novel by Alice Walker, from the library shelves of nine schools in the Grossmont Union High School District. He had read only the first page of the book.

Nov. 16 – A 15-year-old El Cajon girl went to the police and reported her mother's abuse of drugs, the first case of its kind in East County. The girl and her 4-year-old brother were placed in protective custody, and their mother was arrested along with a 28-year-old man who had been staying at their apartment.

Nov. 18 – Ground was broken for the extension of the East Line of the San Diego Trolley to El Cajon. The $93 million trolley extension was expected to be in service by 1989.

Nov. 22 – Beverly Miller, president of the Cajon Valley Union School District Board, requested membership in the all-male El Cajon Rotary Club. This was at a time when Rotary International had attempted to revoke the charter of a club in Duarte, CA, that had admitted three women as members in 1977. The U.S. Supreme Court was expected to rule on the question next summer. . . . Nayoma Raleigh, former manager of the Linda Turman Guest Home in El Cajon where three residents died in a late night fire, was sentenced to two years in state prison on two counts of involuntary manslaughter. The fire alarm system at the home had been shut off.

Dec. 4 – Letters written by Sam Jones of El Cajon in 1944 finally were returned to him – 42 years after they supposedly were processed and dispatched while he was on board the USS Caleb Strong and headed for port at Oran, Algeria. Jones' undelivered mail was part of 235 wartime letters that had been misplaced for more than four decades.

Dec. 9 – Stewart Siegel, 49, of Las Vegas, former bingo manager at Barona Indian Reservation, was sentenced to a year in county jail for rigging games and stealing about $97,000. Eligible for a five-year term in state prison, he received a lighter sentence because he has colon cancer and must undergo chemotherapy.

Dec. 10 – "The Color Purple," a Pulitzer Prize-winning novel by Alice Walker, is to remain on the library shelves of Grossmont Union High School District schools despite parent John Russell's campaign to have it removed. Instead, Russell's daughter, Michelle, 16, will leave El Capitan High School and enroll elsewhere.

Dec. 16 – Captain Sticky, a caped crusader fighting crime in East County, faces a possible misdemeanor charge for renting his home for the filming of a pornographic movie. Sticky's real name is Richard Pesta.

Dec. 18 – Businessman Taylor Whatley filed a disturbing the peace complaint against more than 100 people from a church group that presented a Christmas program at Grossmont Center. Whatley said he supported all religious activities in the church but not in the business district.

Dec. 19 – El Cajon police reported there were 138 abandoned cars littering the city's streets.

Dec. 30 – Cara Knott, 20, of El Cajon was strangled and her body thrown over the railing of a frontage road bridge in the Rancho Penasquitos area. An honor graduate of Valhalla High School and an honor student at San Diego State University, Miss Knott had gone to Escondido to care for her ailing boyfriend, Wayne Bautista, who had the flu. She was returning home at night when she was killed.

1987

Jan. 8 – Beverly Miller, president of the Cajon Valley Union School District Board, abandoned her attempt to become the first woman member of the El Cajon Rotary Club. She went to a meeting with a club member and felt "uncomfortable" being there. She planned to join a Rotary Club in another community.

Jan. 9 – San Diego Glass and Paint, a fixture in San Diego County for 59 years, announced it would close all 18 of its retail stores, including four in East County. "Economic reasons" were cited as the cause of the closings.

Jan. 11 – Sally Lambert of La Mesa, widely known as "The Possum Lady," has been notified she is in violation of zoning ordinances and will have to rid her place of possums. She has cared for as many as 40 sick and injured possums at a time for more than 11 years.

Jan. 14 – Rocky Home Dairy in Lakeside has been sold and the 26-acre property will be used for a 354-unit apartment complex and shopping center.

Jan. 16 – Craig Peyer, 36, a California Highway Patrol officer, was arrested for the slaying of Cara Knott, 20, of El Cajon, whose body was found at the bottom of a ravine off Interstate 15 near Poway.

Jan. 21 – Skyline Wesleyan Church of Lemon Grove proposed to buy 80 acres of Home Capital Development land near Cuyamaca College for a sanctuary to hold as many as 5,000 people and a huge complex of other buildings supporting its ministry.

Jan. 22 – Craig Peyer, 36, who had been a California Highway Patrol officer for 13 years and was father of three children, pleaded not guilty to the murder of Cara Knott, 20, of El Cajon, a junior at San Diego State University.

Feb. 11 – Cajon Valley Union School District Board approved year-round status for four schools – Ballantyne, Lexington, Magnolia and Vista Grande.

Feb. 14 – An $8 million medical office complex is scheduled to open next month across the street from the 50-bed Kaiser Foundation Hospital at 203 TraveLodge Drive in El Cajon. Kaiser Permanente was building an $87 million facility in San Diego.

Feb. 25 – El Cajon City Council forecast a $76,200 debt for the celebration of the city's 75th birthday unless some proposed expenditures were cut. Spending for the birthday bash was pegged at $174,300, with income projected to be $98,100. Some council members objected to the anticipated loss.

Feb. 27 – A Municipal Court judge in San Diego dismissed charges against an El Cajon woman, Pamela Rae Stewart, 28, who gave birth to a brain-damaged baby, allegedly because she ignored her physician's order not to use drugs during her pregnancy.

Mar. 3 – A 24-year-old man whose body was found hanging in a tree near Dulzura last August is believed to have been killed by disgruntled customers who were sold diluted drugs. Travis Baker had been beaten, and investigators suspect he was forced to write in blood a note that would indicate his death was a suicide.

Mar. 5 – California Highway Patrol officer Craig Peyer, who had pleaded not guilty to the murder of Cara Knott, 20, of El Cajon, was released from jail after friends and family posted $1 million bail.

Mar. 6 – Superior Court Judge Milton Milkes ruled that Helen Gary has the right to have the feeding tube removed from her comatose mother, 92, who is in a La Mesa nursing home. It was the first right-to-die case litigated in San Diego County. Milkes wrote in his opinion: "Life is time, and death is always untimely. However, when life has lost all function, it is not life which is extended. Rather it is death which received a reprieve."

Mar. 11 – Toufic Naddi of El Cajon, who is accused of killing his wife and four of her family members at a home in the Fletcher Hills area, was found competent to stand trial by a jury. His trial is to start March 24. The district attorney is seeking the death penalty.

Mar. 18 – El Cajon City Council voted to trim the budget for the city's 75th birthday celebration by $29,459. It canceled the Friendship Festival and the Great Pumpkin Festival.

Mar. 19 – Anacomp Inc. paid $128 million to acquire Datagraphix, Inc. and within 24 hours laid off 225 workers at plants in El Cajon and San Diego. About 90 of those employees worked at the El Cajon plant on West Main Street.

Mar. 20 – Some streets in La Mesa were closed to accommodate the filming of "Little Nikita," a movie starring Sidney Poitier. The closures were needed so a parade scene could be filmed.

Apr. 2 – An Associated Press story featured David Leisure, the El Cajon actor who plays Joe Isuzu in Isuzu TV commercials. The story's lead paragraph: "David Leisure is the only actor who's been caught lying so often on television that it could make him a star." With "snake oil sincerity," the story said, Isuzu declares that Isuzu "gets 94 mpg city, 112 highway" as a disclaimer, "He's lying," flashes on the screen. Leisure, a product of the drama department at Grossmont College, also had roles in "ALF" and "Empty Nest."

Apr. 16 – The outcome of the first right-to-die case in San Diego County remained in doubt. Superior Court Judge Milton Milkes had ruled that the feeding tube of 92-year-old Anna Hirth, lying comatose in a La Mesa nursing home, could be removed. But neither the woman's doctor nor members of the nursing staff wanted to do it. Judge Milkes removed responsibility for enforcement of his order from the doctor and nursing staff, leaving in the hands of Hirth's daughter, Helen Gary, the arrangements for her mother's death.

Apr. 18 – A 36-year-old Santee man pleaded guilty in San Diego Superior Court to encouraging his 14-year-old son to take drugs and have sex with the father's girlfriend. He admitted giving marijuana to his son, then transporting him to various hotels to have sex with women the father was seeing. The encounters had started when the boy was 11. The boy's sister, 16, reported the incidents to sheriff's deputies in Santee, saying their parents bought drugs and alcohol for themselves but no food for their children.

May 1 – Helen Gary, daughter of a semi-comatose 92-year-old woman in a La Mesa nursing home, is appealing a judge's decision to free her mother's doctor and nursing home from the responsibility of removing life support for Anna Hirth. She is appealing to the Fourth District Court of Appeal in San Diego to reinstate Superior Court Judge Milton Milkes' initial order in March directing Hirth's doctor and nursing home to disconnect the woman's feeding tube.

May 5 – CHP Officer Craig Peyer was ordered to stand trial for the slaying of Cara Knott of El Cajon. Municipal Court Judge Frederic Link said in his ruling: "Mr. Peyer's practice of luring young women to a very dark area for supposed safety reasons when they were already very safe on the highway indicated a strong suspicion that he may have committed a crime." Fifty-seven witnesses had been called by the prosecution during the preliminary hearing.

May 24 – The county Department of Health will begin advertising in newspapers next week in the hope of finding an East County site for an emergency shelter for the mentally ill who are homeless.

May 30 – Craig Peyer was fired by the California Highway Patrol. He had been receiving his $3,025 a month salary even though he faced a murder charge. The CHP, relying on an internal investigation, had determined that Peyer killed Cara Knott and was dismissed for "inexcusable neglect of duty, dishonesty . . . willful disobedience" and other charges. There had been 10 incidents between May and December of Peyer pulling female motorists off the road and ordering them to stop on an isolated freeway ramp where he engaged in long personal conversations with them.

June 4 – Grossmont Hospital announced it will stop treating Medi-Cal inpatients after Oct. 1 because the state had refused to consider increasing the hospital's reimbursement rate. Alvarado Hospital had done the same thing.

June 5 – The leader of the God Unlimited Campus of Healing in Campo was sentenced to 42 years in state prison for molesting a 10-year-old boy member of his cult. Herbert Beierle, 60, also was fined $7,000.

June 14 – Santee City Councilman Jim Bartell vowed to risk arrest to save the city's oldest structure from the wrecking ball. Bottroff-Bliss House was scheduled to be demolished in two or three weeks. Harriette Wade, president of Santee Historical Society, pledged to be at Bartell's side.

June 17 – A nationwide meth-making operation, which included five labs in East County, was smashed by San Diego County law enforcement officers after a five-year investigation. Jack Battaglia, 48, of San Diego, and his brother, Manuel "Manny" Battaglia of rural El Cajon, were accused of running the operation.

June 21 – Grossmont Hospital recorded 341 births in May, the highest monthly total in the hospital's history.

July 1 – An $80 million redevelopment project, projected to bring 4,000 jobs to East County, was approved unanimously by the county Board of Supervisors. . . . An attorney whose client was wrongly convicted of murdering his wife was ordered to pay nearly $1 million in damages for providing an inadequate defense for his client. Attorney Otis Jones had to pay Chester Holliday of Lemon Grove $229,194 in special damages and $400,000 in general damages. He also was ordered to pay $150,000 to both of Holliday's teenage children. Holliday, 58, was convicted in 1981 of second-degree murder in the 1980 strangulation death of his wife, Rose. He was cleared in a second trial.

July 14 – Superior Court Judge Wayne Peterson placed a mentally impaired man on five years of probation for his role in the arson deaths of three residents of a board-and-care home in El Cajon. David Allen Giles, 19, admitted setting fire to fingernail polish he had spilled on some newspapers on a sofa at the Linda Turman Guest Home. The home's fire alarm system had been turned off.

July 22 – Michael Bang, the recently resigned president of Associated Students of Grossmont College, Inc., has been accused along with 10 unnamed persons of engaging in a $27,800 spending binge with student funds at a Beverly Hills hotel from June 27 to July 8. Bang, who spoke for 15,000 students as a non-voting member of the Grossmont-Cuyamaca Community College District Board, has dropped out of sight. The accused students used an American Express card to charge room rentals, food, beverages, limos, jewelry and other items.

July 24 – Swallows-Sun Island, a nudist resort in Dehesa Valley, was preparing to host the annual convention of the Western Sunbathing Assn., a nudist organization claiming to have between 5,000 and 6,000 members in California, Nevada, New Mexico, Arizona, Utah, Colorado and Hawaii. The four-day convention was expected to attract about 1,000.

Aug. 8 – An estimated 45,000 retail grocery clerks from San Luis Obispo to the Mexican border went on strike, affecting about 850 stores, including Ralphs, Food Basket, Vons and Safeway in East County. The last strike by retail workers had occurred in 1978.

Aug. 11 – Albert Van Zanten, 66, former El Cajon mayor and councilman who was serving most recently as president of the Grossmont-Cuyamaca Community College District Board, died Aug. 10 of cancer. He was 66.

Aug. 29 – Buck Knives, Inc. of El Cajon plans to open a satellite plant in Tijuana in December to produce some of its outdoor clothing and work on leather goods and pocket knife blades. Labor cost savings were cited as the reason. The Tijuana plant will employ 10 to 15 workers.

Sept. 2 – A freak thunderstorm downed power lines and trees, blew a patio roof away in Santee, caused lightning fires in trees and even produced some tornado sightings. A power outage forced Yogurt Mill in El Cajon to close. The city's high temperature that day was 106.

Sept. 5 – The former owner of an El Cajon aerospace manufacturing firm was convicted of 43 counts of conspiracy, theft of government property, mail fraud and issuing false invoices. Jurors had deliberated three days before convicting George Thomas Straza, 58, of all the charges against him. Corporation secretary Alice Skinner, 57, of Lakeside was convicted of 20 similar counts. A third defendant, Joas Jamie Costa, 50, the company's former vice president and general manager, was acquitted of 20 counts. Jet Air, Inc. had been accused of selling 90 jet engine components for personal profit while under contract to build parts for Pratt & Whitney, a government contractor in Connecticut.

Sept. 10 – Four of the top officials in student government at Grossmont College were recalled during two days of voting. Ousted were Larry Humpal, president of Associated Students of Grossmont College, Inc.; Jeff Farrell, acting vice president; David Brooks, acting executive secretary; and Laura MacFarland, director of publicity. The recall stemmed from a $36,000 spending binge – revised upward from the previous estimate of $27,800 – using student funds at a Beverly Hills hotel. Later in an election, a reform slate took all 21 positions in ASGC government.

Sept. 18 – Federal agents swooped into El Cajon to seize the records of defense contractor Ametek-Straza. The U.S. Justice Department was probing activity that involved two highly classified Navy sonar contracts that the company had been awarded. Brothers John and George Straza started the company in 1951 in Lakeside. They parted ways in the late 1950s. George Straza founded Jet Air, Inc., and recently had been found guilty on 43 counts of illegally selling jet engine parts that were supposed to have gone to the Navy.

Sept. 24 – Sixteen people were taken to area hospitals to be treated for reactions to a chemical that had been released from the Fluid Polymer Systems plant at 10139 Prospect Ave. in Santee. Fifty-one nearby homes were evacuated.

Oct. 2 – The name of the newspaper was changed from *The Daily Californian* to *East County Daily Californian,* presumably to be identified with a larger geographic area.

Oct. 7 – Actor Glenn Ford, 71, was identified as the choice for grand marshal of this year's Mother Goose Parade. . . . Fiesta Dinner Theatre in Casa de Oro announced it would close Jan. 10 at the end of its current production of "Angel Over My Shoulder." The theater had produced more than 100 plays during its 10 years in business.

Oct. 10 – "Valley of Opportunity: The History of El Cajon," written by Eldonna Lay to commemorate the 75th anniversary of the city's incorporation, was coming off the presses. The initial printing was for 2,250 copies.

Oct. 18 – El Cajon launched its 75th birthday celebration the previous day, attracting a crowd of 28,000, about half the size expected by City Councilman Jack Hanson, the event organizer.

Oct. 24 – J. Clifford Wallace of La Mesa is one of four judges the White House has been evaluating for a seat on the U.S. Supreme Court as a substitute for Robert Bork, whose name had been withdrawn. Wallace didn't get the job. Neither did the substitute nominee, Douglas H. Ginsburg, who withdrew his nomination because of the furor over the revelation that he had smoked marijuana. Anthony M. Kennedy of Sacramento, like Wallace a member of the 9th U.S. Circuit Court of Appeals, was ultimately nominated and confirmed.

Oct. 30 – A Spring Valley man from Iraq won a $3.4 million jackpot in the state lottery and promptly quit his job as a liquor store clerk. Hermiz Pauls, 30, had borrowed $5 from his cousin, Sabha Hermiz, 26, to buy quick picks.

Nov. 4 – County voters approved a half-cent increase in the local sales tax, with $500 million of the projected revenue increase to be used for transportation projects in East County. The money would pay for an 8.6-mile extension of Highway 52, a 3.3-mile extension of the San Diego Trolley from El Cajon to Santee, a 3.8-mile extension of Highway 125 from Highway 52 in Santee to Grossmont Summit on Interstate 8, and $140 million for local road improvements.

Nov. 5 – Dorman Owens, senior pastor of Bible Missionary Fellowship in Santee, was indicted by a federal grand jury for an alleged conspiracy to bomb an abortion clinic. The associate pastor and five church members also were indicted.

Nov. 18 – Four local women became members of the previously all-male El Cajon Rotary Club. They were Marge Dean, principal of Emerald Junior High School; Yvonne Johnson, assistant superintendent of Cajon Valley Union School District; Marilynn Linn, city clerk for El Cajon; and JoAnn Smith, principal of Granite Hills High School. Some male members had resigned because of the change in membership rules ordered for all civic organizations by the U.S. Supreme Court.

Dec. 6 – A gunman suspected of killing a San Diego County sheriff's deputy from El Cajon was shot to death by heavily armed police and sheriff's officers during a daylong standoff at an apartment complex in Escondido. The slain gunman was identified as Robert Gary Taschner, 30, of Escondido. Taschner allegedly shot Deputy Lonny G. Brewer, 29, in the chest. Brewer was a SWAT team member and had married a fellow deputy just three weeks earlier.

1988

Jan. 6 – Divers from Arkansas have been hired to probe the El Cajon sewer system near Gillespie Field to remove concrete-like deposits which have halted a major sewer cleaning and sealing project. It's a mystery how the deposits occurred. Some are six inches to a foot high. . . . Marshal Scotty's Playland Park east of El Cajon was preparing to install a $1 million water ride dubbed White Water Rapids.

Jan. 7 – Ted Borkstrom, 82, reputedly the oldest mailman in the United States, was on his route today for the El Cajon Post Office. He started as a mailman when he was 65 and averages 85 miles a day in his postal vehicle. Borkstrom said he might consider retirement when he turns 90. *(He retired in November 1989.)*

Jan. 8 – Elvis Presley's stepbrother, Billy Stanley of El Cajon, is writing a book, "Elvis, My Brother," with the assistance of ghost writer Steve Gruber, also of El Cajon. Stanley, 34, became Elvis' stepbrother in 1960 when the singing idol's father married Dee Stanley. Elvis' mother died in 1958.

Jan. 12 – The name of the newspaper reverted to *The Daily Californian* with "of East County" in much smaller type. The paper had been given a makeover with a drastic change in typography.

Jan. 31 – La Mesa Family Fun Center will vacate its site at the end of the summer to make way for Phase 4 of the Interstate 8-Highway 125 expansion.

Feb. 3 – Child actress Heather O'Rourke, star of the blockbuster film "Poltergeist" and former resident of Santee, had died a day earlier at Children's Hospital in San Diego from complications while undergoing surgery for an intestinal infection. She was 12. Heather recently had completed filming of "Poltergeist III" directed by Steven Spielberg.

Feb. 26 – The trial of former California Highway Patrol Officer Craig Peyer, charged with murdering Cara Knott, 20, of El Cajon, ended in a hung jury. The vote was 7-5 for conviction. District Attorney Ed Miller said the case would be re-tried. Knott, a junior at San Diego State University, was hurled to her death off a bridge at an I-15 exit.

Mar. 2 – Pastor Dorman Owens of Bible Missionary Fellowship in Santee pleaded guilty to witness tampering and concealing a felony in connection with the bombing of an abortion clinic. He faces a maximum sentence of 13 years in prison and a $500,000 fine....A San Mateo firm is to be paid $34,000 to conduct an organization and management study of El Cajon Police Department. Police officers had been at odds with Police Chief Darwin Sinclair. Grievances had been filed against City Manager Bob Acker, Sinclair and the city's personnel department.

Mar. 24 – La Mesa City Manager Ron Bradley, 48, resigned to become city manager of Oceanside. His last day will be May 9.

Mar. 26 – Lori Bartz, 25, of El Cajon, was sentenced to 48 years in prison for molesting four girls and a boy in a bizarre scheme in which she impersonated the devil. A co-defendant, Robert Wilkins Jr., 38, also of El Cajon, had been sentenced earlier to 46 years in prison for similar offenses.

Apr. 3 – Least Bell's vireo, a federally protected songbird, was threatening to delay the completion of Highway 52 into Santee.

Apr. 9 – As many as 75 students at Monte Vista and Valhalla high schools are suspected of participating in a new fad – a scavenger hunt to steal things for fun. Cars had been vandalized and stereo equipment taken. A point value was assigned to each item on the hunt list.

Apr. 27 – Nadia Davies, a veteran Monte Vista High School teacher, and her husband, Thomas, were suing Grossmont Union High School District for $1 million each, charging that Nadia's transfer to Valhalla High School had caused them emotional distress. Nadia Davies, 51, who had taught at Monte Vista for 17 years, was transferred after interrupting an advanced placement test for several of her Spanish students.

Apr. 28 – Olaf Wieghorst, a resident of El Cajon since the 1940s and a celebrated Western artist, died April 27 at Grossmont Hospital. He was 88. His painting, "Navajo Madonna," sold for $450,000 in 1982.

May 4 – Eva M. Quicksall, who had directed the popular Holiday Pageant at Grossmont High School for 40 years, died May 2. She was 90.

May 11 – Students from Emerald Junior High School and their adult chaperones were stranded in Washington, D.C., when it was discovered some of their accommodations, including air fare home, had not been paid for. There were 185 students and 29 adults on the trip. Associated Press reported the travel agency that booked the excursion ran out of money. The trip was salvaged with the aid of Cajon Valley Union School District, parents, local businesses, politicians and civic organizations.

May 12 – AMI Valley Medical Center is one of 37 American Medical

International, Inc. hospitals to be sold to an employee group in a $910 million transaction. AMI has hospitals in 10 states, of which the El Cajon facility is the largest.

May 18 – East West Travel & Tours filed for bankruptcy after leaving 185 students and 29 adult chaperones from Emerald Junior High School in El Cajon stranded in Washington, D.C. The agency had debts of $1.5 million and owes $45,000 to Cajon Valley Union School District for botching a school excursion to the East Coast. . . . Michael Bang, 26, former president of Associated Students of Grossmont College, Inc., pleaded guilty to grand theft in the embezzlement of ASGC funds for a $41,000 spending spree at the Beverly Hills Hotel with fellow officers. Bang, who had changed his last name to "Humbert," faces a maximum term of one year in county jail. Larry Humpal, who succeeded Bang as ASGC president, also pleaded guilty to grand theft.

May 21 – *Daily Californian* senior writer Steve Petix, 31, was stabbed to death at his El Cajon apartment while defending his wife from a sexual attack. He had just arrived home for lunch when he discovered the assault. Petix's action allowed his wife to escape, but he was pronounced dead at the apartment from numerous stab wounds inflicted by the assailant who fled the scene. . . . The City of El Cajon dedicated its $1.2 million multipurpose neighborhood center at 195 E. Douglas Ave. It has 8,600 square feet of space.

May 24 – David Alan Weeding, 38, of Santee, was arrested in connection with the stabbing death of *Daily Californian* senior writer Steve Petix. Weeding, employed as a radiator repairman, had served more than 10 years of a 25-year sentence in Texas for aggravated rape and is on federal parole for two sex offenses. Nearly 400 people attended Petix's funeral. A scholarship in his honor was established with contributions from friends and community members. Petix reported on high schools in the Grossmont Union High School District.

May 27 – Grossmont College released some of the bills racked up during a spending spree by officers of Associated Students of Grossmont College, Inc. at the Beverly Hills Hotel. Among the unauthorized items paid for with a college credit card: $39.94 for duck pate, crab, shrimp and room service; $325.73 for drinks, including a $96 tip; $150 a day for the rental of a cabana at the pool; $170 for manicures and pedicures, plus a $35 tip.

May 28 – Barona Bingo Palace reopened after being closed for two years as a result of a court settlement reached between Barona Indians and a former manager of bingo operations. The previous management company had declared bankruptcy.

June 9 – Toufic "Tom" Naddi, 47, accused of killing his wife and four members of her family at his El Cajon home, was found guilty of five counts of first-degree murder. The slayings occurred June 1, 1985. The sanity phase of his trial was still ahead.

June 10 – Lakeside firefighters risked their lives and successfully rescued a Blossom Valley man and his 17-year-old daughter from a collapsing house engulfed by flames. Firefighters participating in the heroic rescue were Forrest Kahn and David Lones and paramedics Victor Gonzalez and Mark Grow.

June 14 – Michael Bang, 26, former president of Associated Students of Grossmont College, Inc., was sentenced to a year in county jail for a $41,000 spending spree using student funds at the Beverly Hills Hotel. Larry Humpal, 26, who succeeded Bang as president, was sent to jail for six months. Bang and Humpal each were ordered to pay $20,500 in restitution.

June 17 – Theresa Adams, 49, of El Cajon, picked all six numbers in the California Lotto 6/49 game and won $4.7 million, splitting a $23.4 million jackpot with four others.

June 21 – Pastor Dorman Owens of Bible Missionary Fellowship in Santee was sentenced to 21 months in federal prison for concealing a felony and witness tampering in the bombing of an abortion clinic at Alvarado Medical Center in July 1987.

June 23 – At the conclusion of his second trial, former California Highway Patrol officer Craig Peyer was found guilty of first-degree murder in the death of Cara Knott, 20, of El Cajon, who had been strangled and her body hurled off a bridge at an I-15 off-ramp after being directed off the freeway.

July 1 – Fire destroyed the Jack in the Box Restaurant at Broadway and Graves Avenue. Damage was estimated at $475,000.

July 2 – A mistrial was declared in the sanity phase of the murder trial of Toufic "Tom" Naddi, 47, the El Cajon man charged with killing his wife and four of her relatives at a home in Fletcher Hills. The jury split 11-1 for conviction, but a unanimous verdict was required.

July 9 – An El Cajon couple was awarded $4.2 million by a Brooklyn, NY jury in a suit charging an East Coast hospital with neglect that resulted in the couple's now 12-year-old daughter being brain-damaged. Elizabeth and Javier Sastoque filed the suit against Maimonides Medical Center in 1980, alleging the hospital staff failed to provide oxygen to their infant daughter, leaving the baby permanently disabled and unable to care for herself. The girl is mentally retarded and suffered some neurological impairment.

Aug. 4 – Former California Highway Patrol officer Craig Peyer was sentenced to the maximum term of 25 years to life in state prison for the murder of El Cajon resident Cara Knott, 20. Peyer's wife, Karen, told the judge her husband had been "railroaded" and "the wrong man" had been convicted of the crime.

Aug. 5 – An $80 million expansion of Parkway Plaza has begun. The work will nearly double the size of the shopping center and add three new department stores – Mervyn's, J.C. Penney and The Broadway. The expanded center is expected to be completed in 1992.

Sept. 13 – A pilotless F-14 Tomcat fighter jet crashed upside down on a Gillespie Field helicopter hangar and exploded into a huge plume of billowing black smoke just moments after the pilot and his radar intercept officer ejected in the downtown area of El Cajon. Lt. (j.g.) Randall Furtado, 27, the radar officer, was taken to Sharp Memorial Hospital where he died of a broken neck and other injuries the next day. The pilot, Lt. Cmdr. James Barnett, suffered a broken arm, a broken heel and facial cuts and was at Mercy Hospital. William Grant, a civilian worker at the airport, underwent amputation of a leg and was in critical condition at Sharp Hospital. No explanation was given as to why the $44 million jet malfunctioned.

Sept. 17 – Seven thousand signatures were taken to the county administration building in support of making Lakeside a city. Only 6,000 signatures were required. After examining the signatures, however, the incorporation bid failed because too many signatures were invalid.

Sept. 27 – Manuel Battaglia of El Cajon was convicted of heading a nationwide drug syndicate that distributed methamphetamine, marijuana and cocaine. He was sentenced to 20 years in prison.

Sept. 30 – Three meth users had died in the past two weeks at AMI Valley Medical Center, apparently because the drugs they ingested were contaminated. The victims, who were 18, 22 and 32, experienced incredibly high body temperatures and internal bleeding that could not be stopped.

Oct. 13 – An Escondido man, Ronald Elliott Porter, 41, was arrested by sheriff's homicide detectives and questioned about the strangulation of a Texas man in a field near Buckman Springs in East County. Porter was questioned about several similar incidents in the same general area where hitchhikers had been taken, choked into unconsciousness and abandoned in fields. The bodies of three women had been found in the same vicinity. Porter pleaded not guilty to six felony counts.

Oct. 28 – El Cajon Valley High School band members were upset because they were prevented from welcoming President Reagan to San Diego for a campaign stop. District policy forbade the band's participation in political events.

Nov. 6 – The first American to get the world's smallest dual-chamber pacemaker was an 84-year-old former diesel truck mechanic from El Cajon. Dr. Peter Belott installed the pacemaker under the skin of Ferdinand Laux's chest in a one-hour operation. The mechanism is half the size of other dual-chamber systems and weighs just under an ounce.

Nov. 10 – Fifteen prisoners at the East County Detention Facility required hospital treatment after a race riot broke out in the dayroom area of a seventh-floor cellblock. Nearly 140 prisoners participated in the brawl which authorities described as a fight between blacks and Hispanics.

Nov. 22 – The cost of rerouting Highway 52 to protect endangered songbirds was placed at $11 million by the State Department of Transportation. The major portion of the estimated cost was to relocate KFMB's towers.

Dec. 1 – Michael Bang, former president of Associated Students of Grossmont College, Inc. involved in a $41,000 spending spree using a college credit card, was sentenced to two years in state prison for leaving a work furlough center last August and fleeing to Texas. Bang, 27, also was ordered to pay a restitution fine of $8,500 for his part in the embezzlement of student funds. At his sentencing hearing, Bang's attorney said his client had suffered physical and emotional abuse as a child and there was an allegation he had been molested for eight years by the priest who baptized him.

Dec. 6 – Metropolitan Homicide Task Force disclosed that 40 women had been murdered in San Diego County in the past four years. The bodies of at least eight of the victims were found in East County along the Interstate 8 corridor. Authorities have been in touch with the Green River Task Force in Seattle where 40 women had been killed and eight others had disappeared between 1982 and 1984.

Dec. 7 – Gertrude Palmer, at 105 the oldest registered student in the state and who is attending Grossmont Adult School, was to be honored as "The Adult Student of the Year" in California. She was enrolled in the "Effective Living Skills for Seniors" class.

Dec. 29 – Joselito "Gerry" Cinco, on Death Row at San Quentin prison for killing San Diego police officers Kimberly Tonahill of Santee and Timothy Ruopp of National City, committed suicide in his cell by hanging. Ruopp was writing a misdemeanor ticket on Sept. 14 for Cinco, 29, who was drinking alcohol with a friend and two under-age girls in a San Diego park. When Tonahill began frisking Cinco, he pulled a pistol from his jacket and shot her and Ruopp, killing both of them.

1989

Jan. 3 – An explosive device went off at Parkway Plaza last night, forcing the evacuation of about 200 shoppers and 150 store personnel. Police identified the device as a booby trap that malfunctioned but which would have been deadly if it had worked properly.

Jan. 18 – Capt. Jack Smith, head of Los Angeles Police Department's personnel and training bureau, is to be El Cajon's new police chief. The search had taken seven months. Smith will replace Darwin Sinclair who retired.

Jan. 24 – Frances Felio, 70, of El Cajon, won $5.8 million in the California Lotto 6/49 game. She shared a $40.7 million jackpot with six others.

Feb. 3 – Santee City Council hired former State Sen. Bob Wilson to be its lobbyist in Sacramento at a cost of $15,000 this year.

Feb. 7 – A 13-pound, 8-ounce boy was born to Susan and Ernest Mitchell at Grossmont Hospital, one of the largest infants ever delivered at that facility. His father named him Michael after boxer Mike Tyson.

Feb. 18 – Councilman Jim Bartell pushed past a startled sheriff's deputy to prevent workers from razing the 91-year-old Bottroff-Bliss house in Santee, the city's oldest home. It was still to be determined if the house qualifies as an "historical structure."

Feb. 25 – Sixteen children were taken to three area hospitals for treatment after a pickup truck rear-ended a loaded school bus at Dallas Street and Fletcher Parkway. Forty children were in the bus when the accident occurred. Most were checked for neck injuries and released, but two were candidates for admittance and further treatment.

Mar. 1 – The historic Bottroff-Bliss house in Santee was headed for demolition because Superior Court Judge Kevin Midlum ruled that it didn't meet the city's legal definition of an historic landmark. It was the oldest home in Santee.

Mar. 2 – Somebody was stealing ducks from Santee Lakes. In six weeks, the population of domesticated ducks had shrunk from 150 to 10.

Mar. 14 – Ken Overstreet, 51, a Grossmont Union High School District trustee for 17 years and director of Youth for Christ in San Diego for 25 years, died Mar. 11 of AIDS at his home in Newport Beach. He had revealed his condition last July, explaining that he probably contracted the disease through a blood transfusion.

Mar. 16 – U.S. Fish and Wildlife Service determined that the least bell's vireo would not be in jeopardy from the proposed eastern extension of Highway 52 through Santee. Construction had been held up pending a finding that the work would not harm the endangered songbird. Cost of rerouting the highway had been pegged at $21 million.

Mar. 21 – Gene Ainsworth, 68, the first mayor of Santee, died Mar. 20 of acute emphysema.

Mar. 29 – Carbon monoxide fumes sickened 43 girls attending the Cuyamaca Outdoor School camp in the mountains. All were treated and released at area hospitals. A faulty heater was suspected as the cause.

Apr. 4 – Ernest J. Dronenburg of El Cajon, a member of the State Board of Equalization, was under consideration by President George H.W. Bush's administration for appointment as commissioner of the Internal Revenue Service. *(He did not get the job, but now is serving as the elected assessor of San Diego County.)*

Apr. 23-24 – A Molotov cocktail was thrown at the El Cajon office of the *San Diego Jewish Times* newspaper. It caused little damage to the building at 2952 Fletcher Parkway, but there was intense antagonism toward the bomb thrower. In subsequent days, pipe bombs were set off at an apartment complex and the Department of Motor Vehicles.

May 2 – John Mark Hewicker III, 25, formerly of La Mesa and son of a deputy district attorney and grandson of a San Diego County Superior Court judge, was sentenced to state prison for 11 years for robbing two banks and violation of probation imposed for similar crimes committed in 1985. He had a cocaine addiction.

May 3 – The Navy expressed interest in purchasing the 10-acre Aero Drive-in property at 1270 Broadway Ave. in El Cajon for a 150-unit townhouse development costing $12 million.

May 14-15 – A 68-car smashup on fogbound Interstate 8 near Pine Valley sent 50 people to seven area hospitals. Eight had suffered serious injuries.

May 23 – Pathway Bellows, Inc. will close its corporate office July 31 and relocate to the company's manufacturing division in Oakridge, TN. The company had operated in El Cajon more than two decades. Its latest closing here resulted in layoffs for 32 employees.

May 26 – Helix High School's Academic League team won the San Diego County Academic League championship by defeating Gompers Secondary School in San Diego by a score of 90-79.

June 16 – An arsenal of more than 150 guns was seized by El Cajon police after SWAT action at 12224 Lakeside Ave. Lt. Bob Lein of El Cajon Police Department suspected the cache of weapons was linked to the exchange of guns for drugs.

June 22 – David Allen Lucas, 33, a Spring Valley carpet cleaner, was convicted of killing three people, and attempting to kill a fourth person, by slashing their throats. The jury had deliberated for eight days. Lucas was acquitted of one murder and the jury deadlocked 11-1 for his conviction on two murder charges. A survivor of the murder spree identified Lucas as her attacker.

June 24 – The East Line of the San Diego Trolley made its way to El Cajon and was greeted by a choir singing "This Train Is Bound for Glory."

July 5 – The 9th Circuit Court of Appeals reversed the 1987 conviction of Alice Skinner, 59, of Lakeside, who had been imprisoned on charges of mail fraud, conspiracy to defraud a defense contractor and others related to the case against George Straza of Jet Air, Inc., where Skinner worked. The appellate court ruled there was insufficient evidence to sustain the charges against Skinner.

July 7 – Similienne Smith, a 66-year-old La Mesa grandmother, won a $10.5 million jackpot in the California Lotto 6/49 game.

July 18 – The first successful escape from the East County Detention Facility in El Cajon occurred when a prisoner broke through a wall and slid seven stories down knotted sheets to the ground. John J. Pugh, 36, was back in custody a few days later and was sentenced to two additional years in prison for his escape attempt.

Aug. 3 – A Superior Court jury recommended that David Allen Lucas, 34, a Spring Valley carpet cleaner convicted of three throat-slashing murders, should die in the gas chamber.

Aug. 4 – Actor Cliff Robertson, a La Jolla native who won a best-actor Oscar for playing the title role in the movie "Charly," was announced as the lead-off speaker for the Celebrity Authors Series at Grossmont College. He was to speak Sept. 22.

Aug. 8 – Pussycat Theater on West Main Street in El Cajon is showing its last X-rated film and will reopen as a family theater offering second-run movies for $1.99 a seat. The movie house opened shortly after World War II.

Aug. 10 – Full-time nursing care for quadriplegic Kip Hayes was rescinded by his insurance carrier because he recently married his nurse. Hayes, who suffered his paralyzing injuries in a Mt. Miguel High School football game in 1978, had earlier won a lawsuit entitling him to 24-hour, in-home nursing care.

Aug. 30 – Sheriff John Duffy told the county grand jury that the "Rambo squad" at the East County Detention Facility in El Cajon would be disciplined, saying the behavior of some deputies at the jail was "inexcusable, unprofessional and embarrassing to the department." The punishment was to include dismissal, demotion and suspension without pay. Ten deputies had been accused of inmate harassment, which included the trashing of cells and requiring prisoners to lean against walls for extended periods.

Sept. 5 – John Pugh, 36, the first inmate to successfully escape from the East County Detention Facility, was one of two men who escaped from the Central Detention Facility in San Diego using the same method that Pugh had devised for his earlier escapade – rappelling on knotted bed sheets from the eighth-floor exercise room. His companion in his latest escape was convicted child killer Leon Eugene Morris, 35, of Spring Valley. As a side note, two jail trusties walked away from a work assignment on the same day.

Sept. 16 – Jack Battaglia, 50, described by prosecutors as the kingpin of a massive East County-based cocaine and methamphetamine ring, was sentenced to a 29-year term in federal prison and fined $100,000. His brother, Manuel, 46, is serving a 20-year sentence for his part in a multi-million-dollar drug trafficking operation.

Sept. 19 – Superior Court Judge Laura Hammes sentenced David Allen Lucas, 33, to death in the gas chamber as recommended by the jury that convicted him. He was convicted of three murders and the attempted murder of a fourth person.

Sept. 22 – The four-month marriage of paraplegic Kip Hayes to his nurse was annulled to preserve the 24-hour care he requires to remain alive. Hayes' insurance carrier had canceled his insurance after it learned that he had married. His care costs $200,000 a year.

Sept. 29 – Oak Grove Middle School in Jamul was honored at the White House for earning the National School Recognition Award.

Oct. 13 – A 63-year-old tradition came to an end when Grossmont High School canceled its annual Christmas pageant. Rising costs and falling attendance were cited as the reasons.

Oct. 18 – The front page of *The Californian* was devoted entirely to the Oakland area earthquake that had killed more than 279 people and injured hundreds more. The quake collapsed buildings and a section of the San Francisco-Oakland Bay Bridge.

Oct. 19 – An explosion in a transformer room at Santana High School in Santee caused $200,000 in damage about 40 minutes after classes had ended. It took four hours to put out the fire.

Oct. 22-23 – Police arrested 205 protesters in less than four hours at an Operation Rescue anti-abortion demonstration at a La Mesa clinic. Five hundred demonstrators participated.

Nov. 1 – The Rev. Edward "Bud" Kaicher, 34, became the first Catholic priest in San Diego County to be imprisoned for anti-abortion activity. He was sentenced to 45 days in jail for his part in a Feb. 1 protest at a La Mesa family planning clinic.

Nov. 7 – Five of seven inmates who escaped the night before from the East County Detention Facility remained at large. It was reported that seniors in a nearby apartment complex watched the escape while it was in progress but didn't call police. A sheriff's lieutenant said later that jail security had been sacrificed to cut the cost of constructing the jail.

Nov. 23 – David A. Weeding, 40, was convicted of first-degree murder for the stabbing death of *Daily Californian* writer Steve Petix on May 20, 1988. Weeding's defense attorney had attempted to put the blame for the journalist's death on his client's younger brother, Hans.

Nov. 29 – Todd Iseminger, 25, a former three-sport star at Grossmont High School but now a paraplegic, was awarded $3.5 million because doctors at Kaiser Permanente Hospital failed to diagnose a rare spinal cord infection.

Iseminger went to the hospital with a high fever and back pain and was told to go home and take Tylenol. He returned to the hospital the next day with paralysis. Iseminger was a student at San Diego State University majoring in physical education when the disease struck.

Dec. 12 – Convicted killer David A. Weeding, 39, was spared the death penalty for stabbing to death *Daily Californian* writer Steve Petix, 31. The jury recommended he spend the rest of his life in prison without the possibility of parole. His sentencing is Jan. 8.

Daily Californian senior writer Steve Petix, 31, was murdered in 1988 by David Alan Weeding, a federal prison parolee. *Photo: Petix family*

California Highway Patrol officer Craig Peyer is serving a life term in state prison for killing Cara Knott of El Cajon. *Photo: El Cajon Library*

Ted Borkstrom, 83, believed to be the oldest mailman in the United States, was on the job in 1988 at El Cajon Post Office. He retired in 1989. *Photo: El Cajon Library*

Art Decker designed some of El Cajon's most prominent public buildings, including the Superblock. *Photo: El Cajon Library*

El Cajon Councilwoman Beverly Miller made a bid for membership in the El Cajon Rotary Club, an all-men's group.
Photo: El Cajon Library

Michael Bang went to jail for misusing a credit card when he was student leader at Grossmont College.
Photo: El Cajon Library

Santee Councilman Jim Bartell risked arrest to save an old house.
Photo: El Cajon Library

1990-1994

Some highlights ahead:

Mini-tornado at Parkway Plaza . . . President George H.W. Bush names Alpha Project of El Cajon his 185th "Point of Light" . . . Bill Clinton brought his quest for the presidency to El Cajon . . . Four people shot to death at Family Fitness Center in El Cajon by a 19-year-old gunman who then killed himself.

Tom Wigton, founder of the Mother Goose Parade. *Photo: El Cajon Library*

1990

Jan. 20 – El Cajon Municipal Court Judge Larrie Brainard ordered flamboyant defense attorney Cyrus Zal to jail for 45 days and fined him $4,500. Zal is general counsel for Operation Rescue, an organization that demonstrates against abortion at family planning clinics. He was cited for contempt of court for repeatedly asking questions of witnesses when ordered not to do so. . . . The first In-N-Out Burger restaurant in the San Diego area is in the East County community of Lemon Grove. It was doing so much business in its first days after opening that a backup burger unit had to be used.

Jan. 30 – A former San Diego State University professor was sentenced to nearly six years in federal prison for possession of marijuana with intent to distribute. Jack David Mooers, 57, also was fined $50,000 stemming from a raid last summer on his Jamul farm where 614 marijuana plants were confiscated.

Jan. 31 – The American Civil Liberties Union filed two separate "religious liberties" suits in federal court against the City of La Mesa and the County of San Diego challenging the maintenance of the Mt. Helix cross and the cross insignia on a city logo. East County Supervisor George Bailey criticized the ACLU, saying the Mt. Helix cross has been maintained with private, not public, funds for many years.

Feb. 1 – Eight prostitutes had been arrested in the past three weeks by El Cajon police officers posing as johns. It was an attempt by the El Cajon Police Department to reduce prostitution on city streets.

Feb. 14 – A storm from the Bering Sea brought hail and snow flurries to parts of East County, including unofficial sightings of snowflakes in Lakeside, Alpine, Harbison Canyon, Crest, El Cajon and Santee.

Feb. 27 – Twin brothers who operated a tour agency that went broke after 185 El Cajon Junior High School students were stranded on the East Coast pleaded guilty to conspiracy to commit mail fraud. Anthony and Leo Casias, 47, of San Diego, owned East-West Travel and booked thousands of students on group tours in 1988. Sentencing is set for May 14. The defendants could face a maximum sentence of five years in federal prison and a $250,000 fine. *(Update: These same twin brothers, now 64, were again sentenced to prison in 2014 for wire fraud conspiracy involving their company, L&T Sports Events, Inc. U.S. District Court Judge John Houston said: "This was an old-fashioned, salt-of-the-earth swindle.")*

Feb. 28 – Law enforcement officers captured three jail escapees, including one accused of murder, before the fugitives could get away from the East County Regional Center jail. The trio included Raymond Harry Stone, 41, convicted of bilking women in confidence schemes and accused of murdering Anita Dalfoss, 50, of El Cajon.

Mar. 28 – Surgeons at Grossmont Hospital were hopeful that Brian Stowers, 32, would regain the use of his nearly severed thumb and finger after they used a vein graft from his foot to reattach them. Stowers, a carpenter, had been operating a table saw when his hand was caught in the blade.

Apr. 14 – Christina Osborn, an El Cajon police dispatcher, received the top award from the California Public Safety Radio Assn. for talking on the phone with a woman who had been shot by her ex-boyfriend. Osborn was to appear on the Oprah Winfrey Show where the audience would hear the six-minute conversation she had with the gunshot victim. "Rescue 9-1-1," a television show, planned to re-enact the call.

Apr. 25 – Santee City Councilman Roy Woodward was fined $6,000 by the California Fair Political Practices Commission for conflicts of interest. He had voted on routing decisions for the Highway 52 freeway even though he owned property in the corridor planned for the road.

May 5 – The youngest child ever to appear before the East County Student Attendance Review Board was a 6-year-old kindergartener. The mother accepted blame for her daughter's truancy but offered a lot of excuses.

May 19 – Joan Larson claimed that a mini-tornado lifted her off her feet at Parkway Plaza and dropped her a foot and a half, resulting in a broken tooth and causing other injuries. She had witnesses, including shopping center manager Bryan Jenkins who said "some kind of funnel" skittered through the plaza around noon.

May 11 – The state's Department of Food and Agriculture ordered aerial spraying of the controversial pesticide Malathion to repel an infestation of Mexican fruit flies in El Cajon. Spraying was to begin May 21. Legal papers were filed to stop the spraying.

May 15 – The first murder case to be tried in an El Cajon courtroom was assigned. The murder occurred April 11, 1979, and involved the bludgeoning and strangulation death of Debra Owen, 19, whose remains had been found in a ditch in Linda Vista. Jessie Ray Moffett, 31, was accused of the slaying. He also faced another trial for an unrelated murder he allegedly committed more than 11 years ago.

May 23 -- A *Daily Californian* editorial had this to say about the Malathion spraying of El Cajon which occurred May 21: "They came. They sprayed, and they didn't kill anybody." No one was even taken to the hospital.

May 24 – An organization quickly dubbed Stop Malathion Aerial Spraying Here (SMASH) was formed.

June 3-4 – It was announced that El Cajon Cemetery would not be available for burials as of July 1. Some of the remains dated to the 1860s.

June 5 – El Cajon residents by the hundreds were taking their vehicles to car washes to purge them of residue from the second aerial spraying of Malathion on June 4. One facility expected to wash 900 vehicles in one day. Six helicopters had sprayed a 16-square-mile section of the city to eradicate Mexican fruit flies.

June 6 – Councilwoman Joan Shoemaker won her race for mayor of El Cajon, defeating incumbent John Reber and former County Supervisor Lucille Moore.

June 12 – The Sycuan Band of Mission Indians announced plans for completing construction of a $3 million gambling casino by the fall. It would also have off-track betting.

June 14 – The Pointe, a $750 million destination resort with mixed uses planned for Spring Valley, was approved unanimously by the Board of Supervisors. It had been in the planning stage for eight and a half years.

June 18 – Millions of sterile Mexican fruit flies were to be released over El Cajon beginning next week and through the summer, all part of the effort to prevent damage to trees and fruit.

June 22 – Convicted murderer Toufic Naddi of El Cajon was found sane by a jury at the conclusion of his fourth sanity trial. He had been convicted of killing his wife and four of her relatives in his Fletcher Hills home.

June 28 – The Fourth District Court of Appeal upheld the conviction of California Highway Patrol Officer Craig Peyer for the June 22, 1989, killing of Cara Knott, 20, of El Cajon. The ruling required 65 pages dealing with 10 issues that had been raised during the trial.

June 29 – Boys Club of East County and Girls Club of East County announced they would merge to become Boys and Girls Club of East County. There were 2,700 boys and 700 girls in the new organization. Architects of the merger said it would make raising money easier and allow for a unisex recreation program.

July 3 – Alpha Project, an El Cajon-based project assisting the homeless in finding jobs, was cited by President George H.W. Bush as his 185th "point of light." The president inaugurated his "Thousand Points of Light" campaign to publicize what people in the private sector were doing to help their fellow citizens.

July 5 – Penny parking ended in La Mesa when city workers changed 478 parking meters to accept only nickels, dimes and quarters. San Rafael and Newport Beach were the only California cities still accepting pennies in parking meters.

July 10 – A Superior Court jury rejected the death penalty for Toufic Naddi, 49, of El Cajon, who had been convicted of killing his wife and four of her relatives in 1985. Instead, he will serve a life sentence in prison without the possibility of parole. Another jury earlier had found Naddi sane. Over the course of numerous trials, Naddi had dismissed 11 of the 12 attorneys who had been appointed to defend him.

Sept. 5 – El Cajon City Councilwoman Beverly Miller withdrew her proposed gay rights ordinance, saying she did not have the support of her fellow council members to pass it.

Sept. 14 – Rancho San Diego Golf Course, formerly Cottonwood, was sold to Japanese entrepreneur Tomio Nitta, owner of Scripto Corp., the oldest writing instrument manufacturer in the United States. The previous owner was the local law firm of Jennings, Engstrand and Hendrikson. The course reportedly sold for between $30 million and $35 million. . . . It was announced that The Highway Men – a popular country music group featuring Willie Nelson, Johnny Cash, Waylon Jennings and Kris Kristofferson – would perform at the Lakeside Rodeo Grounds.

Sept. 18 – More than five years after he shot and killed five family members, including his wife, Toufic Naddi of El Cajon was sentenced to life in prison without the possibility of parole and an additional 135 years, a procedural move to keep Naddi imprisoned in the event an appellate court struck down his conviction. It required four trials, and the dismissal of 11 attorneys by Naddi, to determine if the defendant was sane enough to stand trial.

Oct. 2 – Charles W. Thomas II, 64, of El Cajon, a professor at the University of California, San Diego known as "the father of black psychology," was fatally stabbed in San Diego. He was founding chairman of the National

Assn. of Black Psychologists. He died at Villa View Community Hospital in east San Diego.

Nov. 3 – Robert Browning, a candidate for El Cajon City Council, decided not to hold a scheduled press conference to refute charges that he had mishandled funds six years ago when he was volunteer treasurer for the San Diego County Council of Real Estate Boards, Inc. He was alleged to have diverted $12,500 in board funds to his personal checking account.

Nov. 7 – Councilman Art Madrid narrowly defeated La Mesa Mayor Fred Nagel in his bid for re-election. Anti-incumbency fervor also took out Dr. Sydney Wiener, a 17-year member of the Grossmont-Cuyamaca Community College District Board, and his fellow trustee, Tom Buchenau; La Mesa Councilman Ed Senechal; and Betty Pengelley and Don Hunsaker, members of the Grossmont Union High School District Board.

Nov. 8 – *The Californian* began running a continuing series of reports listing the yearly salaries of all school and college district employees in East County.

Nov. 13 – Police arrested 16 men in an undercover prostitution sweep over the weekend in the downtown area of El Cajon and at motels in the eastern part of the city.

Nov. 21 – Paul Bresney, 39, was sentenced to 47 years and four months in state prison for committing 51 robberies between January and April 1989. He was called the "Walk to the Back" bandit because he ordered his victims to walk to the back of their stores during his robberies.

Nov. 23 – Sycuan Indian Reservation dedicated its new $3 million casino and donated $30,000 to the San Diego chapter of the Arthritis Foundation.

Dec. 12 – A donated handgun accidentally discharged at a Salvation Army collection trailer in the parking lot of Kaelin's Market, killing 61-year-old James Erwin Brower of Alpine. . . . John "Jack" Hogan of Lakeside arrived Dec. 11 at Lindbergh Field from Kuwait where he and 39 others had been held captive by Iraqi soldiers for three and a half months. Hogan and his wife had lived in Kuwait for 18 months, working on a project he called "Greening of Kuwait." His wife, Roberta, left Kuwait in early September.

Dec. 13 – Thomas P. Davies, newly elected trustee of the Grossmont Union High School District Board, was ordered by a Superior Court judge to step down because his election was a violation of an agreement with the district that neither he nor his wife, Nadia, a district teacher, would work in the district in return for a payment of $39,200.

1991

Jan. 3 – East County gun owners and thousands of others in California were waiting until the last minute to register their assault weapons, swamping the State Department of Justice with applications even though the deadline had passed. Late filers had 90 days to get rid of their weapons if they missed the Dec. 31, 1990, deadline.

Jan. 15 – An Iraqi-owned liquor store at 518 Jamacha Road was torched over the weekend, causing $370,000 in damage. There was speculation the arson fire may have been linked to Iraqi dictator Saddam Hussein's threatened invasion of Kuwait.

Jan. 27 – J.O. Orsborn, 64, retired as La Mesa's fire chief. He had been a firefighter for 46 years.

Feb. 5 – Fred Andrews Jr., 50, a Grossmont Union High School District trustee since 1979, was found dead Feb. 4 in his hotel room in the Los Angeles area. His death left the GUHSD board with only two trustees – June Mott and Ken Whitcomb. Tom Davies had been removed from the board by a circuit court judge for legal reasons, and Dr. Maynard Olsen was an Army reservist who had been sent to the Persian Gulf War. Ada Reep had been appointed to fill Davies' seat, but her appointment had to be put on hold pending the outcome of Davies' appeal.

Feb. 9 – El Cajon's most notorious mass murderer, Carl Eder, was featured on "America's Most Wanted" television show on Channel 6. Eder had received multiple life sentences for the slayings of Lois Pendergast, 37, and her four children, 3, 4, 6 and 9, in 1958 when he was 16. His prison status eventually was reclassified, allowing him to work outside the prison walls. He has been at large since his escape from Tehachapi State Prison in 1974.

Feb. 12 – The 9th U.S. Circuit Court of Appeal ruled that Tom Davies should be reinstated on the Grossmont Union High School District Board, giving the panel a working majority if three members could agree on any recommended action.

Feb. 21 – A San Diego County Superior Court judge ruled that admitted killer Steven Larsen of El Cajon, a dentist, is well enough to be released from Patton State Hospital. Larsen, 40, admitted he shot and killed Escondido physician Dr. Craig Blundell on July 28, 1986, but he was found not guilty by reason of insanity. Larsen suffered from paranoid schizophrenia and after his release must take medication for his illness.

Feb. 27 – Tony Orosco, an industrial designer, was chosen on the 13th ballot to be the first Hispanic on the Grossmont Union High School District Board. He replaces Fred Andrews, Jr. who died in a Los Angeles hotel room. Only Dr. Maynard Olsen, serving in the Persian Gulf War, remains absent from the board.

Mar. 9 – The Feb. 4 death of Fred Andrews Jr., an 11-year member of the Grossmont Union High School District Board, was ruled a suicide by the Los Angeles County coroner's office. Andrews, 50, was thought to have died of a heart attack in a Los Angeles area hotel room, but the coroner's office listed his death as "acute desipromine intoxication," a result of ingesting too much of an anti-depressant drug.

Mar. 14 – Buffum's, one of the anchor stores in Grossmont Shopping Center, will close its doors by late spring, along with 15 other outlets in the Long Beach-based chain.

Mar. 15 – San Diego County Water Authority Board voted unanimously to declare a water emergency in the county and impose a set of 13 prohibited water uses. This was in response to an area-wide drought.

Mar. 20 – The National Weather Service determined that a windstorm which swept through a San Carlos neighborhood was in fact a tornado. Roofs were peeled back, windows smashed and trees uprooted.

Mar. 21 – Confessed murderer Dr. Steven A. Larsen, an El Cajon dentist, is to be released from Patton State Hospital on March 25 when he will continue his treatment for paranoia. Larsen shot and killed Escondido physician Dr. Craig Blundell at his office on July 28, 1986. He pleaded guilty by reason of insanity to the murder.

Apr. 2 – Alfred Charles Buck, 80, founder of Buck Knives in El Cajon, died two days ago of cancer at his home. He had built one of the world's largest and best known knife manufacturing plants.

Apr. 6 – Club Tronix in Casa de Oro was shut down by sheriff's deputies pending an investigation for its failure to comply with the conditions of its license. Grossmont College student Theodros Zeudalem, 18, was killed in a hail of bullets outside the crowded club a week ago. Two other young men were wounded by the gunfire. The club reopened May 3 but was closed permanently on May 16.

May 9 – In a case described as "the biggest single bribery case in the history of the Internal Revenue Service," an El Cajon father and son were charged in a 205-count indictment of taking huge bribes to help people avoid paying taxes. Former IRS auditor Robert A. Morales, Sr., and his son, Robert A. Morales, Jr., a tax preparer, were accused of laundering illegal funds through sham corporations and "ghost employees." Tens of millions of dollars in taxes were evaded.

May 14 – Feed the Hungry, a coalition of church volunteers that had served meals to the needy for five years at Wells Park, folded when the El Cajon Planning Commission denied the group's application for a conditional use permit. Residents of the area had complained that the feeding program lured the homeless and other needy folk to their neighborhood. . . .Dale A. Akiki, 33, was arrested on a 50-count grand jury indictment charging him with child molestation, child abuse and kidnapping while a child care volunteer at Faith Chapel in Spring Valley. Ten children were alleged to have been abused. (*Akiki later was exonerated of all charges, freed from jail and won a huge settlement for having been falsely accused of the criminal acts.*)

May 17 – The 35th anniversary of a sneak preview held at El Cajon Theater for the blockbuster movie "Giant" was noted. The film, starring Rock Hudson, Elizabeth Taylor and James Dean, ran for three hours and 35 minutes without an intermission. Film publicist Bob Warner wrote the reminiscent piece. The sneak preview was held May 28, 1956.

May 19 – A welcome home party for troops returning from Kuwait was held in *The Daily Californian* parking lot. One of the honorees was Dr. Maynard Olsen, a La Mesa physician in the Army reserve and a Grossmont Union High School District Board member.

May 22 – County supervisors voted 3-0 to approve Skyline Wesleyan Church's proposal to build a 345,000-square-foot church and educational facility on a hilltop at Highway 94 and Jamacha Boulevard. The proposed church was said to be comparable in size to the San Diego Convention Center and larger than St. Peter's Cathedral in Vatican City. Plans called for a 3,500-seat sanctuary and 3,550 parking spaces. The project had been reduced by more than 112,000 square feet. . . . The paper's Street Beat question on this day was: "Should Queen Elizabeth step down and let Prince Charles become king of England?" Of the five respondents, three said yes, two said no.

June 14 – Packaged cookies were pulled from 100 vending machines in the county after Eric Munzenmaier of El Cajon bought a pack of Grandma's Nutty Fudge Cookies from a Cuyamaca College vending machine and noticed they smelled like model airplane glue. He nibbled on them and got a headache. The product was sent to a lab in Texas for analysis.

June 20 – Dana Jones, senior class president at El Cajon Valley High School, caused a ruckus when he launched a verbal attack against the school's administration during graduation ceremonies, blaming officials for the lack of school spirit.

June 28 – San Diego Metropolitan Homicide Task Force identified Carol Jane Gushnowski, 31, of El Cajon, as one of an estimated 45 women whose bodies had been buried throughout the county since 1984, many of them in East County. Gushnowski's decomposed body was found in brush near Buckman Springs Road and Old Highway 80.

June 30-July 1 – The U.S. Supreme Court let stand a Feb. 11 decision by the 9th Circuit Court of Appeal that allowed Tom Davies to keep his seat on the Grossmont Union High School District Board despite the fact that he and his wife, Nadia, a former district teacher, had signed a pledge not to seek employment in the district in return for a payment of $39,200. The appellate court ruled the district had no right to take away from Davies his constitutional right to run for a seat on the board.

July 14-15 – The state's sales tax was scheduled to increase by 1.25 percent, giving San Diego County residents a share of the dubious distinction of paying the highest sales and use tax in the state – 8.25 percent. Seven other counties in the state had the same rate.

July 24 – Cycling star Tony Clark, 18, died in a motorcycle accident in the desert near Gordon Wells. He had just graduated from Granite Hills High School where he was homecoming king.

July 31 – Planning commissioner Donna Alm, 52, was appointed to the La Mesa City Council to replace Jerri Lopez, who resigned for health reasons.

Aug. 8 – A gas leak in the air conditioning system at El Cajon Police Department forced evacuation of the building at Fletcher Parkway and Magnolia Avenue.

Aug. 22 – A new 30,000-square-foot El Cajon Regional Branch Library, four times the size of the old one, was opened Aug. 21 and will house 85,000 to 90,000 books. It has a capacity to hold 200,000.

Aug. 29 – The family of a 20-year-old Spring Valley woman who committed suicide while under the influence of the anti-depressant drug Prozac filed suit against Eli Lilly Co., maker of the drug. Jennifer Barrett, an honor student at Monte Vista High School, shot herself in the head, an act the suit alleges was caused by the drug she was taking. The suit contended that Prozac led to Barrett's hostile behavior toward her family and friends, nightmares and other strange behavior.

Sept. 1-2 – El Cajon police officer Dave Turner was watching "America's Most Wanted" on TV and spotted a man he recently had interviewed who was wanted for attempted murder. After all-night surveillance, the suspect – Walter Lee Anderson, 30 – was arrested at a friend's house on East Madison Avenue. *(Anderson had watched the TV program, too.)* Besides attempted murder, Anderson was wanted in Atlanta and Indiana for alleged cocaine trafficking.

Sept. 24 – El Cajon's first International Friendship Festival, a two-day event, attracted a crowd estimated at between 25,000 and 30,000.

Sept. 25 – East County joined the rest of the world in mourning the death of Theodor Geisel, 87, otherwise known as Dr. Seuss, author of such whimsical children's classics as "The Cat in the Hat" and "How the Grinch Stole Christmas." Geisel lived in La Jolla.

Oct. 1 – Elmer Lee Nance, 63, convicted in 1974 of child molestation in El Cajon, was arrested in Barstow in connection with the 1986 murder of Nancy Allison White, 22, a wife and mother whose car had broken down at the map stop on Interstate 8 east of El Cajon. She was returning from El Centro where she celebrated her second wedding anniversary with her husband, Marine Sgt. Milton White.

Oct. 6-7 – A 21-year-old Upland woman crashed her midget race car into a billboard at Cajon Speedway and had to be airlifted to Sharp Memorial Hospital. The victim – Kara Hendrick – died of massive head injuries.

Oct. 20-21 – Flood lights were turned on, sheriff's officers were dispatched, and a sheriff's helicopter hovered overhead – all because it was assumed inmates were breaking out of the East County Detention Facility. False alarm! County workers were washing the jail's windows during early evening hours instead of the daytime.

Oct. 24 – Dianne Jacob, who recently stepped down as chief of staff for Second District Supervisor George Bailey, announced she would be a candidate for supervisor whether or not Bailey decided to seek re-election.

Oct. 30 – Law enforcement officers served simultaneous search warrants at all three Indian gaming casinos in East County – Barona, Sycuan and Viejas. More than 150 machines and their contents were seized in the morning raid. Officers involved in the raid exceeded 80.

Nov. 1 – An article about condom use by high school students, appearing in a free monthly publication called *High School Times* and inserted in high school newspapers in Grossmont Union High School District, caused a rumble and was expected to lead to a change in district policy. The article was written by a student at Bonita Vista High School who claimed that 85 percent of students randomly surveyed at that school were sexually active.

Nov. 27 – El Cajon Councilwoman Beverly Miller criticized the Mother Goose Parade Assn. for allowing two tanks to roll through city streets during the annual parade. "What nursery rhyme highlights a tank?" she wanted to know. Ron Snow, association president, said the parade sponsors were not glorifying warfare. "Kids love them (the tanks)," he said.

Dec. 7 – Matthew Van Loon, 4, was hailed as a hero for dialing 911 when his grandfather, Arthur Van Loon, suffered a stroke at his Alpine home. Matthew did more than make the phone call. He was the only person available who was small enough to squeeze through the crack in the bathroom door and move his grandfather so firefighters could get through the door and assist the elderly man.

Dec. 21 – Second District Supervisor George Bailey announced his retirement, ending a 34-year career in public life that included serving on the La Mesa Planning Commission, the La Mesa City Council and being mayor. "We love you Dad, and we didn't applaud because we wanted you to go," fellow Supervisor Brian Bilbray said as he hugged the departing officeholder.

Dec. 22-23 – The remains of a Jamul woman missing since July 30, 1987, were retrieved from a spot on the property where she, her husband and their three children had lived. Vickie Eddington, 29, was last seen July 30, 1987, at a convenience store after she walked two miles to get help because her car had a flat tire. Her husband, Navy Lt. Cmdr. Leonard Eddington, 43, was arrested and later convicted of her murder. The children were 9, 6 and 4.

Dec. 24 – About 400 protesters carrying candles and flashlights held a late-night rally around the Mt. Helix cross to protest a judge's ruling that the cross should come down. U.S. District Court Judge Gordon Thompson Jr. had ordered the cross removed because it is primarily a religious symbol and violated the law against government favoring a particular religious belief.

1992

Jan. 2 – On the day before he was to be married, 28-year-old Terry L. Davies of El Cajon lost his life while retrieving a hat on Interstate 8 in the Hotel Circle area of San Diego. Davies, on New Year's Day, was driving with his fiancée when a hat containing $100 – money he intended to use for gas to travel to Stockton for his wedding the next day – blew off the dashboard of his car and out the window. Davies, despite being warned not to go on the freeway, climbed over a fence and retrieved his own hat but spotted another hat belonging to his friend and ran onto the freeway to get it. He was struck and killed.

Jan. 28 – An El Cajon Police Department patrol dog was relieved of duty after biting off part of an ear of a handcuffed and prone prisoner, 27-year-old Clayton Meserole of El Cajon. The incident happened when the handler of another dog slipped and lost control of his animal. The detached portion of the man's ear could not be reattached. Police suspended their K-9 program pending a full review of the circumstances that led to the bite.

Feb. 7 – Child pornography valued at $500,000 was taken from a shed in an unincorporated area of El Cajon. It was the largest seizure of its kind in San Diego County history. The confiscated material included 6,000 magazines and instruction manuals. Patrick Albert Dixon, 47, of Santee, was arrested in late February on suspicion of distributing child pornography.

Feb. 18 – Cinema Grossmont, a theater seating 1,000, closed its doors today. It had operated since the 1960s near Grossmont Shopping Center.

Feb. 19 – An 8-year-old boy from El Cajon, molested by his Cub scoutmaster, won a $400,000 judgment against the local and national Boy Scouts of America. Jerry Frazier pleaded guilty to molesting the boy and is serving a 19-year term in state prison. He was ruled 90 percent negligent for his role in the crime.

Feb. 21 – To prevent the Mt. Helix cross from being taken down, county supervisors transferred title to the cross and property on which it is located to the San Diego County Historical Society. Courts ruled the cross had to be taken down because its presence on public land showed a preference for a particular religious faith.

Mar. 12 – Santee City Council voted in principle for an agreement to purchase Magnolia Village Center for the city's administrative offices. The purchase price was $2,050,000 for 9.2 acres at 10601-10629 Magnolia Ave. . . . A letter from President George H.W. Bush was printed on the front page of *The Daily Californian*, congratulating the paper on its 100th anniversary. (*The Daily Californian's* predecessor was *The Valley News*.)

Mar. 25 – Despite emotional pleas to save it, the El Cajon City Council voted 3-2 to allow the El Cajon Theater to be razed. The theater was described as unsafe and riddled with cancer-causing asbestos. El Cajon Theater was built in the art deco style after World War II and had been transformed from a family theater to one featuring X-rated films.

Apr. 1 – El Cajon Mayor Joan Shoemaker filed an official rebuttal to charges by a local attorney trying to drive her from office. Shoemaker, accused by attorney Julian Turner of uprooting residents and businesses by pressing for redevelopment, defended her stance on the subject and vowed to move forward with it. . . . A front-page story focused on a drainage ditch hangout for young people known as Hell's Gate in the vicinity of Parkway Plaza. The ditch was described as a haunt for truants, runaways, transients, graffiti artists, drug users and thieves. The ditch ran behind the shopping center to Johnson Avenue and Fletcher Parkway.

Apr. 23 – An earthquake measuring 6.1 on the Richter scale rattled East County but caused no known injuries or property damage in this area.

Apr. 24 – The execution death of Robert Alton Harris, who killed two teen-age San Diego area boys and mutilated their bodies, led murder defendant Hai Van Nguyen, 19, of Garden Grove, to change his plea to guilty in the death of Iraqi-born Thamir "Tom" Mikheal, 31, owner of The Deliquery Market in El Cajon. Nguyen's attorney said his client feared he would be given the death penalty if convicted rather than life without the possibility of parole. Mikheal's nephew, David Wartan, 18, was wounded in the Aug. 18, 1991, robbery attempt.

May 10-11 – Arkansas Gov. Bill Clinton brought his quest for the presidency to El Cajon on May 9, drawing a crowd of 400 to a town hall meeting in the amphitheater near the city administration building. Clinton, 46, the presumptive favorite for the Democratic presidential nomination, chatted for 90 minutes with supporters and others during his visit.

May 13 – Santee was in the running for a federal project that potentially could lure 7,000 jobs to this area. The city was one of five under consideration by the Department of Defense for a large accounting office.

May 16 – Two women and a man – all serving time in state prisons – were arrested as suspects in the torture-murder four years ago of Irene Melanie May, a 23-year-old mother of three from Lakeside who was described as a narcotics user. It was alleged that the three used electric wires to shock May and injected her with battery acid. The suspects were Kerry Lyn Dalton, 39, of Lakeside; Sheryl Baker, 28, of El Cajon; and Mark Tompkins, 30, of San Diego. May's murder occurred June 26, 1988, in a mobile home in Live Oak Springs, about 50 miles east of El Cajon.

June 3 – El Cajon City Councilman Jack Hanson was defeated in his bid for re-election, ending his 14-year tenure on the council. Bob McClellan and Richard Ramos were the newly elected councilmen. Another prominent loser was Assemblywoman Carol Bentley, R-77th, who lost her race with Assemblyman David Kelley, R-Hemet, to move to the State Senate.

June 11 – An artist's studio used by the late golf legend William "Bill" Casper was demolished at the intersection of Bradley and North Magnolia avenues. Casper, who died at 96, painted Western landscapes, seascapes, nudes and portraits of American Indians. Built around 1941, the studio served as a showplace not only for Casper's paintings but also for those of his longtime friend, Western artist Olaf Wieghorst.

June 14-15 – Black and Hispanic inmates at Descanso Detention Facility rioted over the weekend, a clash inspired by racial slurs that involved an estimated 100 prisoners. The disturbance lasted 20 minutes. Rocks, broomsticks and rakes were used by the battling inmates. Only minor injuries were reported.

June 28-29 – Marguerite L. Patrick, 76, of La Mesa, died a day after two con artists stole $3,200 from her by posing as bank and police officers. The death had to be listed as "natural" because of the difficulty of linking it to stress from the ordeal.

July 7 – Federal regulators took control of insolvent Home Federal, the nation's eighth-largest savings and loan company, but it was business as usual at East County offices in La Mesa, El Cajon, Rancho San Diego, Alpine, Lakeside, Santee, Spring Valley, San Carlos, Del Cerro, Marketplace at the Grove and College Center.

July 8 – An El Cajon resident, William R. Kennedy Jr., was one of three men charged in a 16-count federal indictment alleging the men secretly took $7.7 million from Kuwait to illegally drum up support for U.S. intervention in the Persian Gulf. Kennedy is the former owner of Conservative Digest, a now-defunct political journal. The indictment contends the men diverted $5.7 million from Kuwait for their personal use, hiding the payments to avoid income taxes.

July 12 – Dr. Dale Burke, a dentist who had been a trustee of the Grossmont-Cuyamaca Community College District for 21 years, announced he would not seek re-election.

July 18 – The decomposed body of a La Mesa man suspected in the stabbing death of his mother was found in a Portland, OR park with a gun in one hand and a nearly empty whiskey bottle in the other. Dennis Scott Hulmes, 45, apparently committed suicide and left behind a note saying he was upset with his 73-year-old mother, Anita Hulmes, who was found dead in her bathtub.

July 22 – El Cajon resident Leonard F. Scott, 24, killed his infant daughter, his estranged wife and her stepmother before turning the gun on himself, ending his life. The victims were the man's 4-month-old daughter, Jennifer Shales; the infant's mother, Robin Jean Bergeron, 25; Bergeron's stepmother, Sophia Bergeron, 30; and Scott, who apparently was upset over a child custody battle. Scott suffered from brain damage resulting from accidents when he was a child.

Aug. 7 – Municipal Court Judge Donald Meloche overturned a jury's decision in favor of a sheriff's deputy who attempted to stop a woman driver on a darkened rural road in 1987. Deputy Robert Frausto had tried to pull over Christina King, who was 23 at the time, on Steele Canyon Road, but for her own safety she continued driving until she reached a convenience store about two miles down the road. The jury had voted 11-1 against awarding $25,000 to King. Meloche ordered jurors to return to court for further deliberations. King had been arrested for speeding. Her refusal to stop was described as fear stemming from the case of Cara Knott of El Cajon, who was murdered by California Highway Patrol Officer Craig Peyer after stopping her on Interstate 15 and ordering her to drive to a darkened off-ramp.

Aug. 16-17 – Names of about 1,200 drunken driving offenders were to be printed in *The Daily Californian* in an effort to clear up a backlog of cases left in limbo by the unwillingness of the culprits to step forward and take responsibility for their crimes. Warrants for their arrests had been issued but not enforced. The county had a backlog of nearly 700,000 arrest warrants that were ignored by the defendants because they knew the county didn't have jail space for them. Subsequently, some named offenders came forward and law enforcement sweeps drew others into court, but nowhere near the number of violators on the list.

Sept. 1 – Two sailors accused of the hate-crime murder of El Cajon resident Michael Hamilton, 48, in Balboa Park will serve time in state prison. Todd Fluette, 19, who admitted he used a butterfly knife to slit Hamilton's throat, was given a life term without the possibility of parole. His companion, David Kring, 23, received a term of 25 years to life for his part in the slaying. The sailors were accused of lying in wait to kill Hamilton, a bisexual. Court testimony revealed the sailors had gone to the park "to kill a faggot."

Sept. 10 – Twin brothers, Frank and Brian Pennisi, 16, were killed in a three-car pileup on their way to Santana High School. Four other students in the Pennisi vehicle were injured in addition to three passengers in another vehicle.

Sept. 19 – Chuck Merino, an El Cajon police officer, was rejected by the Boy Scouts as an Explorer post adviser because he is gay. Merino coaches high school football and was a Boy Scout when he was young. Merino disclosed his sexual orientation last December at a public meeting in Hillcrest while helping San Diego police deal with attacks on gays in that part of San Diego.

Sept. 24 – San Diego State University revised its policy on post-game interviews by journalists with athletes by ordering all media interviews to be conducted outside the locker room. The issue had been raised when *Daily Californian* sports correspondent Karen Pearlman and two other female reporters were denied access to a locker room at San Diego Jack Murphy Stadium where the Aztecs played their football games.

Oct. 6 – Sheriff Jim Roache sent four detectives to Alpine to investigate the rape of a white woman and what appears to be a retaliatory attack by bat-wielding white men who assaulted three migrant workers. Roache vowed that vigilante attacks would not be tolerated.

Oct. 9 – A Superior Court jury convicted Navy Lt. Cmdr. Leonard Eddington, 44, of the murder of his wife, Vickie, 29, and burying her body in the yard of their Jamul home in 1987. Vickie's skeletal remains were unearthed Dec. 21, 1991, under 10 feet of dirt. Her husband subsequently was sentenced to life in prison without the possibility of parole. The couple had three children.

Oct. 17 – A *New York Times* reporter attended a candidates' forum in La Mesa featuring candidates for the La Mesa-Spring Valley School District Board, apparently lured by the controversy over representatives of the Christian right-wing running for many elective offices in California and elsewhere. Other national media outlets that had contacted district leaders included *Time* magazine, *Playboy*, the *Wall Street Journal* and the MacNeil-Lehrer News Hour. . . . Tom Wigton, founder of the Mother Goose Parade in El Cajon, died of cancer Oct. 15 in a North Dakota hospital. He was 78.

Nov. 14 – The death penalty will be sought for three defendants accused of slaying a Lakeside mother of three whose body has not been recovered. Special circumstance allegations were filed against Sheryl Baker, 28, of El Cajon; Kerry Dalton, 29, of Lakeside; and Mark Tompkins, 29, of San Diego. Irene May, 23, was killed June 16, 1988, in a mobile home at Live

Oak Springs. The allegations included a claim that May, a drug user, was tortured by having battery acid injected into her veins.

Dec. 4 – A five-year battle by Gavin O'Hara, 31, of La Mesa to regain custody of his five-year-old daughter ended when the Fourth District Court of Appeal ruled in his favor. It took more than 100 court appearances by O'Hara and nearly $60,000 in legal fees and foster care payments to reverse a Department of Social Services ruling that stripped O'Hara of his parental rights. O'Hara, now a law clerk, had been a substance abuser, a factor in his loss of custody, but he has since been rehabilitated. The girlfriend with whom he had the child attempted to place the infant in a "fast-adopt" home, but it was revealed her social worker was a sister-in-law of the foster mother who wanted to adopt the baby.

Dec. 16 – Smith's Food and Drug, Inc. of Utah was awarded a contract by El Cajon Redevelopment Agency to develop an 11.2-acre site at the corner of Main Street and Magnolia Avenue to be called the Corners Project. The Utah company's bid of $6.4 million was chosen over a higher bid of $8 million by Lucky Stores, Inc. The El Cajon City Council doubled as the redevelopment agency.

1993

Jan. 5 – Dianne Jacob of Jamul was sworn in Jan. 4 as the newest Second District supervisor. Jacob, former chief of staff for retiring Supervisor George Bailey, defeated Santee Mayor Jack Doyle for the position.

Jan. 6 – Dr. Donald Coleman, a veterinarian and founder of Grossmont Animal Hospital, was slain over the weekend at his new home in Alamos, Mexico. Coleman had planned to move to what he called his "dream home" in the state of Sonora in northwest Mexico. He was reportedly murdered by masked men who tried to rob him during a dinner party.

Jan. 11 – Darlene Bryant was vowing to keep her pot-bellied pig, Swynonna, despite being ordered by animal control officers to find another home for her outside the city of El Cajon. Claiming that Swynonna – named for singer Wynonna Judd – is one of her "children," Bryant said the pig can eat off a spoon or fork, likes cherry Coke, bounces on a trampoline and shares her owner's bed. Bryant paid $350 for Swynonna, whose estimated lifespan is between 12 and 30 years.

Jan. 27 – Swynonna was spared exile from El Cajon when the City Council voted to allow pet pigs inside the city limits. The vote was 3-1, with

Councilwoman Harriet Stockwell dissenting with the comment "Pigs is pigs." The council's action elevated Swynonna's status from pot-bellied pig to "exotic pet." *The Daily Californian* editorialized: "For now, Swynonna is safe. It's an appropriate reward for a pot-bellied pig who has learned to go to the bathroom in a litter box and who wears a tailored black suede jacket with silver studs when riding in her car seat on afternoon sojourns to the country. Swynonna might be a pig, but she's a pig with manners and class."

Feb. 9 – A 29-year-old Camp Pendleton Marine sergeant fatally shot his wife and her father Feb. 8 in the parking lot of a Lucky shopping center in Casa de Oro, then killed himself. The dead were Olivia Keys Ruis, 29; her father, Antonio Ruiz, Jr., 58, of La Mesa; and the shooter whose wife had a restraining order against him. Found in the sergeant's rental car was an audio cassette tape labeled "The Tape," which revealed why he intended to kill his estranged wife and himself. The shooter later was identified as Marine Sgt. Samuel Keys.

Mar. 5 – Nine East County residents were caught in a massive national raid to crack down on phone sales fraud. At the same time, FBI agents raided a Lakeside home as part of a nationwide effort to put child pornography distributors out of business.

Mar. 6 – Travis Wade Amaral, 17, of Lakeside was ordered to serve at least 55 years in prison for his part in killing two graduate students at an Interstate 8 rest stop near Yuma, AZ. The victims were Bryan and Laura Bernstein, both 22, who were on their way from Alabama to UCLA when they stopped at the roadside rest area near Yuma. Amaral avoided the death penalty by agreeing to testify against his accomplice, Gregory Scott Dickens, 27, of Carlsbad.

Mar. 9 – Henry W. Kozak, 75, founder and owner of Kozak's Restaurant at 401 W. Main St. in El Cajon, died of respiratory failure at Scripps Green Hospital. He opened the first Denny's in San Diego on Pacific HIghway and opened his El Cajon restaurant Jan. 11, 1964.

Mar. 19 – Scripps Health announced it has purchased the Valley Medical Center on East Main Street in El Cajon from Epic Healthcare Group. The 172-bed facility will be called Scripps Hospital – East County.

Mar. 22 – Former San Diego County Sheriff John Duffy, 62, died of a heart attack while serving in El Salvador as a consultant to establish a national all-civilian police force. Duffy was elected sheriff in 1971 and held that office for 20 years. The former resident of El Cajon and Alpine had been with the sheriff's department for 38 years.

Mar. 23 – Archeologists unearthed artifacts from the Hotel del Corona, which was built in 1886 and was destroyed by fire in 1920. It was near what is now the corner of Main Street and Magnolia Avenue in El Cajon. Among the artifacts were purple glass, ceramics, square nails, and fragments of bottles and cans.

Mar. 29 – Retired Army Lt. Col. Oliver North, central figure in the Iran-Contra scandal during the Reagan administration, spoke twice to full houses at Shadow Mountain Community Church in El Cajon. An estimated 5,000 people heard his speeches, which focused on his Christian faith rather than his legal troubles.

Apr. 21 – Work on Cuyamaca College's physical education facility was halted by the U.S. Fish and Wildlife Service to protect a tiny songbird called the gnatcatcher, which had been designated a threatened specie.

Apr. 25 – Citizens for Responsive City Government failed to get enough signatures for a recall election against El Cajon Mayor Joan Shoemaker and council members Harriet Stockwell and Richard Ramos. The issue was a council decision to reverse an earlier vote not to widen Chase Avenue to five lanes.

May 2 – James C. Snapp, 69, the first popularly elected mayor of El Cajon, died May 1 at his home in Lakeside. He was elected in 1968 and re-elected in 1972, serving until 1976. During World War II, he was a U.S. Army Air Corps pilot and suffered severe injuries in a plane accident. Despite that, he served vigorously in civic affairs as a member of the city planning commission from 1961 to 1962, the Gillespie Field Development Council in 1977 and as Gov. Ronald Reagan's appointee to the State Aeronautics Board, of which he was chairman from 1972 to 1973.

May 6 – Sexually explicit material from El Cajon vending machines was ordered by the El Cajon City Council to be shipped to cities throughout California in an effort to bolster support for a legislative measure limiting the availability of such publications in the state's cities and towns.

May 16 – *The Daily Californian* published the first in a series of articles about the San Diego Metropolitan Task Force which since 1988 had been investigating the mysterious murders of 43 women whose bodies had been found throughout the county.

June 10 – A 4-month-old infant girl died of malnutrition and dehydration at Balboa Naval Hospital. Petty Officer Jason Clay Glasgow, 22, of El Cajon, and his wife, Kay, 20, were arrested and charged with involuntary manslaughter. Lt. Bob Lein of El Cajon Police Department said: "This is the worst case of child neglect that this department has investigated." The couple's other daughters, 4 and 2, were taken to Hillcrest Receiving Home for Children. Neighbors of the Glasgows had called Child Protective Services in the middle of May but there was no response until June 3. (*On July 15 it was reported the parents were charged with the murder of their daughter.*)

June 26 – The annual destruction of illegal fireworks seized by authorities went awry when one of the exploding rockets strayed and started a 10-acre grass fire near the sheriff's bomb range at Highway 94 and Jamacha Road.

July 7 – A divorced couple from Lakeside, both remarried, made headlines by agreeing to donate portions of their lungs in an attempt to save the life of their gravely ill son who suffered from cystic fibrosis and was near death. Darlene Pinkerton, divorced from her first husband for 17 years, and Paul Hartup each donated lobes from their lungs to their son, Ty, 21, during a rare operation June 29 at USC University Hospital. The current spouses of Ty's parents also offered to donate lung lobes, but doctors decided to use those of his biological parents. It was the third lung operation of its kind at the hospital and in the world. Ty was reported in guarded but improving condition. (*Ty returned to his home Aug. 28, saying: "I feel really good."*)

July 29 – Ruth Norman, 92, director of the Unarius Academy of Science in El Cajon, was reported to have died in her sleep July 12. She made international headlines in 1976 when she wagered $4,000 with Ladbroke & Co., Ltd. in London that spaceships would land that year in San Diego County. Her organization purchased 70 acres in Jamul in 2001 to accommodate spaceship landings.

Aug. 2 – Two Lakeside boys, both 15, were struck and killed by a hit-and-run driver while they were walking home from El Capitan High School. The victims were Sean McNamer and Tyler "Ty" Cash. Cheryl Diane Garcia, 27, of El Cajon was charged with two counts of felony manslaughter, felony hit and run, felony drunken driving and driving with a suspended license. (*Garcia received the maximum sentence of 13 years in state prison.*)

Aug. 30 – Santee City Council voted to spend $20,000 as a sponsorship fee in support of the Steve Scott Invitational Mile race in Santee in January as part of Holiday Bowl festivities in San Diego. The race would have a purse of $10,000. It is named for an internationally known racer who has run more sub-four minute miles than anyone in the world.

Sept. 28 – The Parent Porn Patrol was activated in El Cajon, with about 15 members of the group keeping vigil on five news racks containing sexually explicit material outside the Bostonia Post Office on Second Street.

Sept. 29 – County supervisors voted to send President Clinton and Congress monthly invoices detailing the cost of undocumented immigrants borne by U.S. citizens in this region. It was estimated the annual bill for services to those immigrants was $146 million or more.

Oct. 11 – Barry Bosworth, drama and world history teacher at Granite Hills High School, was named one of four "Teachers of the Year" in San Diego County. Many of Bosworth's students went on to successful careers in arts, including Melinda Gilb who sang the second lead in "Singin' in the Rain" on Broadway.

Oct. 14 – Five people were known to have died in an early afternoon shooting at Family Fitness Center on Arnele Avenue in El Cajon. Among the dead were two instructors, two customers and the gunman who used a 12-gauge shotgun, later identified as 19-year-old James Buquet of Alpine, a drug user said to have been depressed because of a knee injury that would not heal. The next day the victims were identified: Helen-Mary Spatz, 36, and Rebecca "Becki" Negrete, 31, employees of the health club; and customers Laxmi Patel, 19, and Charles Bradford "Brad" Tucker, 37. In an eerie twist, it was revealed that Buquet had written a story for his creative writing class at Grossmont College that could have been a plot sequence for what happened at the exercise facility.

Oct. 31 – A man shooting from a second-story apartment on Mollison Avenue in El Cajon killed two people and wounded five others Oct. 30, then set his apartment on fire, resulting in his own death. The sniper was identified as Gordon Neuman, 62, who had been a resident of the Key Largo apartment complex at 380 N. Mollison Ave. for 20 years and was described as a loner and a cranky old man.

Nov. 1 –Victims of the Oct. 30 sniper shooting on Mollison Avenue in El Cajon were identified: Virginia Eash, 46, of El Cajon; Jessica Reuhl, 9, a tenant; and Gordon Neuman, the sniper. Neuman had been placed on probation 13 years earlier for the sale of a tear gas canister. Police found a .38-caliber revolver and an M-16 rifle in Neuman's fire-ravaged apartment.

Nov. 20 – A seven-month trial ended with former Sunday school teacher Dale Akiki, 36, found innocent of charges that he raped, sodomized and tortured nine children of parishioners at Faith Chapel in Spring Valley. The children testified that Akiki had killed a baby, sacrificed a rabbit and slaughtered an elephant and a giraffe. The jury said it did not believe the accusations, all of which Akiki denied. Akiki, who had birth defects caused by a rare genetic disorder called Noonan's syndrome, had been in jail for 30 months.

Dec. 4 – Great Western Bank submitted the winning sealed bid to buy 119 branches of the troubled HomeFed Bank in San Diego County.

Dec. 20 – *The Daily Californian's* fund drive for the homeless had reached $9,131.46, more than halfway to the $15,000 goal. The homeless were trekking to the National Guard armory in increasing numbers with nighttime temperatures dropping to as low as 33 degrees.

1994

Jan. 5 – When El Cajon City Council voted against allocating any money to keep the National Guard armory open through the winter for the homeless, *The Daily Californian* challenged the community to raise $25,000 more than the nearly $16,000 already raised from contributions by citizens.

Jan. 7 – Second District Supervisor Dianne Jacob announced that $80,000 in federal money had been allocated for East County emergency homeless shelters but no one had applied for it. Volunteers of America promptly applied for the funds but must wait until Jan. 14 to learn if the organization gets the money.

Jan. 8 – The adobe home of famed Western artist Olaf Wieghorst on Renette Avenue in El Cajon will be preserved as a museum. El Cajon Chamber of Commerce Foundation bought the property from its current owner, Clark Mires, professor of theater arts at Grossmont College.

Jan. 13 – Polly Morris, 107, Santee's oldest resident, died Jan. 6 in her sleep. A sharecropper's daughter, she was born in east Texas and worked in the fields from the age of 8, picking cotton, watermelons and other crops. She married at 12 and had four children.

Feb. 5 – Failure of HomeFed Bank has affected the development of Rancho San Diego in a huge way. Some 2,100 acres formerly owned by HomeFed subsidiary Home Capital Corp. has been turned over to the federal government's Resolution Trust Corp. The property had been reserved for 4,000 homes.

Feb. 22 – Harold G. Hughes, 87, first superintendent of what was then called Grossmont Community College District and a longtime teacher and administrator in Grossmont Union High School District, died of bone cancer in Hawaii where he made his home after retirement. He came to this area in the 1930s and taught chemistry at Grossmont High School.

Mar. 17 – Ex-Padres pitcher Eric Show, 37, was found dead in his bed Mar. 16 at a drug rehabilitation center in Dulzura. He helped lead the San Diego Padres to their only National League pennant in 1984 and held team career marks for wins (100) and for strikeouts (951).

Apr. 6 – A shoeless man tore a crucifix from a casket during a funeral at Our Lady of Grace Catholic Church in Fletcher Hills. Mourners held the man, Glen K. Hall, 42, for police, who discovered this was his third arrest in three days. Hall was booked for robbing a corpse and disrupting a church service. Suspecting Hall was under the influence of drugs, police took him to a psychiatric unit at George Bailey Detention Facility in Otay Mesa.

Apr. 13 – El Cajon mayoral candidate Mark Lewis called for the firing of City Manager Robert Acker and James Griffin, director of community development, during an interview with *The Daily Californian's* editorial board. Lewis accused the two officials of disregarding council directives. Acker invited Lewis to put the matter before the City Council at its next meeting.

Apr. 16 – El Cajon police arrested the mother of a 5-year-old girl who was believed to have been killed in Kansas City more than a year ago because she would not say her ABCs or numbers when awakened from a deep sleep. Angela Lynn Melton, 22, was charged with collecting welfare while knowing her daughter was dead. Melton's boyfriend, Gary Christian, 33, had been arrested a day after Easter on suspicion of beating and drowning the girl on Feb. 24, 1993, in a Kansas City motel room. The body of the girl, named Angel, has not been found despite searches of Arizona and California desert regions where the couple's other children thought she had been buried on the way to their new home in East County.

Apr. 29 – Santee City Council adopted a rent control ordinance governing mobile home parks that rolls back rents to 1989 levels and factors in annual increases based on the Consumer Price Index.

May 1 – Assemblyman Tom Connolly, D-77th, is under investigation by the Assembly Rules Committee for alleged sexual harassment claims made by members of his staff – Dena Holman, his office manager, and aides Meredith Anderson, Lori Arbogast and DeVoe Treadwell. Connolly said the allegations were an orchestrated attempt to ruin his political career. The 77th Assembly District includes much of East County.

May 3 – An El Cajon couple whose 4-month-old daughter died of starvation was found guilty of second-degree murder after three days of deliberation in Superior Court. Jason Glasgow, 23, and his wife, Patricia, 21, also were found guilty of child abuse. They face maximum terms of 15 years to life in prison. Witnesses testified that the infant spent most of her day, up to 22 hours, strapped into a car seat.

June 8 – El Cajon Mayor Joan Shoemaker won re-election, beating challengers Mark Lewis and Peter Chirimbes. In countywide elections, Sheriff Jim Roache was defeated by former San Diego Police Chief Bill Kolender, and attorney Paul Pfingst ousted 24-year incumbent Ed Miller to become district attorney.

June 20 – The U.S. Supreme Court ruled that San Diego County violated the state's constitution by maintaining the Mt. Helix cross, but County Supervisor Dianne Jacob said the decision is irrelevant because of a February 1992 agreement that transfers control of the cross and some mountaintop property to the San Diego Historical Society.

June 21 – Two young Iraqi refugees who fled their native land to avoid torture were killed by a suspected drunken driver while trying to replace a flat tire just off Interstate 8 in La Mesa. The victims were Salam Al Asady, 30, and Ali Hussain Al-Hajam, 25, of El Cajon, both married and fathers of small children. Lisa Louise Rausch, 29, of El Cajon was arrested on suspicion of driving while drunk.

June 25 – An estimated 200 people attended a dinner honoring Harriet Stockwell, longtime civic activist in El Cajon who recently retired after serving since 1980 on the City Council.

July 1 – An El Cajon mother and father found guilty of second-degree murder for the starvation death of their 4-month-old daughter were both sentenced to 15 years to life in prison. Jason Glasgow, 23, and his wife, Patricia, 21, also had been accused of child abuse for keeping their child strapped in a car seat for as many as 22 hours a day. The baby died at a hospital, unable to recover from a massive yeast infection that damaged nearly all of her organs.

July 5 – To avoid paying a $55 a ton tipping fee at Sycamore Canyon landfill in Santee, Universal Refuse was preparing to haul 220 to 300 tons a day of El Cajon's trash to its landfill in Lancaster in Los Angeles County where the tipping fee was $40 a ton.

July 8 – Superior Court Judge Anthony Joseph ruled that state law prohibited the Boy Scouts of America from expelling Chuck Merino, an El Cajon police officer who is gay, from his position as an adviser to an Explorer Scout unit at El Cajon Police Department. It was the first ruling of its kind in the nation.

July 18 – The concluding article of a two-part series based on an interview with the widow of mass murderer James Huberty, who killed 21 people at a McDonald's restaurant in San Ysidro on July 18, 1984, was published in *The Daily Californian*. Etna Huberty, now living in Spring Valley, told reporter Jo Moreland that Huberty had requested counseling the day before the attack but a receptionist had misspelled his name and he was not contacted. Mrs. Huberty said her husband was obsessed by the notion that Nazis were trying to take over the world. Her husband was killed by police responding to the San Ysidro massacre.

July 28 – The Assembly Rules Committee found that aides to Assemblyman Tom Connolly, D-77th, had fabricated claims he or his wife had sexually harassed them. The report said the allegations were part of a plot to coerce Connolly into taking disciplinary action against one member of his office staff.

Aug. 9 – Santee brothers Jeffry and Dale Brown were stabbed to death at a park in Milwaukie, OR, a suburb of Portland. The bodies of Jeffry, 23, and Dale, 22, were found by fishermen. Both had been stabbed multiple times. They had been camping at the park to celebrate Dale's recent birthday.

Aug. 15 – La Mesa Mayor Art Madrid wanted to publish photos of all johns arrested inside the city limits in an attempt to eliminate prostitution on the western edge of the city.

Aug. 20 – Jodie Kirst, a Santee mother whose two children became mysteriously ill over a six-month period and who herself became ill, settled for a payment of about $1 million from her apartment complex, the building contractor and a carpet cleaner. The culprit was found to be a moldy carpet that had not been adequately cleaned after the apartment was flooded.

Aug. 22 – G. Wayne Oetken, 49, assistant superintendent of Cajon Valley Union School District, won a $361,000 out-of-court settlement of his medical malpractice case. The suit was filed because Oetken and his attorney believed he had been improperly treated at Grossmont Hospital when he suffered a heart attack on his way home from a school district meeting on April 8, 1992. It was alleged in the suit that his life was shortened by 10 to 15 years because he did not receive adequate care.

Aug. 27 – Superior Court Judge Anthony Joseph ordered Boy Scouts of America to reinstate gay El Cajon police officer Chuck Merino as its adviser for the El Cajon Explorer Post. Joseph wrote: "The evidence presented at trial does not justify Mr. Merino's expulsion or prohibit his reinstatement as an Explorer Post adviser."

Aug. 29 – Police in Milwaukie, OR, arrested a suspect in the stabbing deaths of two Santee brothers – Jeffry Ray Brown, 23, and Dale Archie Brown, 22 – in a city park. Karl Anthony Terry, 20, who was believed to be a friend of the victims, was charged with two counts of aggravated murder. Police said they found five-point stars associated with Satanism at Terry's home.

Sept. 4 – East County Supervisor Dianne Jacob wants to stop the county's practice of giving free meals to county workers that she says costs taxpayers $1.5 million a year. Most of the free meals are eaten by employees of the sheriff's and probation departments. They are guaranteed by contract negotiations between employee unions and the county.

Sept. 20 – El Cajon civic leader Bob Durrant was found innocent of all sexual battery charges that had been leveled against him. Durrant, owner of Leatherby's Ice Cream and Diner, had been accused of inappropriate touching of a 10-year-old boy on a tour of the ice cream parlor and three former male employees.

Oct. 9 – Judge Joseph Wapner, the no-nonsense judge of television's popular "People's Court," came to El Cajon to deliver a strong message to fight drugs by educating youth. He attended a Drug Abuse Resistance Education (DARE) Family Fun Fair in the Kmart parking lot.

Oct. 12 – El Cajon Police Department was to receive a $694,316 grant from the federal government for more police officers. President Clinton announced $200 million in grants to help more than 300 police departments across the country.

Oct, 26 – The Mother Goose Parade had been threatened with cancellation, so queen candidates squeezed harder for memberships and almost doubled their take from $15,000 to $28,000 in one week. The membership campaign also was aided by more donations from merchants. This year's parade is expected to cost $100,000 to $120,000.

Oct. 28 – Ray Anthony, 55, a music teacher and band leader at Mt. Miguel High School, was honored as one of five "Teachers of the Year" in California.

Nov. 4 – A La Mesa couple who blamed each other for the beating death of their 19-month-old son were both sentenced to 15 years to life in state prison for second-degree murder. The mother, Leeann Nabors, 24, was given an additional four years because she had a prior conviction for child abuse in 1989 when the couple's first child was beaten. Nabors and George Barner III, 30, also were fined $10,000 in the death of George Barner IV who, according to court testimony, was beaten nearly every day.

Nov. 9 – Among the victors in the general election were Pete Wilson who defeated Kathleen Brown for a second term as governor; Republican Steve Baldwin who defeated Democratic incumbent Tom Connolly for the 77th Assembly District seat; attorney Paul Pfingst who ousted 24-year incumbent Ed Miller to become district attorney; Art Madrid who retained his job as mayor of La Mesa, beating Councilman Fred Nagel; and incumbent Dianne Feinstein who was re-elected to the U.S. Senate over Michael Huffington.

Nov. 21 – A 96-year-old motorist, Paul C. Davis, died in a traffic accident when he made a left turn in front of oncoming traffic as he returned home to Highland Mobile Home Park in Santee. He was trying to prove he was a competent driver.

Nov. 23 – Mark B. Casady, 53, fourth of the five sons of former *El Cajon Valley News* owner Simon Casady, died Nov. 18 in Bakerfield of valley fever. He had been a reporter for his father's newspaper, an aide to U.S. Sen. John F. Kennedy when he ran in the presidential primary against Adlai Stevenson, and an aide to former Los Angeles Mayor Tom Bradley. In later years, he had abandoned politics to do agricultural research.

Dec. 9 – Sheriff-elect Bill Kolender selected El Cajon Police Chief Jack Smith to be one of his assistant sheriffs. Smith was to be in charge of personnel matters, training and human resource development.

Dec. 11 – A cougar was believed to have been responsible for the death of Iris Kenna, 58, a San Diego elementary school teacher whose mauled body was found in Cuyamaca Rancho State Park. Later in the week, fish and game officials killed a 125-pound cougar, the fifth to be shot in the vicinity of the park in the last 18 months. The park was closed indefinitely while officials studied the area's mountain lion population.

Dec. 16 – An anonymous donor contributed $25,000 to the lagging East County Toy Drive.

Dec. 22 – Dale Akiki, acquitted of molesting nine children while he was a Sunday school teacher at Faith Chapel in Spring Valley, was to be interviewed on "Prime Time," a nationally distributed TV show on ABC.

Dec. 23 – El Cajon business owner and civic leader Bob Durrant filed a $34 million suit against San Diego County, the City of El Cajon, and several deputy district attorneys. The suit alleges that false accusations of sexual abuse had devastated him and his family. A jury had acquitted Durrant of all charges.

Protesters at Gillespie Field opposed the spraying of Malathion to control fruit flies.
Photo: El Cajon Library

Dianne Jacob of Jamul has been the Second District's representative on the San Diego County Board of Supervisors since Jan. 4, 1993. *Photo: El Cajon Library*

Former San Diego Police Chief Bill Kolender became county sheriff by defeating incumbent Jim Roache. *Photo: City of San Diego*

Mary Howell of Lakeside shared with Daily Californian readers on Nov. 28, 1993, the problems she had with Susie. *Photo: El Cajon Library*

Mabel Bryan at Harry Griffen Park Amphitheater which was named for her. *Photo: El Cajon Library*

Some highlights ahead:

Quadruplets – all girls – were born to an Alpine couple. . . . Santee man arrested in four-year-old mobile-home park murder. . . . Savage attack on black Marine leaves him paralyzed. . . . Two East County couples died in the crash of an EgyptAir jetliner off the coast of Massachusetts while en route to Cairo.

Murder victim Cara Knott's family. *Photo: El Cajon Library*

1995

Jan. 5 – A howling windstorm blew down the walls of a new sanctuary at First Baptist Church in Santee, and Lindbergh Field in San Diego set a new rainfall record for this date of 2.24 inches.

Jan. 27 – Chargermania drew 65,000 fans to San Diego Jack Murphy Stadium this morning (Friday). The Chargers were to play the San Francisco 49ers on Sunday in the Super Bowl in Miami. *(The 49ers won, 49-26).*

Jan. 29 – From more than 600 entries, a five-member panel of judges selected "El Cajon: Hub of East County" as the city's motto.

Feb. 1 – The City of La Mesa's new policy of printing photos of those who buy or sell sex made the latest edition of *Newsweek* magazine. Mayor Art Madrid has been asked for interviews and copies of the city's anti-prostitution resolution since the article was published. . . . U.S. Rep. Duncan Hunter, R-San Diego County, proposed a $1.50 per car border-crossing fee to pay for additional measures to curtail illegal immigration.

Feb. 2 – Lee Ann Stark, widow of Edward Stark, 60, of Lemon Grove, who was murdered and buried in a remote location, called for the execution of the two men charged with killing him – her son, Edward Bergman, 22, and her ex-husband, Lawrence "Ed" Bergman, 46. "I know in my heart they are guilty of his murder," Lee Stark said.

Feb. 17 – Tom Youngholm, 45, of Lemon Grove, was to fly to New York to sign a contract with Dell Publishing for his first book, "The Celestial Bar." He had received a $250,000 advance.

Feb. 23 – Olympic diving gold medalist Greg Louganis, 35, a graduate of Valhalla High School, confirmed that he has AIDS in an interview with Barbara Walters on ABC-TV's program "20/20."

Feb. 25 – Kerry Dalton, 42, of Lakeside, was convicted of first-degree murder for the brutal killing of Irene May, a 23-year-old Lakeside mother of three and a known drug user. It was alleged that Dalton and two other defendants – Sheryl Baker, 28, of El Cajon and Mark Tompkins, 29, of San Diego – took May to a mobile home in Live Oak Springs where they injected her with battery acid and hit her on the head with a frying pan, allegedly because she had stolen some of Dalton's jewelry and did not tell her friends she had hepatitis, an omission of great concern to them because they had shared needles for illicit drug injections. May's body was never found.

Special circumstances applied in Dalton's case because she had previous convictions for burglary, petty theft and forgery. *(Dalton, mother of five, was given the death penalty in early March, the first woman in San Diego County history to receive that punishment.)*

Mar. 6 – Lucille Moore, 67, the first woman elected to El Cajon City Council and also the first woman to chair the San Diego County Board of Supervisors, died Mar. 5 at Grossmont Hospital after undergoing brain surgery for a tumor. Moore had been active in El Cajon civic affairs for 40 years.

Mar. 10 – Sunbelt Publications announced it has moved its $3 million-a-year business from Santee to 1250 Fayette St. in El Cajon. The company distributes more than 4,000 titles and represents 500 American publishers. Owners Lowell and Diana Lindsay started the business 10 years ago.... A five-part series based on the life of Olympic diving champion Greg Louganis, an El Cajon native and graduate of Valhalla High School, was to be published over five days in *The Daily Californian*. The first installment, from his book "Breaking the Surface," appeared in today's edition.

Mar. 16 – Quadruplets, all girls, were born to Alpine residents David and Heidi Waitley at Sharp-Mary Birch Hospital for Women in San Diego. The couple has three other girls – Kaila, 8; McKenna, 6; and Demi, 2. The latest births were achieved without the use of fertility drugs.

Mar. 20 – Law enforcement officers were trying to find out why 18-year-old Jesse Dillon, who recently moved to this area from Michigan, was shot and killed while riding the trolley from La Mesa to Lemon Grove. The suspected assailant, Leneral Deshone Sharpe of San Diego, also 18, was killed in a hail of bullets during a shootout with sheriff's deputies on Skyline Drive.

Mar. 24 – Twenty-three members of El Cajon's homeless population will share an $8,000 award from the City of El Cajon because their possessions were hauled away and apparently destroyed. Amounts received varied from $40 to $1,000.

Mar. 27 – Simon Casady, 87, who owned *The El Cajon Valley News* for 11 years and converted it to a twice-a-week publication and then a daily, died March 26 at the La Jolla home of his eldest son, Derek. He had been in failing health since last August and was suffering from pneumonia. Casady aided the political careers of President Lyndon B. Johnson and U.S. Sen. Lloyd Bentsen of Texas and U.S. Sen. Barry Goldwater of Arizona in his role as a newspaper executive in those states before coming to El Cajon.

Mar. 30 – The San Diego Trolley completed its first test run from El Cajon to Santee. The 3.6-mile line, built at a cost of $114.4 million, had been under construction for two years.

Apr. 30 – Astronaut Dr. Ellen Ochoa, a graduate of Grossmont High School, was named Alumnus of the Year by San Diego State University and had returned to accept the award. Ochoa had been on two space trips.

May 1 – A van carrying 36 undocumented immigrants crashed into a pickup on Highway 94, killing the driver, Richard J. Horton, 32, and two passengers in the van – Roberto Lopez, 38, and Antonio Frias, 40, both from Mexico. Sixteen other passengers were hurt. The packed van crossed the center line into the path of Horton's truck, according to the California Highway Patrol. Horton's wife and 9-month-old son were in a separate vehicle and on their way home from a wedding.

May 3 – *The Daily Californian* announced on the front page that it would change to an all-local news format, effective May 16. Six reporters were being added to the staff to report on local events. All national and international news and sports would be eliminated. Publisher Paul Zindell wrote that in a readership survey 80 percent of respondents had requested the change. Saturday morning and Monday afternoon editions were to be discontinued. . . . Chancellor Jeanne Atherton of the Grossmont-Cuyamaca Community College District wanted to give East County Performing Arts Center to the City of El Cajon on the condition that it allocate $300,000 to $500,000 to improve and maintain the facility.

May 24 – Capt. Bob Moreau, 51, was appointed El Cajon police chief. Moreau, with 26 years on the police force, replaced Jack Smith who quit to become an assistant county sheriff.

May 28-29 – El Cajon Bowl at 215 N. Second St. was closing, citing the public's declining interest in trying to knock down 10 pins at the end of a long alley. The business had been here since 1958.

June 9-10 – Andy Johnson, 15, a Valhalla High School freshman honor student, was suspended and faced expulsion because he was seen using the scissor on his Swiss army knife to cut a rubber band from his finger. Having the knife was a violation of Grossmont Union High School District's zero tolerance policy against bringing weapons of any kind to school.

June 15 – Lakeside Hotel, a 108-year-old landmark with a reputation for the rowdy behavior of its guests, will be converted into a halfway house for recovering drug addicts.

June 23-24 – Grossmont Union High School District trustees voted 3-1 to expel Andy Johnson, 15, from Valhalla High School for bringing a Swiss army knife to school. They suspended the expulsion but refused to let Andy attend any school in the district until certain unannounced conditions are met. Johnson and his father planned to appeal the decision to the San Diego County Board of Education. *(The county board subsequently upheld the decision of the high school district board by a vote of 3-2.)*

July 18 – Leaders of the Barona, Sycuan and Viejas Indian bands announced they would share as much as $6 million a year from video gaming machines with 14 non-gaming tribal governments in the county.

July 19 – Killian Moss, 8, of Scottsdale, AZ arrived in El Cajon with his father and they were to leave from Gillespie Field with Killian at the controls of their plane, hoping to make it into the Guinness Book of World Records as the youngest person ever to fly solo across the United States. His father, Jim, was to accompany him and had installed a camera on board to prove that Killian was at the controls for the entire trip. Killian's aunt, Marge Boone of El Cajon, and her three daughters were present to see the takeoff.

July 21-22 – G. Dennis Adams, 54, a former El Cajon lawyer and Superior Court judge who graduated second in his law school class, was removed from the bench on a 6-1 vote by the California Supreme Court. In a 57-page ruling, the court said Adams was guilty of judicial misconduct for taking gifts from lawyers with cases in his courtroom.

Aug. 4-5 – Controversy swirled around the forthcoming production by Christian Community Theater of "Jesus Christ Superstar" at the Mt. Helix amphitheater. Critics called the musical by Andrew Lloyd Webber "blasphemy."

Aug. 8 – Jimmy's Family Restaurant at 9635 Mission Gorge Rd. in Santee was destroyed by fire over the weekend. The $1 million fire started near the french fryer. Owner Mike Wins vowed he would rebuild.

Aug. 10 – Boots, a 10-foot, 4-inch Burmese python, was returned to its home on Carlton Hills Boulevard in Santee and owner Kathy Sorenson, who said she would get the required conditional use permit to make Boots a legal resident of the city.

Aug. 18-19 – Publisher Paul Zindell wrote a front-page column excoriating representatives of the *San Diego Union-Tribune* for telling prospective subscribers that the El Cajon paper planned to drop its Sunday edition and was going out of business. Not true, Zindell wrote. "*The Daily Californian* has served the community of East County for 103 years, and we intend to be here for at least another 103 years," he wrote. "Be assured, we have fought off past anti-competitive action by the *Union-Tribune* and will do so in this instance. In fact, several months ago, we filed a formal antitrust suit against the *Union-Tribune's* parent company, the Copley Press."

Sept. 1-2 – A speaker who refused to relinquish the microphone at a Grossmont Union High School District Board meeting prompted Michael Harrelson, board president, to clear the meeting room and move the session to a conference room with only board members and the media in attendance. Wayne Robinson, a parent, refused to stop talking about a survey which asked students about their sexual behavior, prompting other parents to loudly state their positions on the matter.

Sept. 19 – Charles Kelly, 19, of El Cajon, a linebacker on the football team at Grossmont High School only a year ago, was shot and killed in the Skyline area of San Diego while standing on a sidewalk where he had gone to visit longtime friends. Kelly hoped to play football at the University of Oregon. He had recently broken up with his girlfriend and had received threatening phone calls.

Sept. 22-23 – Sam and Joyce Knott of El Cajon, whose daughter, Cara, was murdered by California Highway Patrol Officer Craig Peyer, won a $7.5 million judgment in the courtroom of Superior Court Judge Arthur Jones. Cara Knott was killed Dec. 27, 1986, after she was pulled off Interstate 15 by Peyer and directed to a dark exit road.

Sept. 26 – Frances and Donald Brown of Alpine won $4.5 million in the state lottery after spending $5 for quick-pick tickets. Their winnings represented half of the total jackpot.

Sept. 27 – Paul Coronado, 18, a 1995 graduate of El Capitan High School and a highly ranked rodeo bull rider, died of brain injuries suffered when he was trampled by the bull he was riding Sept. 17 at Lakeside Rodeo. Coronado was ranked 10th in bull riding by the Western Region of the International Professional Rodeo Assn. . . . Ownership of the East County Performing Arts Center was transferred from Grossmont-Cuyamaca Community College District to the City of El Cajon by a 3-2 vote of the El Cajon City Council. Proposed improvements to the facility were expected to cost as much as $500,000.

Oct. 1-2 – An estimated 300 sheds at a U-Haul storage complex in Spring Valley were burglarized over the weekend, with losses of electrical equipment, military hardware, weapons and other goods. As many as four unidentified thieves cut the padlocks from a main gate to gain entry.

Oct. 4 – Bill Sturgeon, a Rea Avenue accountant in El Cajon, faced a $100-a-day fine if he continued to allow homeless people to store their belongings and sleep on his property. Neighboring business owners complained that Sturgeon's accommodation of the homeless was creating litter, encouraging loitering and resulting in vulgar behavior.

Oct. 6-7 – Hundreds of U.S. border residents were poised to demonstrate against conditions caused by illegal border crossers. "Operation Line Up the Border" was designed to pressure President Clinton to act against undocumented immigrants making life unbearable for legal residents by burglarizing homes, stealing cars, setting fires, tearing up fences and wasting water.

Oct. 15-16 – Ray Anthony, 55, who helped revive the marching band at Mt. Miguel High School, won $25,000 from the Milken Family Foundation and a National Educator Award. He is a former recipient of a National Distinguished Teacher Award.

Oct. 24 – Dr. Douglas Giles, 63, superintendent of the Santee School District for 14 years, died Oct. 23 at Sharp Memorial Hospital in San Diego after a long battle with cancer.

Nov. 26-27 – Paul Etzel of La Mesa, an astronomer at San Diego State University, is part of a three-man team whose proposal to try to prove the existence of a white dwarf star has been accepted as a project for the Hubble Space Telescope with the approval of the National Space and Aeronautics Administration (NASA). Etzel is working with a professor from the University of Illinois and another from Villanova University.

Nov. 28 – Valentine Watson, 53, a retired San Diego County deputy sheriff, was found guilty of first-degree murder in the fatal baseball bat attack against his wife at their home in Santee. Madeline Watson, 57, was struck 11 times with the wooden bat. *(Watson was sentenced to a 26 years-to-life term in state prison.)*

Dec. 2 – A Spring Valley man who shot and killed a neighbor for driving recklessly in their neighborhood pleaded innocent to a charge of murdering John Harper, Jr., 45, the offending driver. Danny Palm, 51, a retired Navy lieutenant commander, was accused of shooting Harper eight times. Harper, who only a week earlier had been released from jail after pleading guilty to two misdemeanor reckless driving charges and paying a $500 fine, apparently had a habit of driving recklessly in his neighborhood during the last two years. The charges against Palm opened a lengthy public debate about limits on the action a private citizen can take to punish lawbreakers.

Dec. 24-25 – Sheriff's homicide investigators had been working up to 75 hours a week because of a rash of six fatal shootings, stabbings or beatings in the Spring Valley-Lemon Grove area during the past 26 days.

1996

Jan. 5-6 – El Cajon Mayor Joan Shoemaker is proposing that financially troubled East County Performing Arts Center be renamed for any bene-factor who contributes $1 million or more needed for renovations. Repairs are estimated to cost at least $500,000.

Jan. 9 – Lucky Stores, Inc. has acquired Smith's Food and Drug Center in the heart of El Cajon's redevelopment district. Lucky competed for the spot with Smith, Inc. in 1993. Lucky is acquiring Smith properties also in Lincoln, Oxnard and Hemet.

Jan. 10 – Assemblyman Jan Goldsmith, R-75th, was one of five members of an Assembly subcommittee who voted to give judges the authority to punish first-time vandals with a spanking. The legislation would authorize as many as 10 swats with a 24-inch wooden paddle.

Jan. 12-13 – Board member Kevin La Chapelle was censured on a 3-2 vote of his Grossmont Union High School District colleagues for publicly calling Supt. Jo Ann Smith incompetent. The former El Cajon police officer was accused of violating district and state policy for making his comments in a public rather than a private session.

Jan. 23 – Former Spring Valley bankruptcy attorney Walter McElravy III, 46, was sentenced to 46 months in state prison and ordered to repay more than $500,000 in restitution to clients he bilked. He resigned from the bar and pleaded guilty Nov. 6 to mail fraud, money laundering, embezzlement against a bankrupt estate and fraudulent concealment of assets.

Jan. 24 – A former youth leader at First United Methodist Church of El Cajon pleaded guilty to two felony counts of committing lewd acts with a child under 14 and could face up to six years in prison for his crimes. By pleading guilty, Trevor Scott Hanes, 28, avoided prosecution on three addi-tional counts of committing lewd acts with a child. His male victim was 12 when the molestation began. *(Hanes was sentenced to a six-year term in state prison.)*

Feb. 1 – Dr. Nancy Hampel, an El Cajon veterinarian, successfully per-formed a rare surgery to remove a tumor from the brain of a 15-pound poodle named Alex. She was assisted by Dr. Joel West Ray, a neurosurgeon who specializes in treating human patients. Alex's owners are Wendell and Debbie Wye of Carlsbad.

Feb. 22 – Bill Garrett, 51, the city manager of Corona in Riverside County, will take the same position in El Cajon on April 15. He replaces Bob Acker, who retired after serving as El Cajon city manager since 1982.

Feb. 27 – Patrick Ely, 28, an engineer from El Cajon, won a $6,025,201 Megabucks jackpot at Luxor Hotel in Las Vegas. He won the money after putting his last three dollars into the machine to reach the self-imposed maximum amount of $200 that he could spend.

Mar. 1-2 – Herman "Rock" Kreutzer, 59, former owner of the Big Oak Ranch in Dehesa Valley and now serving a 17 years-to-life term in state prison for killing his son-in-law, made his first appearance before the State Parole Board and was told he must serve at least two more years behind bars to be considered for parole. Kreutzer was sent to prison 11 years ago.

Mar. 3-4 – Actor Richard Thomas, who played John-Boy in the long-running TV series "The Waltons," was here to film a scene at the Main Street Café in Lakeside for a CBS television movie titled "What Love Sees." The movie tells the story of a blind young rancher from Ramona, Forrest Holly, who pursues a sightless debutante from Connecticut, Jean Treadway. At Holly's urging in a letter, Treadway visits this area, falls in love, marries the rancher and they make a life together here with their three children.

Mar. 13 – Edward Arrieta, assistant principal at Mt. Miguel High School in Spring Valley, was credited with coaxing a suicidal teenager to surrender his handgun during a tense confrontation at the school. The boy, who attended nearby Monte Vista High School, came to Mt. Miguel to give his former girlfriend some money because her mother had lost her job. He was distraught over the breakup with his girlfriend and announced that he intended to kill himself.

Mar. 19 – Trinity Presbyterian Church at 3902 Kenwood Drive in Spring Valley sustained $1.3 million in damage that investigators said was caused by an arsonist. *(A parishioner, Mark Eliot Stimpson, 26, married and the father of four children, was arrested for the crime a few days later.)*

Mar. 27 – Incumbent Dianne Jacob easily won re-election to represent East County on the San Diego County Board of Supervisors. She received 56 percent of the vote in a race with five challengers. . . . Councilwoman Mary Sessom was elected the first mayor of the newly incorporated city of Lemon Grove, defeating Councilman Craig Lake. She got 62 percent of the vote.

Mar. 28 – Border Patrol agents witnessed a bizarre sight at a checkpoint in Pine Valley: Seventeen illegal aliens climbing out of a one-stall portable toilet placed on the bed of a 1989 Ford F-350.

Apr. 4 – The plane crash that claimed the life of Commerce Secretary Ron Brown also killed Barry L. Conrad, former president of Forte Hotels whose headquarters were in El Cajon. Conrad left Forte, which operated the international chain of TraveLodge Hotels, in 1991 to become president of Burger King Franchise Services in Miami. The plane, with 33 passengers and crew members, went down on a hillside in Croatia during a storm.

May 8 – The case of a bizarre stoning death that occurred near Lakeside on Mar. 15, 1995, ended when a first-degree murder conviction was returned against Michelle Richards, 20, of San Bernardino. She and two accomplices – Nathan Powell, 19, and James Runion, 22, both of Poway – were accused of killing Robert Mott, 30, of San Bernardino in a remote area by repeatedly striking him on the head with rocks, causing 12 facial fractures. Powell and Runion earlier had been convicted of first-degree murder. The motive for the crime: Runion had allegedly spread a rumor that Mott used drugs in the presence of a child.

May 14 – The son of former La Mesa mayor Fred Nagel was sentenced to 41 months in federal prison for conspiracy to defraud thousands of elderly victims in a crooked telemarketing scam. Fred Forrest Nagel III, 35, was corporate counsel for Can-Do World Wide Marketing, a firm headquartered in San Diego before the Federal Trade Commission shut it down in March 1993.

May 30 – Viejas Casino and Turf Club unveiled a $30 million plan for Viejas Springs Village, a complex of 40 shopping outlets expected to be completed by the end of 1997. The plan included a 90,000-square-foot expansion of the casino.

June 6 – Danny Palm, 52, a retired Navy lieutenant commander, was convicted of second-degree murder in the 1995 shooting death of John Harper Jr., 48, whose reckless driving in his Spring Valley neighborhood had provoked Palm to fire nine shots at his annoying neighbor. The circumstances of the crime drew the attention of the nationally broadcast TV program "48 Hours."

June 16-17 – El Cajon Cemetery, in operation since 1903, was expanded by 5.2 acres, enough to accommodate nearly 8,000 more caskets as well as plots for cremains. The addition increased the size of the cemetery to more than 12 acres.

June 18 – Heather Jaehn, 25, was locked out of her Santee home, so she decided to slide down the chimney. Although she weighed only 100 pounds, she got stuck. Her boyfriend tried for three hours to free her from the 16-inch by 10-inch shaft, but at 4:28 a.m. gave up and called the fire department. Firefighters used a pulley system to free the woman.

June 29 – The U.S. Army awarded a nearly $10 million contract to Buck Knives of El Cajon to manufacture about 250,000 M-9 bayonets over the next five years. The company had received an earlier contract to make 350,000 bayonets for the Army between 1986 and 1989.

June 30-July 1 – Santana High School graduate John Macready was one of seven gymnasts selected for the U.S. men's gymnastics team competing in this summer's Olympic Games in Atlanta.

July 3 – El Cajon City Council approved a downtown business management district to raise money for improvements by authorizing an assessment of property within the boundaries of an area bounded by Magnolia Avenue from Interstate 8 to Douglas Avenue and Main Street from Ballantyne Street to El Cajon Boulevard. The first year's budget, starting Jan. 1, will be $325,000.

July 17 – The family of Cara Knott, who was murdered in 1986 by CHP Officer Craig Peyer, accepted a $2.7 million settlement from the State of California. Peyer is serving a 25 years-to-life term for the murder of the 20-year-old El Cajon woman.

July 28-29 – Civic leaders and businesses were in a snit because the Republican National Committee omitted East County from its printed 20-page guide for delegates who were attending the upcoming Republican National Convention that was to be held in San Diego. The guide included South County and North County, but nothing east of Mission Valley was deemed worthy of notice.

Aug. 1 – Former Assemblyman Tom Connolly, who once represented much of East County as a Democrat representing the 77th Assembly District, faced criminal charges of sexual misconduct after being accused of having sex with a 14-year-old girl in a motel room. Since leaving office, he had worked as a lawyer in private practice in Vista.

Aug. 18-19 – Danny Palm, the retired Navy lieutenant commander convicted of killing a reckless driver in his Spring Valley community, fired his trial attorney, Elliott Kanter, and replaced him with attorney Elizabeth Semel to handle the penalty phase of his case.

Aug. 28 – Kevin Charles Fitch, 39, who lived less than 100 feet from the Santee mobile home where 15-year-old Christin Gray was murdered more than four years ago, was arrested and charged with her slaying. His arrest came after another resident of the mobile home park reported seeing Fitch looking into a bedroom window of the mobile home where Christin had lived with her mother, Patti.

Aug. 30-31 – The death of El Cajon civic leader Charles Cordell, 74, was announced. Cordell, an insurance agent and a U.S. Army Air Corps pilot during World War II, promoted the development of Gillespie Field and served as president of the Bicentennial Commission in charge of arranging a celebration of the 200th anniversary of the founding of the City of San Diego.

Sept. 4 – Nearly 2,500 friends and colleagues of three slain San Diego State University professors attended a memorial service for them on campus. The engineering professors – Chen Liang, D. Preston Lowery III and Constantinos Lyrintzis – were shot to death Aug. 15 by a graduate student whose thesis proposal was being reviewed. Frederick Davidson, the alleged shooter, has pleaded not guilty to murder charges.

Oct. 2 – Campus police officers at Grossmont and Cuyamaca colleges were authorized to carry weapons in a unanimous vote by the Grossmont-Cuyamaca Community College District Board.

Oct. 13-14 – Grossmont High School science teacher Susan Emerson was one of four teachers in San Diego County selected as county Teacher of the Year. There were 33 nominees in the county.

Oct. 18-19 – Two Superior Court judges with East County ties – James Malkus who served in El Cajon Superior Court and G. Dennis Adams who sat in San Diego Superior Court – were found guilty of mail fraud and conspiracy for accepting gifts from attorney Patrick Frega who had been charged with operating a racketeering enterprise.

Nov. 1-2 – To thwart drug and people smugglers, the U.S. Forest Service and National Guard engineers teamed up to place gates on four roads commonly used for those purposes in Cleveland National Forest in the Pine Valley area.

Nov. 10-11 – In a front-page story, it was announced that *The Daily Californian* had been sold to Central Valley Publishing Co., Inc., which is managed by USMedia Group, Inc. of Crystal City, MO. *The Daily Californian*, owned by Kendell Communications, Inc., had a circulation of 16,500. The sale included *Express Line,* a 70,000-circulation weekly entertainment newspaper, plus a commercial printing operation at 1000 Pioneer Way in El Cajon.

Dec. 15-16 – An heir to the Laufer Big & Tall Men's Shop fortune was convicted by a Superior Court jury of torturing his wife over a three-day period at their home in Alpine. Edward P. Laufer, 46, had been accused of assault with a firearm, two counts of assault with a deadly weapon (a hammer and a hatchet), spousal battery, making terrorist threats and false imprisonment. He was convicted of all charges. His wife, Martha, 27, a native of Poland, allegedly was assaulted because she would not confirm her husband's story about two Rolex watches he maintained had been stolen. *(Laufer later was sentenced to 10 years in prison despite a tearful appeal by his 75-year-old mother, Fay, who asked for leniency for her son and blamed herself for his actions.)*

Dec. 18 – Mark Elliot Stimpson, 26, of Spring Valley, married and the father of four, pleaded guilty to starting a fire that caused $1.3 million damage to Trinity Presbyterian Church in Spring Valley and was sentenced to nine years and four months in state prison.

Dec. 27-28 – Edward Fletcher, Jr., 96, eldest son of the man who developed the Fletcher Hills area of El Cajon, died Christmas Day of pneumonia. Edward Fletcher, Jr. supervised the construction of Mt. Helix Amphitheater and the installation of a cross that became a county landmark.

1997

Jan. 15 – A $120,000 study that proposed putting the City of San Diego in the driver's seat for economic development in the county was recommended for the trash can by East County Supervisor Dianne Jacob. The study, commissioned by the San Diego Regional Technology Alliance and conducted by an Ohio-based consulting firm, had representatives seething from north, south and east portions of the county.

Jan. 16 – Frigid weather in the mountains was blamed for the deaths of at least nine undocumented immigrants. Nighttime temperatures in the mountain areas had plummeted into the 20s.

Jan. 17-18 – Members of La Mesa and El Cajon chambers of commerce voted overwhelmingly to merge as a single unit under the new name of East County Regional Chamber of Commerce. This will result in bringing 1,200 businesses together with an operating budget of between $500,000 and $800,000.

Jan. 22 – La Mesa Mayor Art Madrid, a Hispanic, found hundreds of white supremacy leaflets in his yard and neighborhood signed by a group called Pro-White Citizens. This apparently was in retaliation for Madrid's criticism of a racist graffiti attack that occurred earlier in the week at La Mesa Community Center.

Feb. 5 – Former El Cajon Superior Court Judge James Malkus was sentenced to 33 months in federal prison for his part in a corruption scandal that involved taking gifts from attorney Patrick Frega. In separate court action, Frega and San Diego Superior Court Judge G. Dennis Adams, a former El Cajon attorney, were sentenced to 41 months in prison.

Feb. 21-22 – Seventeen top administrators in the Grossmont Union High School District, including three assistant superintendents, were targeted for dismissal or reassignment by the end of the school year. Conservative trustees Nadia Davies, Kevin LaChappelle and Dr. Maynard Olsen voted for the plan presented by interim Supt. Jack Tierney; June Mott and Michael Harrelson opposed it.

Feb. 25 – Interim Supt. Jack Tierney of the Grossmont Union High School District stepped down from that position in an agreement between himself, County Supt. Rudy Castruita and the GUHSD board. Tierney had not been given a chance to interview for the superintendent's job.

Mar. 6 – A Lemon Grove father and son were convicted of first-degree murder of the father's ex-wife's new husband on Jan. 15, 1995. Lawrence Bergman, 48, the father, was convicted of three special circumstances in the killing of Edwin Stark, 60, to whom Bergman's former wife had been married for only three months. Edward Bergman, 26, was convicted by a separate jury. According to the deputy district attorney who prosecuted the case, the father and son were motivated by "greed and evil." Stark's severely beaten body was found Jan. 20, 1995, in a remote area of Alpine. He had been handcuffed at some point during the attack and his head was covered with a plastic bag. His ribs and skull were fractured. Coins and currency belonging to Stark were found in Bergman's hotel room. (*In April, a jury sentenced the elder Bergman to death and a separate jury ruled his son should spend the rest of his life in prison.*)

Mar. 25 – Gillespie Court near the Gillespie Field Airport was renamed Cordell Court in honor of the late Charles Cordell, former chairman of the Gillespie Field Development Council and a driving force in the development of Cuyamaca West Industrial Park.

Apr. 11-12 – David Wayne Anderson, 36, of San Diego, convicted of second-degree murder and other charges in connection with the death of a young man lured to an El Cajon motel room on July 17, 1980, was reported to have escaped from the AIDS unit of the California Medical Facility at Vacaville State Prison north of San Francisco. Anderson and his wife, Linda, 40, had been accused of enticing James Willis, 21, of the Hillcrest area of San Diego, to their motel where Linda allegedly beat him with a lead pipe and Anderson forced a towel rack down his throat. Willis' body was found wrapped in a hotel bedspread on an embankment off I-8 near College Avenue. Prosecutor Frank Brown, now a Municipal Court judge, described Anderson as "one sick puppy."

Apr. 18-19 – Superior Court Judge William Mudd reduced a Spring Valley man's murder conviction to manslaughter and imposed a 10-year prison term instead of the 15 years-to-life term that had originally been given. The beneficiary of the judge's action was Danny Palm, 53, a retired Navy lieutenant commander, who had been accused of shooting to death John Harper Jr., 48, a neighbor with a reputation for driving recklessly in the Spring Valley neighborhood where both men lived. Palm had been convicted of second-degree murder on June 5, 1995, but the verdict split his community, with many people defending Palm's action. Mudd apparently was influenced to change the sentence by a letter he received from Palm's wife of 32 years, Carol Palm.

Apr. 29 – An escapee from Vacaville State Prison with a tie to El Cajon had sent a postcard to his former jailers after being on the lam for more than two weeks. David Anderson, 36, described as a cross-dresser and HIV-positive, mailed the card in Santa Clarita, about 50 miles north of Los Angeles. Anderson had been convicted of second-degree murder in the 1980 death of a 21-year-old San Diegan lured to an El Cajon motel room where he was beaten and killed by Anderson and his wife, Linda. *(In early May, Anderson was taken into custody by San Diego police after he allegedly robbed a diner on El Cajon Boulevard using a sawed-off shotgun. A waitress at Rudford Restaurant ducked into the kitchen and called 911.)*

May 14 – In a dramatic confrontation in Superior Court, Lee Ann Stark faced her 27-year-old son, Edward Bergman, and told him she wished she had the power to take his life for his part in the beating death of her second husband, Edwin Stark, 60. "You took away my happiness . . . and crushed a family's future," Stark told her son. "I gave you life, but if I had the power to take it away, I'd do so." Bergman had been sentenced to life in prison without the possibility of parole. His father, Lawrence Bergman, had been convicted of the same murder and sentenced to death.

May 18-19 – El Cajon City Clerk Marilyn Linn, who joined the previously all-male El Cajon Rotary Club with three other women after the U.S. Supreme Court ruled that all-male clubs had to accept women, was installed as the club's first woman president. She joined the club in 1987, the year the court's ruling was issued.

May 23-24 – The Fourth District Court of Appeal unanimously reversed a 1994 ruling by a San Diego Superior Court judge who had ordered the Boy Scouts to reinstate El Cajon Police Department Officer Chuck Merino, a homosexual, as leader of the department's Explorer unit. Merino's attorney, Everett Bobbitt, said: "No matter who wins or loses today, (the case) will go on to the U.S. Supreme Court." Merino, 41, had been a police officer for 20 years and had worked with Explorers, 16-year-olds and older, for five years. The appellate court said state law prohibited businesses from discriminating on the basis of sexuality, but it held that the Explorer group was not a business.

May 28 – Frederick Davidson, a graduate student at San Diego State University who confessed to shooting to death three professors discussing his thesis proposal, was sentenced to three consecutive life terms in state prison.

June 19 – Regal Cinemas announced its plan to build an 18-theater multiplex at Parkway Plaza, with opening scheduled by the end of next summer.

July 3 – El Cajon police arrested 32 men on various solicitation charges in what was billed as the city's most vigorous attack yet on prostitution. Three female officers had been used as decoys in the sting operation.

July 4-5 – Former Democratic Assemblyman Tom Connolly III, 51, was sentenced to two years in state prison for a sexual encounter with a 14-year-old girl. Connolly represented the 77th Assembly District, which included much of East County, before his 1994 defeat by Republican Steve Baldwin.

July 16 – On a 3-2 vote, Cajon Valley Union School District trustees demoted Supt. John Costello to a teaching position, action that immediately sparked a recall petition against the board majority. Costello had responded to 50 charges during a marathon six-hour session with trustees.

Aug. 3-4 – Grossmont-Cuyamaca Community College District trustees voted 3-2 not to renew the contract of Grossmont College President Richard Sanchez after a three-hour closed session. He had been president of the college for seven years.

Aug. 15-16 – Chris Scobba, 33, an El Cajon engineer, rode his mountain bike across the United States to honor Constantinos Lyrintzis, one of three San Diego State University engineering professors shot to death by a graduate student whose thesis proposal was being reviewed. Scobba described the professor as one who treated his students with respect. Bob Calvin, who accompanied Scobba on the trip, took a tumble and cracked two ribs, forcing him to fly home. Scobba's trip lasted from June 2 to July 15.

Sept. 11 – A 60-ton bulldozer broke free from its support chain while being towed up Center Drive in La Mesa, then rolled down a hill, clipping a traffic pole and rolling over two cars. Passengers in the demolished vehicles were taken to Sharp Memorial Hospital for treatment.

Sept. 17 – In response to a public outcry over the termination of his contract, Grossmont-Cuyamaca Community College District trustees voted unanimously to allow Grossmont College President Richard Sanchez to serve an additional year in that position. Sanchez had received a poor evaluation from District Chancellor Jeanne Atherton.

Oct. 1 – The County Board of Supervisors gave final approval to the construction of a 68-acre shopping and entertainment center in Rancho San Diego south of El Cajon. The project included an 18-screen Edwards Theater, a Lucky Food store, a Sav-on Drug, Target, restaurants and smaller shops. It will be the largest commercial retail outlet in the county's unincorporated area.

Oct. 16 – The owner and an employee of a La Mesa medical supply company surrendered to federal agents to face charges that they were part of a massive international insurance scam in cahoots with 17 Tijuana doctors. David Palmer, 38, owner of Medical Repair Center, Inc. in La Mesa, met authorities at the border after FBI agents contacted him in Tijuana. An employee, Salvador Vega, 24, of Chula Vista, turned himself over to U.S. marshals. Palmer and Vega are suspected of overbilling for medical equipment. Medical offices in Tijuana either didn't exist or were unequipped to provide services that were being billed. The insurance company paid out $800,000 in claims it knew to be false just to aid in catching the alleged thieves.

Oct. 17-18 – A jury awarded Marta Laufer $1.75 million for the beatings and other mistreatment she endured at the hands of her husband, Edward, an heir to the Laufer Big & Tall Men's Shop fortune. The mistreatment occurred over three days at the couple's Alpine home in January 1996.

Oct. 31-Nov. 1 – A two-alarm fire destroyed six science classrooms at Mt. Miguel High School, forcing cancellation of classes and causing $1 million in damage. Portable classrooms were to be brought to the campus.

Nov. 4 – Kaelin's Market, a fixture for 46 years on the corner of Madison Avenue and Main Street in El Cajon, was to be closed by owner John Kaelin, whose 25,000-square-foot emporium started as a liquor store and was expanded over the years to a store with a little bit of everything. Kaelin was applauded by the community when he voluntarily refunded $150,000 to customers after a money order firm he used went bankrupt. Money orders were one of the items that could be purchased at the store. *(New owners chose to keep the Kaelin's Market name and the store at this time is still selling a variety of products in addition to groceries.)*

Nov. 5 – Voters in Lakeside rejected a unification plan that would have taken El Capitan High School out of the Grossmont Union High School District and made it a part of a unified Lakeside Union School District. The unification plan was rejected by a 55-44 percent margin.

Nov. 18 – A three-alarm fire destroyed Payton True Value Hardware in Lakeside. Owners Jim and Diane El-Hay vowed to rebuild.

Nov. 21-22 – A 23-year-old woman and two teen-age boys from El Cajon face maximum terms of life in prison for conspiring, even though unsuccessful, to murder the woman's identical twin who had been her co-valedictorian at Mt. Empire Junior-Senior High School. Jeen Han, 23; Archie Bryant, 17; and John Sayarath, 16, were found guilty of the crimes in a Santa Ana courtroom. Known as the "Evil Twin Case," Jeen Han allegedly became enraged when her twin sister, Sunny, turned her in on a bad check charge. Jeen Han left a work furlough program in San Diego, where she was serving her sentence, and recruited the two boys to kill her sister. The twins were born in Korea but grew up in East County. Sunny Han survived what was to have been a fatal attack and testified in court.

Nov. 26 – Two small planes collided near Gillespie Field while the student pilots were practicing flight maneuvers. Mark Francis, 25, from South Wales, was killed when his plane plummeted into a house on Valley Mill Road. The other student pilot, Robert Blanken, 33, of El Cajon, and his instructor, Danielle Boettcher, 19, crash-landed on Fanita Drive. Blanken was hospitalized for treatment of an injury and released the next day.

Dec. 21-22 – Police officers from La Mesa and El Cajon combined forces for the largest vice sweep in El Cajon history. They arrested 44 men in the downtown area on prostitution solicitation charges.

Dec. 30 – Fire in a Santee strip mall destroyed three businesses, causing an estimated $1.5 million in damages. The businesses were Max's 99 Cents store, where the fire started; the Chic-N-Pigg Restaurant; and Al's Sports Shop. The businesses were located near Jimmy's Restaurant which was destroyed by fire Aug. 6, 1995.

1998

Jan. 6 – The Sports Pub, a small bar adjacent to Denny's Restaurant on North Mollison Avenue in El Cajon, closed its doors, an early casualty of the new state law banning smoking in bars. The bar had been at that location for 26 years.

Jan. 8 – Word reached here that Bob Applegate, 75, city manager of El Cajon from 1958 until his retirement in 1982, had suffered a fatal heart attack in Palm Desert.

Jan. 14 – Four school board members in Dehesa School District were recalled. They were Cheryl Minshew, Gloria Chadwick, Loretta Belt and Irene Harper.

Jan. 25-26 – An El Cajon couple who said they wanted "a skinny baby" are in protective custody, accused of starving their 2-year-old child to death. Jennifer Mayer, 21, and her husband, David Mayer, 30, pleaded innocent to the murder of their son, Zechariah. The toddler weighed only 19 pounds when he died a month before his third birthday. The baby had last eaten, according to his father, eight weeks before his death.

Feb. 12 – All seven massage parlors in La Mesa agreed to cease operations by April 1999. Prostitution allegedly had been a problem in some of the parlors.

Feb. 17 – Dismissal of El Capitan High School principal Mark Lindsay prompted a protest march in the rain at the headquarters of the Grossmont Union High School District Board. Supt. Thomas Godley had placed Lindsay on paid administrative leave, citing a poor evaluation. *(Weeks later, Lindsay was reinstated to his job after an outpouring of public support by Lakeside residents.)*

Feb. 28-Mar. 1 – Actor J.T. Walsh, 54, who played Jack Nicholson's suicidal lieutenant in "A Few Good Men" and more recently had starred as the villain in the thriller "Breakdown," died at Grossmont Hospital of a heart attack. He had been on vacation in this area.

Mar. 19 – Dr. William C. Herrick, a retired Grossmont Hospital pathologist who served as a trustee of Grossmont Health Care District, died in the facility where he spent 35 years of his medical career. He was 75.

Mar. 24 – A drug-sniffing dog being used in a methamphetamine investigation led El Cajon detectives to a cache of cocaine worth $1 million on the street. The discovery occurred at a motel parking lot near Magnolia and Madison avenues. . . . Police Officer Chuck Merino, ousted as leader of El Cajon Police Department's Explorer Post because he is gay, lost his appeal to the California Supreme Court, which ruled that Boy Scouts of America is a private organization and can establish its own membership policies. Merino and his attorney, Everett Bobbitt, vowed to carry their fight to the U.S. Supreme Court.

Apr. 2 – Embattled trustees Nadia Davies and Dr. Maynard Olsen, who had been facing a potential recall election, resigned from the Grossmont Union High School District Board effective May 15. Olsen had moved his medical practice to Utah, and Davies had been accused of living outside the district since before her 1996 election.

Apr. 7 – Parkway Plaza in El Cajon is one of 20 regional shopping centers sold by Canada-based Trizec Hahn Corp. in a deal worth nearly $2.5 billion. Westfield America, Inc. of Los Angeles is the new owner of Parkway Plaza as well as Horton Plaza in downtown San Diego, University Towne Center in La Jolla, North County Fair in Escondido and nine centers elsewhere.

Apr. 25-26 – Singer Patti Page's concert May 22 at East County Performing Arts Center will be taped by the Public Broadcasting System for inclusion in a TV special about the crooner's 50-year career in show business. Page, whose hits include "Tennessee Waltz" and "How Much Is That Doggie in the Window?," has sold more than 100 million records and had more than 160 singles on the music charts.

May 1 – Former La Mesa Mayor Julius Acevez, 91, received accolades for never missing a weekly Rotary Club meeting during half a century as a member. Once in Hawaii he hired a limousine to get him to a Rotary Club meeting on the coast opposite from where he was staying.

May 9-10 – Jeen "Gina" Han, 23, was sentenced to 26 years to life in prison in a Santa Ana courtroom for conspiring in a failed 1996 plan to kill her twin sister, Sunny, who had been her co-valedictorian at Mt. Empire Junior-Senior High School. Jeen Han recruited two teen-age boys to kill her sister who had turned her in for writing bad checks.

May 13 – El Cajon City Council approved moving the adobe home of famed Western painter Olaf Wieghorst from Renette Avenue to a spot on Rea Street in the downtown area.

May 23-24 – A $30 million outlet center with 174,000 square feet of commercial space opened on the Viejas Indian Reservation near Alpine.

May 26 – Sara Bolin, an eighth-grader at Cajon Valley Middle School, won a national letter-writing contest with a submission on child molestation. Her letter was chosen from more than 13,500 submitted nationally in a contest sponsored by the Lutheran Brotherhood.

June 3 – Tom Page, former chief executive officer of San Diego Gas & Electric Co., won a seat on the Grossmont Union High School District Board to replace trustee Nadia Davies. Even though she had resigned earlier, the recall election showed Davies would have lost her seat by a decisive margin. Page had 48,672 votes to 15,189 for Davies with nearly all precincts tallied.

June 6-7 – California Highway Patrol Officer Chris Lydon, 27, was killed in a rollover crash on Route 67, the first fatal accident involving a CHP officer serving the El Cajon area. Lydon was responding to a call about a possible drunk driver when his car left the road and struck a tree. His partner, Jeff Jenkins, 33, of El Cajon, was injured. Lydon's younger brother, Rob, his only sibling, was killed in a car crash in the early 1990s just before his 19th birthday.

June 18 – The Sycuan band of Kumeyaay Indians fired two marketing executives, including the tribal chairwoman's husband, and is investigating the loss of millions of dollars from concert promotions during the past 18 months. More than 40 employees have been terminated during the past two months for budgetary reasons.

July 2 – Kevin Fitch, 41, was found guilty of the April 9, 1992, rape and murder of Christin Gray, 15, in a Santee mobile home park unit she shared with her mother. The Santana High School cheerleader suffered 36 stab wounds. Fitch was not a suspect in the six-year-old case until a resident of the mobile home park saw him looking through the window of the unit where the murder occurred. He lived only a short distance from the site of the murder.

July 29 – A jury took just 75 minutes to convict Alpine nurse Melvenia Martin, 39, of assault and felony abuse that led to the death of her 2-year-old nephew, Anthony Wyche. The trial began July 6 and included a claim by Martin that her nephew had suffered a fatal skull fracture when he hit his head on a concrete basketball pole, a statement one investigator labeled "a fairy tale." Martin faces a maximum term of 34 years to life in prison. Joshua Martin, 15, the defendant's stepson, testified he had seen his step-mother abuse her nephew and call him a "retard."

Aug. 1-2 – Crest resident Mike Mahnke, 35, honoring a death-bed promise to his wife who lost her battle with cancer, pedaled his bike the 3,135 miles separating San Diego from St. Augustine, FL. Mahnke, a correctional officer at Las Colinas Women's Detention Facility in Santee, began the trek June 23 and ended it July 19 in the company of his brother, Bill, of Applegate, CA. Temperatures reached as high as 118 degrees in the shade at Gila Bend, AZ. Mahnke and his brother raised $5,000 for the American Cancer Society while making the trip.

Aug. 7 – Jeanvieve and Art Lamoureaux-Allen of Santee came forward to claim the $4.5 million they won in the bi-weekly state lottery drawing. The couple purchased the winning ticket at Vintage Wine & Liquor. They have three children, 20 months through 10.

Aug. 26 – Tom Davies, representing East County, resigned from the San Diego County Board of Education three months before the expiration of his term. In a four-page letter, he objected to a trip to Cuba taken by fellow trustee Nick Aguilar who represents South County. The county paid $2,300 for Aguilar's expenses but was reimbursed by the World Affairs Council of San Diego.

Sept. 1 – A late-evening wildfire forced the evacuation of the Barona Casino north of Lakeside and burned more than 2,000 acres before it was brought under control. The fire apparently was started by lightning. The casino re-opened the next day.

Sept. 7 – Kevin Fitch, 41, will be sentenced to life in prison without possibility of parole for the murder and rape of Christin Gray, 15, who lived with her mother in a Santee mobile home park. The jury split 11-1 in favor of the death penalty but Christin's mother, Patti, requested that the penalty phase not be retried. The murder occurred in 1992 but was not solved until this year when a resident of the park saw Fitch looking into a window of the home where the slaying occurred. Fitch lived close to the unit where Christin was killed.

Sept. 25 – Four East County men were arrested for the severe beating of a black Marine, who was paralyzed in an attack at a house in Santee. Marine Lance Cpl. Carlos Gilbert, 21, suffered a broken neck during the beating that occurred May 30. The four men, 18 to 21, allegedly shouted racial slurs, and a Dago Mob cap was found at the scene bearing the words: "When in doubt, knock 'em out." A nationwide bulletin was circulated for the arrest of a fifth man. Three of the suspects had been students at West Hills High School in Santee.

Oct. 1 – District Attorney Paul Pfingst, unopposed for re-election, blasted Proposition 5 on the November ballot which supports Indian gaming in California, saying it is "dangerous to California and to our community."

Oct. 2 – Kaiser Permanente is earmarking $100 million to launch a low-cost health care program for 2,500 uninsured children in San Diego County. Insurance premiums will go for $25 to $35 a month, depending on a family's income.

Oct. 9 – Matthew Ward, 21, of El Cajon, won a $10,000 grand prize in a national contest sponsored by Mothers Against Drunk Driving and Dep Gel. It took six days to make the nearly four-minute video that was declared the contest winner.

Oct. 12 – Jack Walker, 78, a P-38 combat pilot during World War II and a member of Confederate Air Force Group One based at Gillespie Field in El Cajon, joined the elite group of pilots known as "Aces." The tribute came 53 years after he shot down an enemy plane over Yugoslavia to score his fifth kill. The War Confirmation Board finally accepted the account of the shoot-down offered by Al Schneider of Phoenix, AZ, the pilot who was behind Walker on the mission.

Oct. 19 – Antonio's Hacienda, a Mexican restaurant on Johnson Avenue near Parkway Plaza in El Cajon, announced it would close. Antonio Sanchez, the owner, said he is ill and unable to operate the restaurant any longer. (*The restaurant reopened as Antonio's in January under new ownership.*)

Nov. 10 – Councilman Mark Lewis was declared the winner in the race for El Cajon mayor, defeating two-term incumbent Joan Shoemaker by 142 votes.

Nov. 11 – Marvin L. Brown, 89, a survivor of the Bataan Death March in World War II and a resident of Magnolia Care Center in El Cajon, is sending a photograph of his 200th Battery B unit to a museum in Santa Fe, NM. The photograph was described as "the missing link" for an exhibit at the Bataan Memorial Museum.

Nov. 24 – The Barona Band of Kumeyaay Indians is proposing a $130 million expansion that calls for a resort hotel and golf course at the reservation's casino site.

Nov. 25 – The widow of a Santee man killed in 1980 pleaded guilty to second-degree murder and faces a 15 years-to-life term in prison. Glenna Faye Brown, 58, hired two men to kill her husband, Walter Brown, 44, to collect on his life insurance policy. She received $125,000 and moved to a ranch in Boulevard with one of the killers, Courday Chinchillas. Court testimony revealed that Brown's husband was lured to Coronado on a ruse that a friend's car had broken down. Chinchillas and Christopher Wahoski, 40, beat Walter Brown to death with a tire iron and a wine bottle. A prison inmate who had lived in the Brown house when he was 16 provided the information that led to reopening the case.

Nov. 28 – Frederick "Ricky" Sturckow, 37, a decorated U.S. Marine Corps major and former all-star catcher on the 1978 Grossmont High School baseball team, will be one of six astronauts hurtling through space aboard the shuttle Endeavor. He is from Lakeside.

Nov. 30 – The U.S. Supreme Court refused to review a California Supreme Court ruling that gay El Cajon Police Officer Chuck Merino's suspension as leader of his department's Explorer Post violated no law. The effect was to uphold Merino's dismissal as leader of the co-educational program for 14- to 20-year-olds interested in law enforcement careers.

Dec. 10 – Grossmont Union High School District Supt. Tom Godley confirmed that FBI agents have taken business records from administration offices dating from the late 1980s through the mid-1990s. The records seizure was first disclosed by trustee-elect Gary Cass, one of three new board members who were to take their seats today.

Dec. 12-13 – Winds gusting up to 70 mph forced closure of a portion of Interstate 8 after three big rigs were overturned in the Pine Valley area. One hurricane-force gust on the Pine Valley Bridge was clocked at 96 mph. The high winds also tore the roof off the Mt. Empire School District administration building, forcing district schools to close.

Dec. 16 – Second-degree murder charges were to be filed against Richard Alan Clements, 18, of El Cajon, who allegedly struck two elementary school students with his truck while trying to evade California Highway Patrol officers in the Lakeside area. Adina Gonzalez, 9, and Christine Turner, 9, died of their injuries. They attended Lemon Crest School in Lakeside.

1999

Jan. 4 – Fire destroyed a 10,000-square-foot mansion valued at $1 million on the 830-acre Spencer Ranch near Campo.

Jan. 5 – Five East County men pleaded guilty to felony assault on a black Marine who was left paralyzed after being beaten at a Santee house where a party was in progress. Jesse Brian Lawson, 20, of El Cajon, faced up to 11 years in prison after pleading guilty to a hate crime in which a felonious assault caused grave bodily harm to black Marine Cpl. Carlos Gilbert, 21, whose neck was broken in the attack. Lawson's four accomplices, all from Santee, face up to a year in county jail and five years on probation.

Jan. 27 – El Cajon Police Chief Bob Moreau told the City Council that 211 residents had been identified as gang members. There were six Hispanic gangs, one black gang, one white supremacy group and one outlaw motorcycle clan.

Feb. 4 – Astronaut Rick Sturckow, who rode the Endeavor shuttle through space, returned to Grossmont High School for a visit. The former Lakeside resident graduated from the school at 16 in 1978. . . . Krista Funk of El Cajon, accused of killing her 5-year-old son with poison, was spared a death sentence but faced a life sentence without the possibility of parole. Funk, 34, was convicted of giving her son, Nicholas, an overdose of phenobarbital. She had taken the drug herself in an apparent suicide attempt, but she survived.

Feb. 5 – Construction delays forced the Grossmont Union High School District Board to postpone the opening of Steele Canyon High School until the summer of 2000. The $33 million school had been scheduled to open this fall.

Feb. 9 – El Cajon City Hall modified its ban on allowing city residents to use restrooms by requiring visitors to ask for a token that opened restroom doors on the second through fifth floors of the building. Previously, the restrooms had been designated for the use of employees only. The policy had been adopted to prevent homeless people from using the restrooms.

Feb. 15 – Por Favor, a restaurant city officials hope will be an anchor for downtown redevelopment, had opened at 148 E. Main St. in El Cajon.

Feb. 18 – Five men involved in a vicious physical attack that paralyzed a black Marine during a party in Santee were sentenced. The longest term was nine years in state prison for Jessie Lawson, 21, of El Cajon. Four other defendants from Santee – Trenton Solis, 19; Jed Jones, 21; Robert Rio, 23; and Steve Newark – were sentenced to a year in county jail. The victim – Lance Cpl. Carlos Colbert – was in the courtroom when his attackers were sentenced.

Feb. 27-28 – Helix High School alum Bill Walton, now a National Basketball Assn. legend, returned to his alma mater to address 400 students on the topic "Life's Playbook" as a representative of the GTE Academic Hall of Fame. "The biggest winners are the ones (who) win with their minds," Walton told the students. "The worst thing you can do in life is not dream enough."

(I could find only the January, February and July microfilm copies of The Daily Californian for 1999. No others exist at the El Cajon Library, the State Library in Sacramento, or the newspaper archives at UC Riverside. So I am grateful to have permission from the San Diego Union-Tribune to extract from its accounts of East County-related news events brief excerpts for the months that The Daily Californian newspapers apparently were not preserved. Items from March, April, May, June, August, September, October, November and December are from the Union-Tribune files.)

Mar. 3 – Two women released on bail from the Las Colinas Women's Detention Center in Santee begged to be returned to the jail because of mistreatment by a bail bond agency owner and his agents. The women said they were held against their will, one for five nights and the other for two nights. They allegedly were handcuffed to chairs, denied food and were forbidden to make phone calls. The mistreatment apparently was "retaliation" for a jury verdict of $129,000 against the bonding agency's owner. ... Regional transportation planners have endorsed spending $23 million for right-of-way acquisitions for Highway 52 from Fanita Drive east to Cuyamaca Street in Santee.

Mar. 4 – Toufic Naddi, 58, the El Cajon man who killed his wife, her parents and two other relatives in his Fletcher Hills home in 1985, was back in court. He was convicted in 1988 of first-degree murder, but it had taken four trials to determine if he was legally sane when he committed the crimes. A jury in 1990 found Naddi sane, but he pummeled his attorney in the courtroom and had to be restrained by bailiffs. Naddi was sentenced to life in prison without the possibility of parole, but a federal judge overturned that conviction, ruling that Naddi's request to represent himself should have been granted. The question before the court now is whether Naddi should be permitted to represent himself in yet another trial.

Mar. 9 – Howard Edmond Pritchett, 47, of Boulevard, who had no criminal record until he shot at a woman on horseback rather than respond to her request for directions, agreed in El Cajon Superior Court to accept a 29-year prison term. The woman used a cell phone to contact the sheriff's department, which dispatched officers to the ranch, one of whom – Ron Hobson – suffered a gunshot wound in the thigh. Pritchett told deputies he "always wanted to do something like this" because his ex-wife married an El Centro police officer. Pritchett said he had dreamed of killing his ex-wife, her new husband and any police officers he encountered.

Mar. 10 – Toufic Naddi of El Cajon has been told he is entitled to represent himself in a fifth trial on charges he shot and killed his wife and four members of her family in his Fletcher Hills home on June 1, 1985. Naddi, a Lebanese immigrant, was convicted of the murders in 1988, but jurors deadlocked over whether Naddi was sane when he killed his relatives. Four sanity trials had ended in mistrials.

Mar. 16 – Medicare fraud charges were filed against an El Cajon ambulance company and a Spring Valley billing service. Indicted were Stat Medical Transport, Inc.; its president, Jeffrey Strange; and its former general manager, Bruce McAvinew. Also indicted were Nutcracker Business Services; its managers, Kenneth Blankenship and Ruth Blankenship; and its owner, Dennis Bates. Medicare paid about $5.8 million to Stat Medical from 1993 through 1997. Stat Medical and Nutcracker Business Services are accused of misrepresenting the destinations of ambulance trips and billing Medicare for ambulance trips when only a van was used or no trip was provided.

Mar. 19 – Deep Sea Research, Inc. of El Cajon will be allowed to keep more than 1,000 gold coins it recovered from the wreckage of the ship, *Brother Jonathan*, which sank in 1865 off the coast of California near Crescent City. The El Cajon firm was authorized by the court to continue retrieving objects from the wreckage and is permitted to keep 80 percent of the worth of what it finds. The sunken vessel lies 250 feet below the ocean surface.

Mar. 24 – Two brothers were sentenced to 25 years to life for the murder of a La Mesa postal worker whose head and hands were cut off. James Dulaney, 29, and Rozell Dulaney, 28, were accused of luring James Desmond, 46, to Compton for a drug deal, then killing him on Dec. 17, 1992. Desmond's missing body parts were never found, but the rest of his body was discovered wrapped in a blanket in an alley less than half a mile from where James Dulaney lived in Compton. Though the brothers denied the killing, court testimony revealed they had bragged about the slaying to relatives and acquaintances in Arkansas. Rozell Delaney, a former El Cajon resident, posed as a bus driver, but prosecutor Jim Oliphant said during trial that he actually was a pimp who employed prostitutes and that Desmond was interfering with his business. Both defendants had criminal records dating back to their teenage years.

Mar. 25 – Friends of 17-year-old Derrick Green, a Granite Hills High School student, were making twice-weekly trips to UCSD Regional Burn Center to pray and offer support for the young man who suffered devastating burns over most of his body in a gas explosion at his father's home in Lakeside on Feb. 16. Derrick had been transferring gas from one container to another inside a dark storage shed and flicked a lighter to better see what he was doing. His father, Darrell, 45, heard the explosion, ran outside, saw his son enveloped in flames and doused him with water from a garden hose to put out the fire. Derrick suffered second- and third-degree burns over 85 percent of his body. Several fund-raisers were planned in the community to assist Derrick's recovery. . . .El Cajon City Council voted not to allow Foothills Bible Fellowship to resume feeding the poor at Wells Park. The church's pastor, the Rev. Larry Deason, had been cited by police for failing to obtain the required conditional use permit for the feeding program.

Mar. 28 – A Border Patrol agent and three undocumented immigrants were killed March 27 when their vehicle plunged more than 1,000 feet into a ravine near Dulzura. The Ford Bronco ran off Otay Mountain Truck Trail. Four other men – also undocumented immigrants – were injured. None were immediately identified. *(The Border Patrol agent killed in the crash later was identified as Stephen M. Sullivan, 27, of San Diego. He had been with the Border Patrol less than two years and was engaged to be married.)*

Mar. 30 – Max Goodwin, who owned the weekly *Lemon Grove Review* and whose newspaper career spanned nearly 50 years, died March 23 of complications from Alzheimer's disease. He was born Mortimer Maxwell Gutman in Sylacauga, AL, but changed his name to Goodwin in 1950. Goodwin would have been 90 had he lived until April 6. He owned and operated the *Lemon Grove Review* for 37 years. . . . Robert Morse of La Mesa is to be reunited with his three children who were abducted by their mother and taken to Texas after a bitter custody battle. The abduction occurred Dec. 13, 1996, when the children – now 12, 10 and 7 – stepped off a school bus at Murdock Elementary School in La Mesa. Morse, who had been awarded full custody of his children, has since remarried. Eugia Morse, 36, the children's mother, was charged with child abduction. Authorities found the children huddled in a closet in a house near Houston after a tipster saw their pictures on the Internet.

Mar. 31 – El Cajon Mayor Mark Lewis' proposal to turn Rea Avenue into a "Wild West" venue with wooden walkways, hitching posts and staged gunfire was bushwhacked by other community leaders who agree the street needs to be transformed but oppose doing it in a Western theme.

Apr. 3 – An overnight snowstorm killed nine Mexicans who crossed the border illegally. Bodies of seven men in their 20s or early 30s were found in rugged terrain near Descanso. Two more bodies were found near Tecate in Mexico. Another body was found later in the week near Pine Valley. Temperatures had plummeted into the 20s. More than 140 people were rescued from the freezing cold on this side of the border.

Apr. 23 – Ex-Padres player Gene Locklear will display some of his Western paintings at the fifth annual Magnolia Festival of the Arts in El Cajon. Locklear specialized in sports and American Indian art. He grew up as a member of the Lumbee Indian Nation in North Carolina before playing for Cincinnati, San Diego and the New York Yankees. He hit at a .321 pace in 1975 and retired in 1978 after playing one season for Japan.

May 1 – Absenteeism was running high in area schools in the aftermath of the April 20 shooting deaths at Columbine High School in Littleton, CO. At Granite Hills High School in El Cajon, 38 percent of its students were absent April 30. Ramona High School estimated absenteeism at between 35 and 40 percent.

May 11 – The new owner of Valle de Oro Bank in El Cajon is Community First Bankshares headquartered in North Dakota. The selling price was $65 million. Valle de Oro Bank has $241 million in assets.

May 17 – Elizabeth Adams of Santana High School in Santee was one of 21 students in San Diego County to receive the gold medal for academic achievement from the National Merit Scholarship Corp. She was among the 2,000 students nationwide who won a $2,000 National Merit Scholarship underwritten by about 600 sponsoring groups and institutions. Elizabeth's intended field of study is computer science.

May 18 – Cpl. Carlos Gilbert, a black Marine whose neck was broken and who was made a paraplegic in a savage attack at a party in Santee, has filed a multimillion-dollar suit against his assailants. Among his claims: He was the victim of assault and battery and defamation, had his civil rights violated, suffered emotional distress and false imprisonment. The suit was filed against Jed Allen Jones, Jessie Brian Lawson, Steven Lawson Newark, Robert Alan Rio and Trenton Joe Solis. Owners of the property where the assault took place also were named defendants and accused of negligence. Three of the five assailants, all white, already have been freed. James McElroy is the attorney who filed the suit. He won a $12.5 million verdict against white supremacist Tom Metzger nine years ago for inciting a racially motivated murder in another state.

May 19 – Dr. John S. Videen, 39, a medical doctor, and his stripper girl-friend, Bobbie Jo Smith, 23, were convicted in El Cajon Superior Court of a crime related to home burglaries and the theft of property. Sheriff's detectives had found rooms filled with stolen jewelry, furniture, purses and computer parts at a house in Santee shared by the defendants. Videen, who faces a three-year prison term, is a kidney specialist at UCSD Medical Center. Smith pleaded guilty to three counts of burglary and was sentenced to 18 years and four months in prison. She is a former dancer at Cheetah's night club in San Diego. Houses where stolen items were found are in El Cajon, Santee, La Mesa and Spring Valley as well as the North County communities of Carlsbad and Encinitas.

May 22 – Opponents of a policy to protect gays and lesbians adopted by the Grossmont Union High School District Board were threatening to recall trustees who voted for it and pull their children out of district schools. Trustees voted 3-2 to add "actual or perceived sexual orientation" to the list of protections in the policy that already includes race, religion, gender or disability. Ted Crooks, Michael Harrelson and Tom Page voted for the change; Gary Cass and Dan McGeorge were opposed.

June 1 – Ron Christman, 48, a high school dropout who received his General Education Diploma in the Army, was awarded an honorary doctoral degree by the California School of Professional Psychology. Christman works as a Kumeyaay Indian medicine man on the Viejas Indian Reservation near Alpine, using a sweat lodge, herbs and prayer rituals to help treat people with physical, mental and emotional problems. . . . James Pernicano, 86, of La Mesa, who opened one of the seven Pernicano chain of restaurants in El Cajon in 1953, died May 29 of cancer.

June 2 – A rumored bomb threat at West Hills High School in Santee kept almost half of its students from classes June 1. About 400 Helix High School students in La Mesa skipped classes the same day and for the same reason.

June 4 – More than 14 percent of students in the Grossmont Union High School District boycotted classes a day earlier to protest passage of a new district policy that gives special protection to gay and lesbian students.

June 9 – The 9th U.S. District Court of Appeal ruled 2-1 that the racketeering conspiracy convictions of two former San Diego judges – both with

East County connections – should be dismissed. But the court also upheld other convictions against former Superior Court judges G. Dennis Adams and James Malkus, whose attorney says he will take the case to the U.S. Supreme Court. Both Adams and Malkus had been convicted of taking gifts from attorney Patrick Frega in what was called a "gifts for favors" scandal. Malkus served as a judge in El Cajon Superior Court; Adams is a former El Cajon attorney who sat in San Diego Superior Court. . . . Toufic Naddi, 58, formerly of El Cajon, was convicted of five counts of first-degree murder in San Diego Superior Court. Naddi, who shot to death his wife, her parents and two other relatives in his Fletcher Hills home on June 1, 1985, will return to court for another jury to determine if he was sane when he committed the killings. He has been granted permission to represent himself with the aid of an attorney.

June 10 – The Viejas band of Kumeyaay Indians near Alpine was prepared to pay between $3 million and $5 million to purchase a low-wattage TV station, KDI-TV Channel 17 in National City. The Viejas band was the first in California to buy a bank and build a factory outlet center.

June 17 – A Superior Court jury found that Toufic Naddi, 58, formerly of El Cajon, was sane when he killed five members of his family at his Fletcher Hills home on June 1, 1985. This was his fifth sanity trial. He will be sentenced July 28.

June 23 – Santee resident Shawn Carlson was awarded one of 32 prestigious MacArthur Foundation "genius grants" for his work with the Society for Amateur Scientists, an organization he started with $4,000 of his own money. The national award is worth $290,000. Carlson is an adjunct professor at San Diego State University who promotes the amateur's role in scientific discoveries. . . . A recall campaign against Ted Crooks, president of the Grossmont Union High School District Board, has begun with recall supporters required to get 22,568 signatures to force a recall election. Crooks is being targeted because he voted with two other trustees to expand civil rights protection for gay and lesbian students.

July 8 – Charles "Chuck" Ferree, who managed the El Cajon Chamber of Commerce for two decades, died at his home in Eugene, OR. He was 75. Ferree was credited with luring many businesses to El Cajon and spearheaded the creation of People for People, an organization dedicated to repairing racial divisions during the turbulent 1960s and 1970s. He was named Citizen of the Year in 1978.

July 16 – An invitation to Valhalla High School to be part of the opening ceremony for the 2000 Summer Olympics in Australia has been rescinded.

Band leader Ray Anthony, who had anticipated taking musicians from six high schools to the Olympics, said the school had been "dis-invited." Attorney Gary Mobley said he would explore the band's legal options.

July 30 – Wild Oats Markets, Inc. of Boulder, CO will spend $46 million to acquire 11 stores or franchises controlled by Henry's Marketplace. Henry's has stores in El Cajon, La Mesa and Santee. The Henry's name is to be retained for the empire founded as Boney's in the early 1980s. Henry Boney, who began with a roadside produce stand in 1943 and created Speedee Mart, Inc. in 1956, also was Second District supervisor on the San Diego County Board of Supervisors.

Aug. 4 – Richard Alan Clements II, 19, was convicted of second-degree murder in the deaths of two 9-year-old girls on their way home from their Lakeside school. He faces 34 years to life in prison for the deaths of Christie Turner and Adina Gonzalez, students at Lemon Crest Elementary School, who were struck and killed by Clements' truck on Dec. 9 last year. Clements was driving his truck at 60 mph and was being chased by a California Highway Patrol officer. He went through stop signs and spun out once during the 90-second chase. . . . Earl Thomas Schultz, 65, of La Mesa, longtime curator of reptiles at San Diego Zoo, admitted in federal court that he embezzled more than $70,000 by selling rare zoo reptiles.

Aug. 14 – U.S. Rep. Bob Wilson, a Republican who represented much of East County during his 28 years in the U.S. House of Representatives, died Aug. 12 from the complications of Alzheimer's disease at Sharp Chula Vista Medical Center. He was 83.

Aug. 21 – Carol Sing, 57, of El Cajon, made history by becoming the oldest woman to swim the 21.5 miles from England to France. Her time was 12 hours and 32 minutes. At the end of the record-setting swim, she was bloated, shivering and suffering from jellyfish stings. "I'm never going to do that again," she said. "That was hard."

Sept. 1 – Former Assemblyman Tom Connolly, who represented parts of East County in the state Legislature, is back in state prison less than a year after his release, this time for violating a condition of his parole which forbade him to interact with young children. Connolly, 53, has been sent to the Richard J. Donovan State Correctional Facility in Otay Mesa until mid-November. He was convicted in 1997 on felony charges of oral copulation with a person under 16 and committing a lewd act with a minor. . . . A man who pelted Border Patrol agents with baseball-sized rocks was shot and killed by one of the agents after a two-hour confrontation. The incident occurred near Loveland Reservoir on Japatul Valley Road southeast of Alpine. The victim was identified only as a "6-foot Hispanic man."

Sept. 3 – About 100 people rallied Sept. 2 in support of Indian gaming outside the East County Chamber of Commerce office. Second District Supervisor Dianne Jacob called on the governor and Legislature to "put a constitutional amendment on the ballot that is fair to gaming tribes – and do it now."

Sept. 4 – After battling for nearly 10 years, the American Civil Liberties Union and the county have reached an agreement in the Mt. Helix cross controversy. The cross can stay, but the county will have to surrender ownership of the park where the cross has stood since 1929 and transfer its interest to the Mt. Helix Improvement Assn. . . . Two 11-year-old boys who were best friends died two days earlier in a fire that trapped them inside a motor home traveling on Interstate 8 near Alpine on their way to hunt doves in Imperial Valley. The victims were Anthony Pongracz and Ryan Reyes. The boys had climbed into an overhead sleeping compartment to escape the fire, which blocked the rear door exit that was their only way to safety. The boys attended different schools in the Santee-Lakeside area. Ryan's grandfather, James Vicars, and his uncle, Danny Brewer, suffered minor injuries.

Sept. 11 – After 10 years of controversy, the California Legislature and Gov. Gray Davis signed the documents that will enable 60 Indian tribes in the state to legally provide casino-style gambling. Viejas near Alpine, Barona near Lakeside and Sycuan southeast of El Cajon were among the 60 reservations that signed compacts with the state. . . . Evan Scheingross, 17, who attends Helix High School in La Mesa and the High School of Jewish Studies in Del Cerro, was credited with successfully lobbying for an indoor skateboard park at the Salvation Army's Ray and Joan Kroc Community Center near the border of San Diego and La Mesa.

Sept. 15 – Chris Miller, 37, an El Cajon bookkeeper, admitted stealing more than $119,000 from the campaign coffers of several local politicians and political campaign committees. He must spend four weekends in county jail and repay the politicians who hired him. If he violates probation, he will be sent to state prison for four years. His victims included Assemblyman Steve Baldwin, former Assemblyman Jan Goldsmith, County Supervisor Ron Roberts and San Diego City Councilwoman Christine Kehoe as well as a number of political organizations.

Sept. 16 – Randy Ashdown, 18, pleaded guilty to a single act of felony vandalism at Valhalla High School that caused an estimated $383,000 in damage. El Cajon Superior Court Judge Lance Lewis sentenced Ashdown to probation and a work furlough program despite an appeal by the prosecution that he be sent to state prison. Ashdown and a friend entered the school at 3 a.m. on June 12, turned on an emergency shower system and sprayed rooms with fire extinguishers. The judge said Ashdown had volunteered 76 hours since the incident and had a clean school record. Ashdown was ordered to pay restitution to the school at a rate of $200 a month.

Sept. 23 – Harold "Hal" Logan, 88, first general manager of Grossmont Center in La Mesa, died Sept. 5 at his home in Santa Barbara. Grossmont Center opened in the fall of 1961 and was the third mall in the county after Mission Valley Center and College Grove.

Sept. 27 – Frank Dillman, 79, of La Mesa, a former Marine who spent 42 months in a Japanese prisoner-of-war camp during World War II, is suing with other POWs two Japanese companies – Mitsubishi and Misui – alleging they profited from the slave labor of people like them who were forced to work in mines, shipyards and factories. The plaintiffs are using a California law which took effect last July – apparently the only one of its kind in the nation – that allows such suits to be heard in state courts. Dillman said prisoners were fed only enough to keep them working another day and had to walk five miles every day to a mine, even in winter, wearing only sandals made from grass.

Oct. 1 – A weeklong search for a volunteer Santee girls' basketball coach and the 16-year-old girl he ran off with ended at the San Ysidro border crossing Sept. 30. Jeffrey Purcell Gagne, 43, was apprehended while crossing into the United States from Mexico. The girl, a student at West Hills High School and a member of the basketball team, was released to her parents. Gagne, married and the father of two, was booked on suspicion of felony child abduction and faces up to three years in state prison and a $10,000 fine if he's convicted.

Oct. 5 – A Flinn Springs mother was sentenced to 25 years to life in prison for the poisoning death of her 5-year-old son. Krista Funk apologized for causing the death of Nicholas Mertens on Oct. 14, 1998, by giving him a lethal dose of phenobarbital and ingesting enough of the drug herself to be comatose when she was found side by side on the bed with him. Nicholas was born with massive congenital hydrocephalus – a brain condition that left him blind, severely disabled and unable to walk, talk or crawl. Funk used drugs and alcohol while she was pregnant and did not get any prenatal care. She had been diagnosed with bipolar disorder and told a neighbor she "would rather see Nicholas dead than have his father get him."

Oct. 7 – Jennifer Mayer, 23, of El Cajon, faces 15 years to life in prison for the starvation death of her son, Zechariah, who was 3 and weighed just 19 pounds when he died of chronic malnutrition on Jan. 20, 1998. During the trial, prosecutor Colin Murray said Mayer and her common-law husband, David, allowed the child to waste away because, according to the father, "God did not like fat babies."

Oct. 8 – Chuck and Penny Hauer of Rancho San Diego were honored in Washington, D.C., last week for adopting 35 physically and mentally challenged children of various ethnic backgrounds over the last 20 years. They were among 10 recipients of America's Award for Unsung Heroes, sometimes called the Nobel Prize for Goodness. Eight of the 21 children now in the Hauer home must use a wheelchair. The Hauers have five children of their own.

Oct. 9 – Melvenia Martin, 40, of Alpine, was sentenced to life in prison for the fatal beating of her 2-year-old nephew, Anthony Wyche. The former emergency room nurse was convicted in July 1998 of assault on a child under 8 resulting in death. Anthony's skull was fractured during the beating.

Oct. 19 – The obituary of Dr. William Soldmann, 87, who spearheaded the building of Grossmont Hospital and was its first chief of staff, appeared in this edition of the *U-T*. Known as "the father of Grossmont Hospital" because of his work to get it built, Soldmann was elected to the hospital board in 1966 and became an inspector for the California Medical Assn. He died of complications from Parkinson's disease.

Oct. 21 – Nearly 250 seniors at El Capitan High School in Lakeside staged a brief walkout a day earlier to protest the discontinuation of a tradition that allowed seniors to comment in the yearbook on their experiences. This year's yearbook staff, all underclassmen, dropped the custom because it would have cost $3,500 to print the extra pages. The issue was resolved by discussions between seniors and administrators. The comments will appear but in a different format. . . . Bob Rundell, longtime member of the Helix Water District Board, had died recently. He was 87.

Oct. 22 – An adobe house built and occupied by famed Western artist Olaf Wieghorst was moved from Renette Avenue in El Cajon, where it had been since 1944, to Rea Avenue where it will be refurbished and opened as a museum. The dwelling has 1,331 square feet of space.

Oct. 23 – David Kirsten, 42, of Santee, spent $10 a week on lottery tickets but had routinely lost his money until this week when he won $8 million in the California Lottery. He and his family will receive annual payments of between $200,000 and $404,000 for the next 26 years.

Oct. 26 – Richard Alan Clements II of El Cajon was sentenced to 34 years to life in prison for killing two Lakeside girls while trying to elude a California Highway Patrol officer who was chasing him. Clements, 18 at the time of the incident, was convicted of two counts of second-degree murder. The victims were Adina Gonzalez, 9, and Christine Turner, 9, who attended Lemon Crest School in Lakeside and were walking home when they were killed.

Oct. 28 – The tiny Jamul Indian Band with 56 members has signed a gambling pact with Gov. Gray Davis. The signing, which means a casino could be built on Indian land, caused a furor in the rural community.

Nov. 1 – Jerry and Barbara Freeman of Alpine and Robert and Mary Rice of La Mesa were among 217 people who died when EgyptAir Flight 990 crashed into waters off Nantucket, MA, en route to Cairo for a tour of the Near East. David and Betty Van Buskirk of the College area of San Diego, friends of the Freemans, also died in the crash. Their plane went down in the same general area of other crashes, including TWA Flight 800 off Long Island in July 1997, Swissair Flight 111 off Nova Scotia in September 1998, and the single-engine plane carrying John F. Kennedy Jr., his wife and her sister off Martha's Vineyard. *(Days later, the Associated Press said a voice and data recorder aboard the ill-fated plane indicated one of the relief pilots had seized the controls of the jet and forced the plane into a steep dive, shouting in Arabic a phrase translated as "I put my faith in God" or "I entrust myself to God.")*

Nov. 9 – Laura Akers, a deputy district attorney assigned to the district attorney's office in El Cajon, was awarded $250,000 by a Superior Court jury which found that District Attorney Paul Pfingst retaliated against her when she complained about a job transfer while she was pregnant. It was the second time a jury had found Pfingst's office retaliated against a pregnant employee. In June a jury awarded $1.5 million to Susan Sergojan, who also worked in the El Cajon office of the district attorney, but that judgment was overturned by a federal judge and a new trial was ordered.

Nov. 10 – Santee voters overwhelmingly rejected a ballot proposal to build Fanita Ranch, a 2,988-home project. Voters spurned three measures dealing with amending the general plan. The percentage of voter opposition to the measures varied from 65 to 85 percent. . . . Jeffrey Gagne, 43, former volunteer girls' basketball coach at West Hills High School in Santee, pleaded no contest to charges of child abduction and having sex with a minor. He was accused of taking a 16-year-old girl on his basketball team to Mexico for a week.

Nov. 13 – David James Casper, 27, son of professional golfer Billy Casper who owned property in El Cajon and had business interests there, was arrested in Las Vegas and will be returned to San Diego to face charges for at least 30 armed robberies. Casper is a suspect in what was called by police the "Anything Goes" series of robberies because of the variety of businesses and individuals targeted. The robberies occurred in La Mesa, Lemon Grove and Spring Valley as well as South Bay cities. Casper was charged in Las Vegas with possession of a controlled substance, possession of stolen vehicles, being an ex-felon in possession of a firearm and being a fugitive in violation of state parole.

Nov. 16 – East County political leaders have agreed to open a cold-weather shelter at the National Guard Armory in El Cajon. The armory had not been used as a shelter for the homeless since the winter of 1994-95. East County Supervisor Dianne Jacob said little of the $48 million received annually by the county for social services has been requested by cities in her Second District.

Nov. 17 – *The Daily Californian* in El Cajon has confirmed it will scale back publication from six days to two days a week on Dec. 1, eliminating about a dozen jobs. The newspaper will publish only on Wednesdays and Saturdays, according to Danny Dean, publisher. Dean said *The Daily Californian*, the *Chula Vista Star-News* and the *La Jolla Light*, all owned by Central Valley Publishing Co. of Merced, were put up for sale several months ago and are still for sale.

Nov. 20 – Santee City Manager George Tockstein, dogged by questions about his supplemental part-time employment, has announced he will retire March 1 or when the City Council finds his replacement. Tockstein is under investigation by the state attorney general's office for his financial ties to a company that trains firefighters, which he helped found. The probe is expected to answer the question whether Tockstein profited illegally by the sale of the company's assets, a charitable trust he established with nine partners.

Nov. 23 – Sharp HealthCare Foundation has agreed to pay $825,000 to settle claims that Grossmont Hospital, which is leased to Sharp, often described patient symptoms as complex and severe in order to bill at a higher rate when the actual diagnosis was simpler and more routine. Sharp HealthCare admitted no wrongdoing and says the government accepts that position.

Nov. 30 – Recall Crooks Committee, a group that wants to oust Ted Crooks as a member of the Grossmont Union High School District Board for supporting a measure to protect gay students in the district from discrimination, submitted 31,000 signatures to the county's Registrar of Voters office. The board passed the measure on a 3-2 vote, but the recall action targets only Crooks. The terms of Michael Harrelson and Tom Page, who also voted for the policy change, expire next year. *(The recall effort failed because many of the signatures were those of people living outside the district and therefore were invalid.)*

Nov. 25 – The mother of a 16-year-old Santee girl who accompanied her West Hills High School basketball coach to Mexico for a week has filed a $1 million claim against Grossmont Union High School District. Anita Miller, mother of Chelsea Olayan, who was a junior at the time, declined to comment on the case on the advice of her attorney. Miller said she was unaware that Santee resident Carol Kaske had complained earlier about the attention Jeffrey Gagne, 43, was paying to a 14-year-old girl on his basketball team. The girl was a friend of Kaske's daughter. . . .Clarence R. Brown, Sr., 71, former tribal chairman of the Viejas Indian Reservation near Alpine, died Nov. 20 in a San Diego hospital from complications of diabetes. Brown started the reservation's fire department and promoted education opportunities for the reservation's children.

Dec. 1 – El Cajon City Council voted to spend up to $9,000 to provide cold-weather shelter for the homeless at the National Guard armory on Pierce Street. Councilman Richard Ramos voted against the action. . . . Vernon Leroy Barker, 36, was sentenced to life in prison without parole for the murder of John M. Simpson, 53, a British tourist who was killed at Rodeway Inn in La Mesa. Simpson was slain for his car and credit cards, according to the testimony of a female witness who knew Barker.

Dec. 3 – David Mayer, 32, of El Cajon, was convicted of first-degree murder in the starvation death of his 3-year-old son, Zechariah. The boy starved to death because Mayer contended that God didn't like fat children. The jury deadlocked 10-2 on a special count of torture. The boy's mother, Jennifer Mayer, 23, was convicted earlier by a different jury of second-degree murder. Both are to be sentenced Jan. 6. At the time of his death, Zechariah weighed only 19 pounds. Investigators said the family's refrigerator was filled with food.

Dec. 8 – Toufic Naddi, formerly of El Cajon, was sentenced to life in prison without parole for murdering his wife and four of her relatives at his El Cajon home 15 years ago. It required five trials to establish that Naddi, a Lebanese immigrant, was sane when he committed the crimes. Naddi said during trial he had been "commanded by God" to slaughter his wife and her relatives.

Dec. 10 – Joe Sandoval, 48, of El Cajon, won $8.5 million as his share of a $34 million lottery jackpot. He shared the jackpot with three others who had the winning numbers. Sandoval, a Pacific Bell employee, is the second East County lottery winner in two months. Santee resident David Kirsten, 42, had a winning ticket in October that was worth $8 million.

Dec. 11 – Jeffrey Gagne, 43, pleaded guilty to one count of child abduction and one count of sexual contact with a minor and was sentenced to nine months in jail. Gagne, former coach of the West Hills High School girls' basketball team, took a 16-year-old member of his team to Mexico for a week. In addition to the jail time, the married father of two was placed on probation for five years.

Dec. 17 – A. Milton Paris, 90, co-founder of Dixon-Paris Mortuary in El Cajon who later built Paris Mortuary in 1942, died Dec. 14 from complications of a stroke. Paris was active in civic affairs, helping to start El Cajon Boys Club and El Cajon Elks Lodge. He also was active in the El Cajon Chamber of Commerce and served as president of El Cajon Rotary Club for one term. . . . Grossmont Union High School District trustees rejected a $1 million claim filed by the mother of a teen-age girl who ran off to Mexico with her West Hills High School basketball team's coach, Jeffrey Gagne, 43.

Dec. 21 – Two San Diego gang members were convicted of murdering store clerk Adrian Garmo on Feb. 18, 1998, at his family's La Mesa liquor store where he worked. Marquell Smith and Lazair Carter were found guilty of more than 75 counts of murder, robbery and assault stemming from a wave of robberies at small businesses . . . . A woman whose husband was shot to death 13 years ago publicly forgave the killer during an emotional meeting in a San Diego Superior Court. Kay Stuckart, who remarried, listened to Steve Larsen's expression of remorse, then tearfully offered her forgiveness. Larsen, an El Cajon dentist, shot to death Dr. Craig Blundell in his Escondido office on July 28, 1986. Larsen, who claimed to have been treated unsuccessfully by a number of doctors, was sent to Patton State Hospital where he was treated for paranoid schizophrenia and was released in 1991. Superior Court Judge David Gill found Larsen, now 44, had proved "that he is no longer a danger to the health or safety of himself or others." Larsen had been found guilty of the crime by reason of insanity.

Dec. 22 – The recall effort against Ted Crooks, a member of the Grossmont Union High School District Board, was 2,822 signatures short of the number required to schedule an election. The signature-by-signature examination of petition signers' names was triggered by the discovery of a single valid vote that had been invalidated because the signer used his middle name instead of his first name when signing a petition.

Dec. 24 – In a blow to downtown redevelopment in El Cajon, the owner of Howard's Bakery withdrew from negotiations to relocate the popular business from Broadway to the center of the city's redevelopment district. Ty Tonnessen, the bakery owner, said he will sell the business on Broadway rather than relocate. . . . The seventh Steven Scott Festival of Races in Santee was canceled because not enough money could be raised to stage the event. The celebration was budgeted to cost more than $105,000.

Dec. 25 – The death of former El Cajon Councilman Jack Hanson, 70, was noted in an obituary published today. Hanson, who died Dec. 21 of esophageal cancer, served 14 years on the council and was known for his long-time civic involvement in youth sports and community service organizations. The one-time first lieutenant in the U.S. Army during World War II and former deputy in the Los Angeles County sheriff's department arrived here as a representative of Hamm's Brewing Co., a beer manufacturer and distributor. Jack Hanson Lane was named for him.

Dec. 31 – Charles Louis Spiegel, 78, successor to Ruth Norman as director of the Unarius Academy of Science in El Cajon, died Dec. 22 at his Mt. Helix home. Like his flamboyant predecessor, who once made headlines around the world by placing bets on the arrival time of aliens to our planet, Spiegel prophesied that as many as 33 spaceships carrying extraterrestrials would land on Earth sometime in 2001. Norman, who died in 1993, had purchased 67 acres in Jamul to accommodate the landing.

Postscript: The last issue of *The Californian* as a daily newspaper was published Jan. 29, 2000. It had been sold by Central Valley Publishing, Inc. of Merced, CA to East County Newspapers, Inc. of Alpine, owned by Jay and Teresa Harn, who also owned the *Alpine Sun* and six other community newspapers in the region. Front-page headlines that day: "Megadevelopment targeted for Jacumba"; "ECCN buys paper"; "Kumeyaay museum opens at Barona cultural center"; "Santee, YMCA to jointly build athletics center": and "Woman blames drug problems on school shooting," a story about an El Cajon woman, 29, who had been wounded Jan. 29, 1979, when Patrick Henry High School student Brenda Spencer, 16, used a rifle to fire shots into the school yard at Cleveland Elementary School, killing the principal and a custodian. The woman, who as a child had been struck in the stomach by a bullet fired by Spencer, now was facing drug possession charges because, according to her attorney, she could not cope with the emotional wounds of that tragic event.

Art Madrid served 34 years on the La Mesa City Council, 10 years as a councilman and 24 years as mayor.
Photo: El Cajon Library

John Kaelin of Kaelin's Market was acclaimed for reimbursing customers when a money order firm went bankrupt.
Photo: San Diego History Center

Ray Anthony, high school band instructor who won state and national teaching awards. *Photo: El Cajon Library*

Tom Connolly, former assemblyman, went to prison for sexual misconduct.
Photo: El Cajon Library

Long-time El Cajon resident Olaf Wieghorst achieved fame as a Western artist. His "Navajo Madonna" sold for $450,000, and President Dwight Eisenhower bought some of his art.
Photo: Olaf Wieghorst Museum

Dennis Adams, a Superior Court judge, disbarred for judicial misconduct.
Photo: El Cajon Library

Buck Knives started in San Diego as a small family business in 1947. In 1969 it moved to El Cajon.
Photo: San Diego History Center

Acknowledgments

I am deeply indebted to El Cajon Historical Society for making the bound volumes of *The El Cajon Valley News* and *The Daily Californian* available to me. A special thank-you to Jonna Waite, who kept the museum open on Tuesdays so I and other researchers could do our work. She and I — and sometimes her husband, Ken – made numerous trips to a storage facility to retrieve the bound volumes, and when I was finished we returned them to their safe haven. The El Cajon Historical Society, El Cajon Library, City of El Cajon, Grossmont-Cuyamaca Community College District and the Grossmont High School Museum also contributed greatly by making pictures in their archives available for the book.

My thanks to El Cajon Library and its reference desk staff for use of the microfilm reader. I was incredibly fortunate to have access to that machine almost every time I wanted to use it. This project would have taken much longer had there been more library patrons asking to use the machine. The reference desk staff was enormously helpful when something on the microfilm reader needed to be adjusted or fixed.

I am especially grateful to Nancy St. John, former librarian, for budgeting money to purchase microfilm of the many issues of *The Daily Californian* that were missing. I would be remiss if I did not also acknowledge the assistance of the California State Library for sending to El Cajon many reels containing microfilm of missing copies of *The Daily Californian*. It would have been impossible to complete this project without that institution's cooperation.

I must also express great appreciation to all the reporters and editors who contributed to the news content of *The El Cajon Valley News* and *The Daily Californian*. It is their stories that I have condensed to put together the compilation of the most notable events of a 50-year span in the life of El Cajon Valley and surrounding areas.

Finally, I want to thank my wife, Sandra, for using her computer skills to cleanse the manuscript of typographical errors and to place copy where it belonged in a format that was consistent and readable.

Del Hood

San Diego Zoo goodwill ambassador Joan Embery and husband, Duane Pillsbury, on their wagon with Clydesdales in 1993. *Photo: Joan Embery*